Beyond nationalism

Manchester University Press

Series Editors: Professor Dimitris Papadimitriou (University of Manchester), Dr Kathryn Simpson (Keele University) and Dr Paul Tobin (University of Manchester).

The *European Politics* series seeks to tackle the biggest issues facing Europe in the twenty-first century.

Previously published under the *European Policy Research Unit (EPRU)* name, this long-established and highly respected series combines an important scholarly legacy with an ambitious outlook on European Studies at a time of rapid change for the discipline. Its geographical coverage encompasses the European Union, its existing and aspiring members, and "wider Europe", including Russia and Turkey, and the series actively promotes disciplinary, theoretical and methodological diversity.

The editors particularly welcome critical scholarship on the politics and policy making of the European Union, on comparative European politics, and on contemporary issues and debates affecting the future of Europe's socio-political and security outlook. Key areas of interest include Brexit, the environment, migration, identity politics and the ever-changing face of European integration.

To buy or to find out more about the books currently available in this series, please go to: https://manchesteruniversitypress.co.uk/series/european-politics/

Beyond nationalism

Acting and thinking for the common good in the European Union

João Labareda

MANCHESTER UNIVERSITY PRESS

Copyright © João Labareda 2024

The right of João Labareda to be identified as the author of this work has been asserted in accordance with the Copyright, Designs and Patents Act 1988.

Published by Manchester University Press
Oxford Road, Manchester, M13 9PL

www.manchesteruniversitypress.co.uk

British Library Cataloguing-in-Publication Data
A catalogue record for this book is available from the British Library

ISBN 978 1 5261 6909 9 hardback

First published 2024

The publisher has no responsibility for the persistence or accuracy of URLs for any external or third-party internet websites referred to in this book, and does not guarantee that any content on such websites is, or will remain, accurate or appropriate.

Typeset by Newgen Publishing UK

Disclaimer

The information and views set out in this publication are those of the author and do not necessarily reflect the official opinion of the European Commission.

Contents

Acknowledgements *page* viii

Introduction: Acting and thinking for the common good in the
   European Union 1
1 What is the common good? 21
2 Understanding EU values 52
3 National interests versus the common good: A way forward
   for the European Union 85
4 EU institutions for the common good 112
5 Building civic friendship in the European Union 134
Conclusion 173

Bibliography 176
Index 200

Acknowledgements

This book has benefited from a large number of instructive conversations with colleagues from academia and the European Commission. I am specially indebted to Rainer Bauböck, Patrice Wangen and Francesco di Comite, who provided highly valuable comments on large parts of the manuscript. Rob Byron, Commissioning Editor at Manchester University Press, supported this project from the start with enthusiasm, for which I am grateful. My family and friends have encouraged me to carry on along the way with patience and love. A very special thanks to my parents, my wife and my daughter, to whom I dedicate this book.

Introduction: Acting and thinking for the common good in the European Union

"The greatest challenge of our times"

In recent years, references to the common good have become increasingly present in the discourse of the leaders of the European Union (EU). For example, the French president, Emmanuel Macron, has condemned the "selfishness of nations only looking after their own interests", calling for a revival of the "spirit of cooperation" that has long "defended the common good of the world".[1] Similarly, the former German chancellor, Angela Merkel, has stated that the primary purpose of the EU "is to come to results which are to the benefit of our community", emphasising the need to overcome "national egoisms".[2] Several other national leaders have made calls and pledges in favour of "the greater good" in areas as varied as accessing COVID-19 vaccines and responding to Russia's invasion of Ukraine. At the EU level, the former president of the European Commission, Jean-Claude Juncker, warned against the "poison and deceit of nationalism" and stated that "Europe must move forward as one".[3] His successor, Ursula von der Leyen, has, in turn, issued a call for the member states "to join forces for our common good".[4] In his capacity as president of the European Council, Donald Tusk went as far as to say that acting and thinking for the common good "may perhaps be the greatest challenge of our times".[5]

Yet anyone contrasting this discursive concern for the common good with the reality of EU politics may be somewhat disappointed. The many crises that have befallen Europe in the last decade have unveiled sharp differences of opinion and considerable power struggles among member states. For example, EU member states have failed to agree on quotas to allocate refugees, fallen short of establishing a permanent financial mechanism with sufficient firepower to address future economic crises and viewed with suspicion large-scale EU defence cooperation initiatives responding to the United States' retrenchment from some aspects of global security. The fragmentation of the political scene is also apparent in the sharp divides between north and south, west and east, which have become increasingly evident in member states' sub-groupings, the Visegrad Group and the so-called "PIGS" being two illustrative examples.[6] This fragmentation has triggered debates about a "two-speed EU" and even a "multispeed Europe".[7] At the same time, the unprecedented event of Brexit has increased the threat of EU fragmentation and has generated fears that it could be followed by a "Frexit, Nexit or Oexit".[8] Given this political landscape, is there room to seek an EU-wide common good? If so, how can it be effectively pursued?

The emergence of nationalist discourse in several member states has jeopardised a robust understanding of the common good in at least three ways.[9] To begin with, nationalist leaders have consistently challenged what seemed to be widely shared EU values, including the rule of law, freedom of speech and equal treatment of citizens. By emphasising the cultural diversity across European states, these leaders have made many EU citizens lose sight of their common values and goals. For example, Prime Minister Viktor Orbán has vowed "to protect Hungary's Christian culture" from "any supranational business or political empire".[10] Second, nationalist parties tend to assess the merits of EU policies exclusively from the standpoint of national gains and losses at the expense of a broader European perspective. According to this view, a desirable EU policy is a policy that serves national agendas. All too often, this leaves EU institutions and their decision-making processes helpless in the face of powerful national interests. Third, nationalist governments have focused on promoting the well-being of their citizens while disregarding the well-being of citizens of other member states. Despite covering a diverse spectrum of ideals, nationalist platforms share a scepticism towards multilateralism, particularly in its most advanced form of political and economic integration.[11] Therefore, nationalist leaders have aimed at regaining sovereign control and have rejected further European integration.

Against this background, the following questions arise: Is there a "European common good" in any meaningful sense?[12] What values, if any, are shared by all member states? What consequences should there be if a member state (or its government) no longer shares the set of common values? How should EU institutions put EU values into practice? How can decision-making at the EU level move further beyond the logic of national interests? Finally, how can EU citizens acquire a greater "concern for the whole, a dedication to the common good"?[13]

To approach these questions in the political and legal language of the EU, the research puzzle presented in the following sections draws on three undertheorised notions from the Treaty on European Union (TEU). These are (i) *EU values*, (ii) *an institutional framework to promote EU values* and (iii) *creating an ever closer Union*.[14] Why do these notions matter? In the first instance, EU values can help us understand what goods the EU seeks to realise. They constitute the moral DNA of the Union, structuring its collective choices and offering practical guidance in the face of difficult trade-offs. Therefore, clarifying the substantive content and practical implications of EU values is essential. Second, despite the endorsement of common values, the predominance of national interests has prevented collective action in critical fields, such as tax competition and tax avoidance. This prevalence means that, under the current EU institutional framework, the pursuit of the common good is not always safeguarded. Thus, the question of what institutional arrangements, if any, could facilitate the adoption of policies for the common good deserves careful treatment. Third, it is likely that EU citizens will only be willing to mobilise the means to seek the common good together if they become ever closer. This prospect raises the question of what conditions might strengthen the civic bonds among Europeans.

Before getting into each of these issues in detail, I should clarify what I mean by "common good" in the context of EU membership.

What is the common good?

By the common good, I mean the conditions and goals that benefit *the EU as a whole*, not just a limited group of member states or EU citizens. Note that this definition should not be swiftly equated with the rule of maximising aggregate utility, which could generate highly uneven distributions of well-being across member states.[15] A question that follows is how much well-being the common good should entail for *each* individual unit of concern. The answer is not straightforward. On the one hand, realising the common good may entail costs in terms of individual welfare. Consider the cases of nurses, firefighters and police officers, who often risk their lives for the sake of the common good. These examples suggest that, at least under certain conditions, the common good has priority over individual well-being. On the other hand, certain types of involuntary sacrifices seem incompatible with the ideal of the common good. Consider the case of carrying out promising but unethical medical experiments on patients. This example suggests that the common good is not an ultimate good – that is, it should not be sought at any cost. For these reasons, this book will rely on the following definition of the common good: *the conditions and goals that benefit the EU as a whole without imposing impermissible harm on some EU citizens or member states.*[16]

A key challenge addressed in this book is how EU politics could tackle these conditions and goals more consistently.[17] However, it should be acknowledged that the issue of what policies are desirable from the standpoint of the common good is not always straightforward. To begin with, the pursuit of the common good is underpinned by a high level of epistemic uncertainty. For example, when civil authorities commit to reforming the financial system to prevent future economic crises, it may not be clear what policy package will produce the intended effects. Crucially, the pursuit of the common good implies difficult normative choices. Consider the case of climate change. Even if member states agreed on the need to address this pressing issue, they would still be faced with complex trade-offs that cannot be readily adjudicated through scientific criteria alone. In other words, determining desirable policy requires value-based judgements.[18] This conclusion suggests that however committed to the pursuit of the common good member states are, they will likely have conflicting views on what it actually entails. In the context of EU membership, this predicament seems to be recurrent, given the diversity of political models, social practices and cultural backgrounds across the member states. Therefore, the following question is unavoidable: Does diversity within the Union warrant talk of a common good of the whole EU?

I shall argue that diversity is not a definitive objection against a shared understanding of the common good in the EU. In Chapter 1, I will argue that *public values* – understood as the values enshrined in the fundamental laws of a polity, such as constitutions and international treaties – provide actionable guidelines regarding what conditions and goals a society considers desirable. For example, public values such as the rule of law, pluralism and accountability, endorsed by many liberal democracies, ought to be translated into a set of concrete requirements regarding the functioning of public administration and the judicial system. Note that all citizens of a given polity are expected to uphold its public values, regardless of their individual preferences and worldviews. By bridging the substantial moral differences amongst citizens, public values create a *common standpoint* against which both individual conduct and public policies ought to be assessed. I shall claim that when the public values endorsed by a group of states overlap or when they explicitly endorse common values through international agreements (as in the EU), it is possible to derive a *transnational* understanding of the common good. I shall add that it is plausible to articulate at least a minimalistic *global common good*, whereby very diverse states share some basic conditions and goals, such as preserving the international system and protecting the planet.[19]

I have suggested that EU values offer guidelines regarding *what types* of conditions and goals *ought* to be pursued by the Union.[20] A question that follows is *how* these conditions and goals *can* be fulfilled in the present-day EU. Any compelling answer needs to accomplish at least two important tasks. The first is to identify the *institutions* through which the common good can be pursued at the EU level. Indeed, the configuration of competences and decision-making rules of EU bodies has a decisive impact on the shape of EU policy outcomes.[21] An illustrative example is the unanimity rule applied by the Council of the European Union ("the Council") in certain policy areas. Under this rule, the interests of a single member state can defeat those of the entire Union without needing to provide any reasonable justification. For example, in order to shield its nuclear energy sector from competition, successive French governments have barred the electrical grids and gas pipelines of central Europe from being connected to Spanish ones through French territory. This ban has meant the EU is much more vulnerable to disruptions of energy supply, as the acute energy crisis triggered by the invasion of Ukraine by Russia later came to demonstrate. How could the authorities of member states think and act more consistently beyond national interests? What institutional reforms, if any, could facilitate the adoption of EU policies for the common good?

The second task involves advancing effective strategies by which the civic bonds among EU citizens could be consolidated. Aristotle famously argued that the common good presupposes a background of "civic friendship", understood as "a bond of reciprocal good-will between fellow citizens, expressed through norms of civic behaviour, such as mutual recognition of moral equality, mutual concern and mutual defence and support".[22] This bond ensures that citizens consider the impact of their preferences on one other's well-being while deliberating on alternative courses of action. Furthermore, individuals who regard themselves as connected by civic bonds are typically more willing to accept sacrifices for the sake of their community than those who feel like distant strangers. This willingness is important because, as we shall see, advancing the common good of the whole EU may come with a cost for the citizens of some member states.

However, the EU political landscape described above seems to reveal a great deal of mistrust rather than civic friendship. Jeroen Dijsselbloem, in his capacity as president of the Eurogroup (the meeting of finance ministers of the Eurozone member states), made this lack of social empathy particularly clear when he stated that financially distressed member states should not expect to be assisted after having spent all their money "on drinks and women".[23] How can civic bonds amongst Europeans be strengthened?

Three contested concepts in the Treaty on European Union

EU values

In this section, I will briefly outline the tensions underpinning the three disputed concepts mentioned above. Let us begin with *EU values*. The TEU states that "[t]he Union's aim is to promote peace, *its values* and the well-being of its peoples".[24] Yet what are these values? The TEU lists several, including "respect for human dignity, freedom, democracy, equality, the rule of law and respect for human rights".[25] According to the TEU, "[t]hese values are common to the member states in a society in which pluralism, non-discrimination, tolerance, justice, solidarity and equality between women and men prevail".[26] However, this direct equivalence between EU values and national values seems puzzling. If EU values are so similar to national values, why do they sometimes clash? Even when member states formally subscribe to common values, such as solidarity and non-discrimination, they seem to disagree regarding their meaning and policy implications. For instance, some member states have referred to the programme of financial assistance to Greece as a clear demonstration of European solidarity, while others cite it as evidence of an absence of solidarity.[27] Thus, despite European leaders' recurrent appeals to EU values, this notion remains ambiguous and under-theorised. In what sense, if any, can we speak of EU values? What conditions need to be fulfilled for EU values to be realised?

While the EU seems eager to export its moral standards through policy instruments such as trade deals and association agreements, member states' basic moral consensus has been called into question in recent years. Indeed, the EU openly states that "[o]ne of the most important aspect of EU trade policy is that – alongside protecting European businesses and consumers – it is promoting the EU's principles and values".[28] However, in recent years, the multiple episodes of noncompliance with EU values involving the governments of Hungary and Poland have shown that the authority of EU values can be challenged. Indeed, Hungary has been charged with a "serious breach of the values on which the Union is founded", notably freedom of speech, freedom of association and equal treatment of individuals.[29] In view of this and other challenges to what Ian Manners has dubbed the "normative power" of the EU, President Ursula von der Leyen considered the goal of "promoting the European way of life" as one of her six political priorities.[30] However, her choice attracted sharp criticism, raising additional questions. Are EU values European by definition? What should the relevant test for compliance with EU values be? What measures should be taken if a member state (or its government) no longer shares EU values?

An institutional framework to promote EU values

The TEU also states that "[t]he Union shall have an institutional framework which shall aim to promote its values, advance its objectives, serve its interests, those of its citizens and those of the member states".[31] A question that follows is what type of institutional framework can best implement EU values, particularly in areas where national interests appear to be divergent?[32] Note that adopting ambitious EU policies for the common good requires not only the endorsement of common values but also a pragmatic agreement regarding what resources are to be mobilised and what interests are to be compromised to achieve this purpose. Achieving such an agreement can be particularly challenging when the distribution of the costs and benefits of policy proposals that promote the common good is asymmetrical. For instance, in the domain of agriculture policy, member states frequently team up in terms of winners and losers, funders and recipients, generating power struggles that jeopardise crucial EU reforms. Consider the case of the Common Agriculture Policy (CAP), where a few member states with powerful farming interests delayed for decades a reform that was widely regarded as much needed. How, then, can EU institutions effectively prevent, or move beyond, these deadlocks with a view to achieving the common good?

According to the TEU, the responsibility to promote the common good of the whole EU lies with the European Commission.[33] However, its ability to achieve this goal is clearly limited under the current institutional setting. An episode related to COVID-19 crisis management can illustrate this point. In April 2020, the Commission presented a roadmap for a coordinated lifting of the containment measures against the pandemic.[34] Note that, in the context of freedom of movement, coordination is critical to ensure that any pandemic is successfully contained. Yet, eager to manage the crisis without EU interference, several member states discredited the Commission's initiative and pursued their own plans instead.[35] Similar episodes have been observed in a number of policy fields where the Commission's powers are limited or non-existent.[36] However, the way forward to unblock important reforms conducive to the common good is not obvious, at least if the path towards political centralisation is to be avoided. In fact, the Commission is already charged with being too powerful and undemocratic.[37] This judgement suggests that increasing its powers might be normatively undesirable and politically unfeasible. How can EU institutions effectively overcome internal divisions and political deadlocks? What institutional reforms, if any, could bring the pursuit of the common good to the heart of EU policymaking?

Creating an ever closer Europe

A question that follows from the previous sections is the following: Why would national governments accept making further sacrifices for the common good of the entire EU? The answer seems ultimately contingent on whether their national constituencies can develop a greater concern for each other's well-being, thus supporting such collective efforts. Thus, the preamble of the TEU established the goal of "creating an ever closer Union among the peoples of Europe".[38] According to the Schuman Declaration of

1950, this goal is to be attained gradually "through concrete achievements" that "create a de facto solidarity" amongst Europeans.[39] Yet, despite several arguably remarkable EU achievements – including the period of peace since 1945, the longest in the history of the European continent – the bonds among EU citizens are currently fragile, if not fraying. This limited level of solidarity is illustrated by the rise of nationalist platforms in the member states. By the end of 2019, nationalist parties had collected at least 15% of the votes in nine member states and participated in several government coalitions.[40] This political landscape has led Jean-Claude Juncker to speak accurately of a "retreat into our own corners".[41] Is this development an inescapable consequence of growing individualism in Western societies and the loss of a sense of community membership?[42] Or can EU leaders do something to reverse this tendency? If so, what "concrete achievements" could bring Europeans ever closer?

In the face of high levels of Euroscepticism, in 2020, President Von der Leyen launched a Conference on the Future of Europe aimed at building "a joint vision of the direction the EU should take in the next decade and beyond".[43] A bold and widely endorsed agenda seems critical to mobilising EU citizens around the pursuit of the common good. I will argue that this vision should address a number of social arrangements that currently prevent the emergence of stronger civic bonds amongst EU citizens. Indeed, in Chapter 4, I shall argue that the following conditions jeopardise civic friendship within the EU polity: (i) fierce competition amongst individuals, leading them to see each other as competitors rather than fellow citizens; (ii) pronounced socioeconomic inequalities, creating cleavages within society; (iii) scarcity of meaningful opportunities for political participation in EU politics, leading to a widespread sense of disempowerment by the citizens; (iv) multiple barriers against freedom of movement, restraining cross-border social interactions; (v) limited information regarding the functioning of EU institutions and the rights and duties linked to EU citizenship, and; (vi) lack of clear guarantees of mutual assistance in the event of an armed conflict. I will claim that appropriate EU policies could overcome these conditions. Before overviewing the arguments presented in this book, I should briefly introduce the scholarly literature with which the latter is in dialogue.

Unanswered questions in the literature

This project is situated within two key branches of literature: (i) communitarianism and (ii) EU normative studies. While the notion of the common good has been present throughout the history of political thought, its implications for modern liberal democracies have been addressed notably by scholars of communitarianism.[44] In a variety of approaches, communitarians stress the importance of social bonds, criticising an atomistic understanding of civil society whereby the interests of individuals have precedence over the common good.[45] Communitarian accounts are usually articulated on the grounds of self-governing communities, such as the city-state and the nation-state. For communitarian authors, these delimited political units provide two critical elements: (i) the background of social relations that shape individuals' identity and (ii) the democratic institutions that allow for a meaningful deliberation concerning the common good. Most communitarians have strikingly avoided passing judgement on the EU case.[46] However, a communitarian reading would typically question whether the EU qualifies as a community, given the lack of a shared European identity and the disempowerment of citizens resulting from the supranational EU institutions.[47] Therefore, so the communitarian argument would go, the pursuit of a European common good may be both normatively undesirable and politically unfeasible.

However, the view that the EU does not qualify as a community disregards salient facts about the Union and presupposes an overly narrow understanding of community. First, the claim that EU citizens do not share a common identity has been challenged. For some authors, European identity encompasses Roman and Christian heritage, the collective memory of the struggle against totalitarianism, and shared symbols and meanings, such as Mediterranean cuisine.[48] Second, as I shall argue, the idea of community does not necessarily need to be conceived in terms of language, culture and history. Alternatively, it can be articulated on the grounds of normative bonds constructed by like-minded states. As I shall claim, states with overlapping moral outlooks share common values, rules and principles despite their citizens' sociological and cultural diversity. Finally, the supranational character of EU institutions may be more of an advantage than an obstacle when it comes to empowering citizens and "restoring control over the forces that govern our lives".[49] Indeed, the interdependencies resulting from economic integration and globalisation imply that member states have a very limited capacity to achieve their own goals alone. Acting at the EU level, as I shall argue, has the potential to empower member states to pursue effective policies that more closely translate the will of their citizens.

Similarly, the ongoing "normative turn" in EU studies has not yet sparked a debate about the common good in the EU.[50] Normative works on the EU have addressed issues such as democratic legitimacy, EU citizenship and constitutionalism, which are related to, but not substitutes for, a debate on the common good.[51] As an illustrative example, the most significant collection of essays addressing the philosophical foundations of the EU contains no reference to the notion of the common good.[52] This lack of interest is striking, at least if we assume, as does John Rawls, that the pursuit of the common good is the ultimate purpose of government.[53] The need to address this issue is even more pressing if we consider the degree of cross-border interdependence in the context of EU membership. Why, then, have EU scholars not examined this topic? In addition to the pervasive influence of rational choice theory and neoliberalism, which have been sceptical towards the notion of the common good, there are conceptual difficulties in articulating this notion beyond the nation-state. Consider, for example, the following questions: On what grounds can we speak of a regional or global common good? Can we distinguish the European common good from, say, the South American common good? What if realising the common good of the EU would jeopardise the pursuit of the common good of other regions?

This book will address these questions in depth. I will argue that shared understandings of the common good within groups of two or more states will be thicker or thinner depending on the extent to which their public values overlap. For instance, Spain admittedly has more in common with France than with North Korea. This moral proximity should make it easier for the Spanish and French authorities to examine transnational challenges from a common normative standpoint, as well as to agree on what should be done to address them. However, I will claim that a basic level of moral agreement between states as different as Spain and North Korea can still be found when it comes to addressing certain fundamental global challenges, such as climate change and HIV/AIDS. I will argue that regional associations play a leading role in realising the global common good since they foster cooperation between neighbouring states that face similar geopolitical challenges and are in a privileged position to assist each other. I will claim that EU values are distinctive because they translate particular understandings of liberal democracy, social welfare and environmental protection. Furthermore, I will argue that it is impermissible to pursue the common good of a state or a region by critically endangering the common good of other states or regions. In the next section, I explain how I intend to solve the puzzle that I have been outlining.

How to solve the puzzle?

The questions I have raised can be summarised as follows: *How can the common good be realised in the present-day EU?* I have also introduced three sub-questions: (i) On what grounds, if any, can EU values be regarded as a meaningful and common moral standpoint amongst the member states? (ii) What type of institutional framework could best realise the common good in the EU? (iii) What conditions can foster (or jeopardise) the development of stronger civic bonds amongst EU citizens?

To address these questions, I will be seeking *normative guidelines* concerning the Union's political configuration, namely its decision-making rules, the allocation of competences across different levels of government, the rules governing the relations between the EU and the member states, the public reasons that can be used to justify EU policies, and so on. The caveat "present-day EU" indicates that this book takes the current configuration of the EU as its starting point, following the so-called practice-dependence approach.[54] Accordingly, my proposals will be articulated in terms of *incremental change* to the status quo instead of assuming that the EU could be redesigned from scratch through exhaustive social engineering. Doing so should improve their feasibility while providing a concrete roadmap for action.[55]

The structure of the book follows closely the research agenda that I have outlined. The first two chapters focus on the question of *what the common good means* in the context of EU membership. The first chapter develops a conceptual framework to analyse the problem of the common good in the EU. I thoroughly discuss the notion of public values, and I explain the advantages of my approach with a view to articulating the common good beyond borders. The second chapter focuses on EU values. I explain why the EU should be regarded as a normative community and analyse the distinctive features of EU values. I discuss several recent challenges against EU values, as well as the appropriate EU response to them. I also explore a few key preconditions for EU values to be realised in a globalised world. The last three chapters address the question of *how the common good can be realised* in the EU. Chapter 3 analyses the challenge that divergent national interests pose to achieving the common good of the Union and presents two complementary strategies to deal with this problem. Chapter 4 introduces a few proposals for EU institutional reform to advance the common good. Finally, Chapter 5 discusses a set of "concrete achievements" that could strengthen the civic bonds among Europeans. I thus discuss the conditions that can either foster or jeopardise a concern for the community, and I present a roadmap for action.

An overview of the argument

Let me now summarise the main arguments presented in the following chapters. This book presents the EU as a community of states that have endorsed a set of shared public values through voluntarily ratifying the EU treaties. I argue that EU values allow for the mapping of certain key conditions and goals that member states jointly consider desirable, thus translating a shared conception of the common good. Notably, these include consolidating liberal democracy, enabling decent standards of social welfare and ensuring a high level of environmental protection. I claim that EU values are not European by definition; they have been built through decades of public debates, policymaking and judicial decisions and have been gradually translated into concrete institutional practices, such as universal access to healthcare and education.

However, I claim that EU values face a number of serious challenges. Under conditions of contemporary globalisation, much of the power to shape the EU's future has been transferred to non-state actors, which pursue agendas that are often at odds with the common good. For example, it has been reported that large data analytics firms played a role in influencing the outcome of the Brexit referendum. In a similar vein, credit rating agencies wield considerable power over some member states by evaluating their debt using methods that are rarely (if ever) subjected to public scrutiny. At the same time, EU-based multinational corporations that shift their manufacturing to countries with weak welfare systems pose a threat to the viability of decent standards of social welfare as this outsourcing often leads to lower labour standards and significant reductions in tax revenue. These and other challenges have clearly jeopardised the EU common good.

I argue that the most effective and desirable way for European states to address these challenges is not to reclaim sovereign control, as many nationalist platforms have suggested, but to join forces to restructure the international environment in which they are embedded. The scope of its political institutions and the size of its common market empower the EU to realise the common good beyond borders in at least three ways. First, representative institutions such as the European Parliament and the Council can host transnational debates on cross-border interdependencies that cannot be effectively addressed by national democracies, such as those related to climate change, food supply and energy security. Second, the European Commission and the Court of Justice of the European Union (CJEU) provide supranational enforcement mechanisms that can be used to implement ambitious agendas for the common good. Third, economic integration gives EU member states higher leverage to persuade business and investment actors that jeopardise the public interest through the threat of restricting their operations in the world's largest internal market.

In view of these potentials, I claim that EU member states could jointly establish a set of bodies with the critical mass to shape globalisation, enabling EU institutions and member states to realise EU values and contributing to the global common good. Focusing on the social dimension of the European Model, I propose the creation of three institutions: (i) a European

Transnational Tax Authority; (ii) a European Credit Rating Agency; and (iii) a European Agency for Fair Trade. Furthermore, I argue that the EU should put in place more robust safeguards against internal breaches of EU values, including enforcing the TEU provision regarding the suspension of the voting rights of non-compliant member states in the Council of the European Union and creating a procedure through which chronically non-compliant member states could be ejected from the Union.

However, I claim that to pursue the common good of the whole EU effectively, EU institutions will also need to be better equipped to promote the convergence of national interests and solve political deadlocks. I argue that two complementary strategies should be pursued to achieve these ends. First, building on Robert Putnam's two-level game theory, I claim that EU actors should play a more active role in the processes through which national interests are formed at the domestic level.[56] By giving the EU a stronger voice in national debates – where the broader European picture often remains underrepresented – the perspective of other member states might be more smoothly incorporated into national positions and might also recruit broader public support. In practice, this would mean that the Representations of the Commission in the member states would act as the face of the EU at the national level, representing the general interest of the EU in the domestic public spheres.

Second, I claim that Brussels' policymaking needs to be reformed to facilitate the resolution of conflicts of national interests and to prioritise the pursuit of the common good. Concrete proposals presented in this book include: (i) directly electing the presidents of the European Council and the European Commission; (ii) abolishing the unanimity rule in the Council; (iii) creating an EU Citizens' Assembly with agenda-setting powers; (iv) adopting transnational lists for the elections for the European Parliament and upgrading the institutional links between the European Parliament and national parliaments; (v) ensuring the impartiality of the bureaucratic apparatus of the European Commission with regards to interstate disputes; and (vi) creating an advisory body of former presidents of EU institutions. Altogether, these institutional reforms could bring the common good to the heart of EU policymaking.

Furthermore, I argue that the EU should establish the conditions that would permit concern for the common good to flourish amongst EU citizens. I present an agenda aimed at strengthening the bonds of civic friendship in the EU, which includes the following proposals: (i) establishing a robust social level playing field to moderate competition among EU workers, notably by launching an EU labour code; (ii) reducing socioeconomic inequalities in the EU; (iii) enhancing the opportunities for citizens' participation, namely through the aforementioned Representations of the Commission and the EU Citizens' Assembly; (iv) reducing barriers against freedom of movement, notably by launching an EU-wide programme of administrative simplification regarding free movers; (v) creating a common curriculum in all EU schools, which would allow EU citizens to acquire knowledge of their rights and duties and develop competences which are crucial for being politically engaged members of the EU polity; and (vi) strengthening the bonds of mutual military assistance and scaling up the existing programmes of defence cooperation. By delivering this set of concrete achievements, the EU could be a solution for, rather than a cause of, the current anxieties at the national level.

Notes

1 Emmanuel Macron, "Macron Denounces Nationalism as a 'Betrayal of Patriotism' in Rebuke to Trump at WWI Remembrance", *The Washington Post* (11 November 2018), www.washingtonpost.com/world/europe/to-mark-end-of-world-war-i-frances-macron-denounces-nationalism-as-a-betrayal-of-patriotism/2018/11/11/aab65aa4-e1ec-11e8-ba30-a7ded04d8fac_story.html (accessed 4 January 2021).
2 Angela Merkel, *Debate on the Future of Europe: Opening Statement by Angela Merkel, German Federal Chancellor*, 13 November 2018, https://multimedia.europarl.europa.eu/en/debate-on-the-future-of-europe-opening-statement-by-angela-merkel-german-federal-chancellor-_I162933-V_v (accessed 4 January 2021).
3 Jean-Claude Juncker, "The Hour of European Sovereignty", *State of the Union Address 2018*, 12 September 2018, https://ec.europa.eu/commission/sites/beta-political/files/soteu2018-speech_en_0.pdf (accessed 4 January 2021).
4 Ursula Von der Leyen, "The World in 2021: Ursula von der Leyen on Teamwork Solving Global Problems", *The Economist* (17 November 2020), www.economist.com/the-world-ahead/2020/11/17/ursula-von-der-leyen-on-teamwork-solving-global-problems (accessed 4 January 2021).
5 Donald Tusk, *Speech by President Donald Tusk at the Athens Democracy Forum 2019* (9 October 2019), www.consilium.europa.eu/en/press/press-releases/2019/10/09/speech-by-president-donald-tusk-at-the-athens-democracy-forum-2019/ (accessed 4 January 2021).
6 "PIGS" refers to Portugal, Italy, Greece and Spain. This designation was used most widely during the sovereign debt crisis. Although the Visegrad Group was created before the 2004 enlargement, its role in EU politics has been expanding in recent years.
7 Jean-Claude Piris, *The Future of Europe: Towards a Two-Speed EU?* (Cambridge, 2021); Valentina Pop, "Once Scorned, 'Multispeed Europe' Is Back", *The Wall Street Journal* (1 March 2017), www.wsj.com/articles/once-scorned-multispeed-europe-is-back-1488388260 (accessed 4 November 2022).

8 Frexit, Nexit and Oexit refer, respectively, to the hypothetical withdrawal of France, Netherlands, and Austria. See Kate Lyons and Gordon Darroch, "Frexit, Nexit or Oexit? Who Will Be Next to Leave the EU", *The Guardian* (27 June 2016), www.theguardian.com/politics/2016/jun/27/frexit-nexit-or-oexit-who-will-be-next-to-leave-the-eu (accessed 31 August 2018).
9 In this book, I refer to nationalism not as a historical process, but as "[a]dvocacy of or support for the interests of one's own nation, especially to the exclusion or detriment of the interests of other nations". See "Nationalism", *Oxford English Dictionary* (2022), www.oed.com/view/Entry/125289 (accessed 8 November 2022).
10 Reuters, "Viktor Orbán: Our Duty Is to Protect Hungary's Christian Culture", *The Guardian* (7 May 2018), www.theguardian.com/world/2018/may/07/viktor-orban-hungary-preserve-christian-culture (accessed 8 November 2022). This path towards political isolation has been observed in several other member states. For an overview, see Stephen Holmes and Ivan Krastev, *The Light That Failed: Why the West Is Losing the Fight for Democracy* (London, 2020).
11 Note that the rejection of transnational integration has drawn support from across the political spectrum. For example, in the case of the United Kingdom, the option to withdraw from the EU recruited support not only on the right but also on the left. This is consistent with Siniša Malešević's claim that nationalism is an "operational" ideology that can be appropriated by distinctive "normative" ideologies. See Siniša Malešević, *Nation-States and Nationalisms: Organization, Ideology and Solidarity* (Cambridge, 2013).
12 Sonja Puntscher Riekmann, Alexander Somek and Doris Wydra (eds), *Is there a European Common Good?* (Baden-Baden, 2013).
13 Michael J. Sandel, *Justice: What's the Right Thing to Do?* (London, 2010), p. 263.
14 EU values are listed in *Treaty on European Union*, article 2. In turn, article 13 states that "[t]he Union shall have an institutional framework which shall aim to promote its values". Finally, the goal of achieving "an ever closer union" is set out in the preamble.
15 For the view that utilitarianism is a sound public philosophy, see Robert E. Goodin, *Utilitarianism as a Public Philosophy* (Cambridge, 1995).
16 Chapter 3 will discuss what should count as impermissible harm in the context of EU membership.
17 For simplicity, I shall refer to this process interchangeably as "realising", "pursuing" or "seeking" the common good. Note that this wording does not suggest that the common good should be taken as given. As I claim in Chapter 1, any understanding of the common good is socially constructed. In other words, it is not grounded on an independent standard of truth, but on conditions and goals that a given community regards as desirable.
18 For example, consider a hypothetical choice to be made between two equally environmentally friendly and economically costly measures vis-à-vis air travel: (i) setting quotas for all citizens, allowing everyone a chance to fly but restraining individual liberty, or (ii) taxing air travel more heavily, charging

users for the pollution they cause but making flying unaffordable to many citizens. A choice between the two options can only be justified on the grounds of normative arguments.

19 It should be added that diversity does not preclude leaders and citizens at the nation-state level referring to the common good as a recognisable standpoint. For instance, President Macron of France often speaks of the common good of France, despite the incommensurable diversity that can be found amongst 67 million French citizens. If one considers the standpoint of the common good plausible in a large pluralist state, then one should not dismiss too quickly its application to the EU.

20 In a variety of approaches, scholars have advanced causal explanations for why we have certain forms of integration rather than others. However, the problem of the EU's rightful purpose has attracted considerably less attention. For influential explanatory accounts, see Karen J. Alter, "Who are the 'Masters of the Treaty'? European Governments and the European Court of Justice", *International Organization* 52 (1998), pp. 121–147; Ernst B. Haas, "Turbulent Fields and the Theory of Regional Integration", *International Organization* 30 (1976), pp. 173–212; Stanley Hoffmann, "Obstinate or Obsolete? The Fate of the Nation-State and the Case of Western Europe", *Daedalus* 95 (1966), pp. 862–915; Paul Pierson, "The Path to European Integration: A Historical-Institutionalist Analysis", in Wayne Sandholtz and Alec Stone Sweet (eds), *European Integration and Supranational Governance* (Oxford, 1998), pp. 28–59; Andrew Moravcsik and F. Schimmelfennig, "Liberal Intergovernmentalism", in A. Wiener and T. Diez (eds), *European Integration Theory* (Oxford, 2009), pp. 67–87; J.H.H. Weiler, "The Transformation of Europe", *The Yale Law Journal* 100 (1991), pp. 2403–2483.

21 See Simon Hix and Bjørn Høyland, *The Political System of the European Union* (New York, 2011).

22 Jason A. Scorza, "Civic Friendship", *The International Encyclopaedia of Ethics* (2013).

23 Mehreen Khan and Paul McClean, "Dijsselbloem under Fire after Saying Eurozone Countries Wasted Money on 'Alcohol and Women'", *Financial Times* (21 March 2017), www.ft.com/content/2498740e-b911-3dbf-942d-ecce511a351e (accessed 31 January 2022).

24 *Treaty on European Union*, article 2. Italics added.

25 *Treaty on European Union*, article 2.

26 *Treaty on European Union*, article 2.

27 On this issue, see Stefan Wallaschek, "The Framing of Solidarity in the Euro Crisis", *Sheffield Political Economy Research Institute* (22 May 2019), http://speri.dept.shef.ac.uk/2019/05/22/the-framing-of-solidarity-in-the-euro-crisis/ (accessed 4 June 2021).

28 See European Council, "Promoting EU Values through Trade", www.consilium.europa.eu/en/ policies/trade-policy/promoting-eu-values/ (accessed 21 September 2020).

29 European Parliament, *Draft Report on a Proposal Calling on the Council to Determine, Pursuant to Article 7(1) of the Treaty on European Union, the*

Existence of a Clear Risk of a Serious Breach by Hungary of the Values on which the Union is Founded (11 April 2018).

30 See Ian Manners, "The Normative Ethics of the European Union", *International Affairs* 84 (2008), pp. 45–60 and European Commission, "6 Commission Priorities for 2019–2024", https://ec.europa.eu/info/strategy/priorities-2019-2024_en (accessed 21 September 2020).

31 *Treaty on European Union*, article 13.

32 Here I understand "national interests" as a set of political goals defined by the member states at the domestic level. As the constructivist school of International Relations theory has highlighted, these goals are socially constructed – that is, they should not be taken as given. Thus, when saying that member state X has a national interest Y or Z I do not assume that it is *objectively* in the best interest of X to pursue Y or Z. Rather, I mean that state X has *expressed* interest in pursuing Y or Z. At the EU level, the expression of national interests takes place notably in the form of "national positions" in the Council of the European Union. In turn, the "general interest of the Union" is understood here as the interest of the EU as a whole as defined by EU institutions. I will discuss these concepts in detail in Chapter 3.

33 *Treaty on European Union*, article 17.

34 European Commission, *Joint European Roadmap towards Lifting COVID-19 Containment Measures* (2020).

35 Lili Bayer, "Brussels Drops Lockdown Exit Plan after Anger from Capitals, *Politico* (8 April 2020), www.politico.eu/article/commission-to-unveil-exit-strategy-as-countries-push-to-lift-coronameasures/ (accessed 28 August 2020).

36 Consider the cases of tax avoidance and climate change. See Rupert Neate, "12 EU States Reject Move to Expose Companies' Tax Avoidance, *The Guardian* (28 November 2019), www.theguardian.com/business/2019/nov/28/12-eu-states-reject-move-to-expose-companies-tax-avoidance (accessed 18 September 2020); and Paola Tamma, "EU Leaders Fail to Commit to Climate Neutrality in 2050", *Politico* (22 June 2019), www.politico.eu/article/eu-leaders-fail-to-commit-to-climate-neutrality-by-2050/ (accessed 18 September 2020).

37 See, for instance, Larry Siedentop, *Democracy in Europe* (New York, 2001) and John R. Gillingham, *The EU: An Obituary* (London, 2016).

38 *Treaty on European Union*, article 1. Note that, in some analyses, the concept "ever closer Union" has been understood in terms of a telos of ever-increasing competencies for the Union, or a functional imperative of political integration emerging from economic integration. However, as I shall claim in Chapter 5, the perspective of civic amity is more useful in making this expression meaningful in the present-day EU.

39 Robert Schuman, *The Schuman Declaration* (9 May 1950).

40 BBC, "Europe and Right-Wing Nationalism: A Country-by-Country Guide" (13 November 2019), www.bbc.com/news/world-europe-36130006 (accessed 26 April 2022).

41 Jean-Claude Junker, *State of the Union Address 2017* (13 September 2017), https://ec.europa.eu/commission/presscorner/detail/en/SPEECH_17_3165 (accessed 27 July 2023).

42 A few authors have pointed to a decreasing concern for the common good in modern societies. For instance, Robert Putnam has conducted empirical research on the weakening of the sense of membership of communities in the United States. In the field of moral philosophy, Gertrude Himmelfarb has claimed that the moral standards of modern societies have been deteriorating. See Robert D. Putnam, *Bowling Alone: The Collapse and Revival of American Community* (New York, 2001) and Gertrude Himmelfarb, *The De-Moralization of Society: From Victorian Virtues to Modern Values* (New York, 1996).

43 Council of the European Union, *Conference on the Future of Europe* (24 June 2020), www.consilium.europa.eu/media/44679/st09102-en20.pdf (accessed 22 September 2020).

44 For influential accounts of the common good in the history of political thought, see Aristotle, *The Politics*, ed. R.F. Stalley (Oxford, 2009); Aquinas, *Political Writings*, ed. R.W. Dyson (Cambridge, 2002); Jean-Jacques Rousseau, *The Social Contract and Other Later Political Writings*, ed. Victor Gourevitch (Cambridge, 2018).

45 See, among others, Michael Walzer, *Spheres of Justice: A Defence of Pluralism and Equality* (New York, 1983); Charles Taylor, "Atomism", in Shlomo Avineri and Avner de-Shalit (eds), *Communitarianism and Individualism* (Oxford, 1992); Amitai Etzioni, *The Spirit of Community* (New York, 1993). As Daniel Bell points out, a few influential authors such as Alasdair MacIntyre and Michael Sandel do not regard themselves as communitarians, yet have been labelled as such by their critics because they share "certain core arguments meant to contrast with liberalism's devaluation of community". See Alasdair MacIntyre, *After Virtue* (Notre-Dame, 1984) and Michael J. Sandel, *Liberalism and the Limits of Justice* (Cambridge, 1998). For the quote, see Daniel Bell, "Communitarianism", *The Stanford Encyclopedia of Philosophy* (Fall 2022 Edition), Edward N. Zalta and Uri Nodelman (eds), https://plato.stanford.edu/archives/fall2022/entries/communitarianism/ (accessed 27 July 2023).

46 References to the EU by communitarian scholars are relatively loose and unsystematic. For instance, in an interview where he discussed the withdrawal of the United Kingdom from the EU, Michael Sandel expressed "some sympathy" for the goal of "taking back control, restoring control over the forces that govern our lives and giving people a voice", claiming that Brexit has been better for the UK than for the EU. However, no general analysis of the merits of regional integration is presented. More generally, communitarianism seems to have a blind spot vis-à-vis the EU. See Michael Sandel, "The Energy of the Brexiteers and Trump is Born of the Failure of Elites", *The New Statesman* (13 June 2016), www.newstatesman.com/politics/2016/06/michael-sandel-the-energy-of-the-brexiteers-and-trump-is-born-of-the-failure-of-elites (accessed 16 June 2022).

47 The point that the EU does not qualify as a community has been made by Amitai Etzioni, perhaps the only influential communitarian who has openly discussed the EU case. According to Etzioni, the EU has a "communitarian deficit". See Amitai Etzioni, "The EU: The Communitarian Deficit", *European Societies* 15 (2013), pp. 312–330.

48 See, for instance, George Steiner, *The Idea of Europe: An Essay* (New York, 2015); Thomas Risse, *A Community of Europeans? Transnational Identities and Public Spheres* (Ithaca, 2010); Étienne François and Thomas Serrier (eds), *Europa: Notre Histoire* (Paris, 2019); Stefan Berger, "Remembering the Second World War in Western Europe, 1945–2005", in M. Pakier and B. Stråth (eds), *A European Memory: Contested Histories and Politics of Remembrance* (2010); Claus Leggewie, "Equally Criminal? Totalitarian Experience and European Memory", *Transit Online* (2007), www.iwm.at/transit-online/equally-criminal-totalitarian-experience-and-european-memory (accessed 28 August 2023).
49 Sandel, "The Energy of the Brexiteers and Trump Is Born of the Failure of the Elites.
50 For an overview of the normative turn in EU studies, see Heidrun Friese and Peter Wagner, "Survey Article: The Nascent Political Philosophy of the European Polity", *Journal of Political Philosophy* 10 (2002), pp. 342–364.
51 See, among others, Rainer Bauböck, "Why European Citizenship? Normative Approaches to Supranational Union", *Theoretical Inquiries in Law* 8 (2007), pp. 453–488; Richard Bellamy, *A Republican Europe of States: Cosmopolitanism, Intergovernmentalism, and Democracy in the EU* (Cambridge, 1999); Richard Bellamy and Dario Castiglione, "Between Cosmopolis and Community: Three Models of Rights and Democracy within the European Union", in Daniele Archibugi, David Held and Martin Köhler (eds), *Re-imagining Political Community: Studies in Cosmopolitan Democracy* (Stanford, 1998); F. Cheneval and F. Schimmelfennig, "The Case for Demoicracy in the European Union", *Journal of Common Market Studies* 51 (2013), pp. 334–350; Dieter Grimm, "The Democratic Costs of Constitutionalisation: The European Case", *European Law Journal* 21 (2015), pp. 460–473; Jürgen Habermas, "Why Europe Needs a Constitution", *New Left Review* 11 (2001), pp. 5–26; Andrew Moravcsik, "In Defence of the Democratic Deficit: Reassessing Legitimacy in the European Union", *Journal of Common Market Studies* 40 (2002), pp. 603–624; Kalypso Nicolaidis, "Demoicracy and its Critics", *Journal of Common Market Studies* 51 (2013), pp. 351–369; Miriam Ronzoni, "The European Union as a Demoicracy: Really a Third Way?", *European Journal of Political Theory* 16 (2017), pp. 210–234.
52 See Julie Dickson and Pavlos Eleftheriadis (eds), *Philosophical Foundations of European Union Law* (Oxford, 2012).
53 John Rawls, *A Theory of Justice: Revised Edition* (Cambridge MA, 1999), p. 205.
54 See Andrea Sangiovanni, "How Practices Matter", *Journal of Political Philosophy* (2016), pp. 3–23.
55 There has been an ongoing debate as to whether feasibility is a relevant attribute of a given political theory. To address this question, I have distinguished elsewhere "pervasive unfeasibility" from "temporary unfeasibility". Pervasive unfeasibility is linked to barriers that human agency cannot reasonably be expected to overcome, such as the high efficiency costs associated with certain policy proposals. In turn, temporary unfeasibility results from circumstances

that can arguably be overcome, such as the preferences of voters at a specific moment of time. I argue that political theorists should take "pervasive unfeasibility" into account, while disregarding "temporary unfeasibility". I discuss the reasons why in João Labareda, *Towards a Just Europe: A Theory of Distributive Justice for the European Union* (Manchester, 2021).
56 See Robert D. Putnam, "Diplomacy and Domestic Politics: The Logic of Two-Level Games", *International Organization* 42 (1988), pp. 427–460.

1

What is the common good?

Introduction

This chapter develops a conceptual framework to analyse the problem of the common good in a morally and culturally diverse European Union (EU). It addresses the following questions: What is the common good? On what philosophical grounds, if any, can a diverse group of states, such as Denmark, Italy and Poland, speak of their common good? What are public values? Can public values translate a shared conception of the common good in a diverse polity? I claim that public values – understood as the values endorsed by the fundamental laws of a polity, such as constitutions and international treaties – provide guidance regarding what fundamental conditions and goals a society considers desirable. All citizens of a given polity are expected to uphold its public values, regardless of their individual preferences and worldviews. By bridging the substantial moral differences amongst citizens, public values create a common standpoint against which both individual conduct and public policies ought to be assessed. I argue that this critical role of public values does not apply exclusively within the nation-state. When the public values endorsed by a given group of states overlap significantly or when they explicitly endorse common values through international agreements (as in the EU), it is plausible to speak of transnational conceptions of the common good. I suggest that shared understandings of the common good within groups of states will be thicker or thinner depending on the extent to which their public values overlap. Regarding the relations between polities with clashing conceptions of the common good, such as the United States and Iran, I claim that states should, in principle, respect each other's conception, provided that they do not perform gross and systemic violations of the fundamental rights enshrined in international law. However, I argue that even highly diverse political communities can usually reach a basic level of moral agreement when it comes to addressing certain fundamental global challenges, including climate change and HIV/AIDS, warranting talk of a *global* common good.

I begin by defining the concept of the common good and situating it within the landscape of contemporary political theory. I also identify a few key challenges to which the common good has recently been exposed. Then, I introduce the notion of public values and discuss their main features. Subsequently, I investigate whether and to what extent public values may apply beyond the nation-state. I discuss two moral principles to guide the relations between states and regions that have clashing conceptions of the common good. Furthermore, I present a few trade-offs linked to the transnational pursuit of the common good that may imply sacrificing some national interests. Finally, I briefly outline a strategy to advance the common good beyond borders.

The common good: a conceptual framework

The common good: still a useful concept?

Since the concept of the common good is simultaneously "self-evident and confused", it pays to begin with a definition.[1] By common good, I mean the conditions and goals that benefit a community as a whole without imposing impermissible harm on some of its members. This definition emphasises two critical aspects. To begin with, the common good refers to conditions and goals that benefit a political community at large, as opposed to limited groups of individuals. While, as we shall see, pursuing the common good does not always mean improving the well-being of *all* citizens, policies for the common good are expected to generate benefits for at least the large majority of them and provide a compelling justification for the sacrifices they may require from the remaining groups.[2] Note that, as has rightly been argued, these widespread benefits cannot always be captured by means of summing individual utilities in a narrow utilitarian fashion.[3] For example, investing in a public school system benefits not only students who attend better-equipped schools but also the broader community by improving literacy levels, enhancing innovation capacity and promoting social mobility. Indeed, these are conditions and goals that most societies consider desirable. Therefore, the notion of the common good is not normatively redundant on a purely aggregative moral doctrine.[4]

Second, this definition emphasises the point that the common good should not be advanced at any cost.[5] As I will claim, the pursuit of the common good provides moral grounds to demand certain sacrifices from some citizens and social groups, but there are limits as to what should be asked on behalf of the greater good. For instance, redistributing wealth and income typically reduces socioeconomic inequalities within a community. Reduced inequality, in turn, improves the physical and mental health of citizens, strengthens the educational performance of children and diminishes the level of violence, thereby contributing to the common good.[6] However, if scaled up to a degree in which the marginal utilities of individuals would be equalised, as Peter Singer has famously suggested, redistribution may jeopardise certain fundamental individual rights, notably the right to property.[7] Crucially, certain policies that may enhance the common good imply morally unacceptable bodily or psychological harm. Consider, for example, the use of torture to obtain information about the location of the members of a terrorist group. These cases suggest that the common good is not an *ultimate* goal – that is, it should be weighed against other relevant considerations. Therefore, pursuing the common good is incompatible with imposing *morally impermissible harm*, which this book shall equate with gross violations of fundamental rights.[8]

So why does the common good matter at all? As will become apparent, this concept is particularly relevant as a means to provide justification for much-needed yet politically and economically demanding reforms, as well as to contest policy agendas that only serve the interests of small and privileged groups. This point has been forcefully made within the "contractarian" tradition, for whom the primary purpose of creating a network of shared political institutions supported by a monopoly of force is to improve the *general* welfare – not just that of a few individuals. Relying on the idea of the social contract – either in an explicit, tacit, or hypothetical format – contractarian authors have argued that citizens would only consent to the creation of a coercive state if this would allow collective action problems to be solved and the provision of certain goods that improve everyone's living standards.[9] Accordingly, John Rawls has stated that "[g]overnment is assumed to aim at the common good".[10] Yet, as has been widely documented, contemporary policymaking processes are to a large extent shaped by well-organised private interests, which have a disproportional capacity to influence policy outcomes.[11] All too often, the agendas of certain political parties, business conglomerates, and religious groups are prioritised over the common good in domains as varied as public health, education and environmental protection. This state of affairs calls for a renewed debate about the pursuit of the common good.[12]

However, contemporary political theorists have increasingly regarded this concept as problematic. In their view, the following question has become unavoidable: How can there be a *common* good in highly diverse societies? For authors such as Aristotle and Jean-Jacques Rousseau, moral diversity did not present itself as a major challenge against the pursuit of the common good since the content of public policies would be determined by relatively small city-states and republics where a consensus was usually in reach through effective public deliberation.[13] In turn, for a medieval philosopher such as St. Thomas Aquinas, the shared ethical framework provided by a common religion under Christendom would leave no room for fundamental disagreements about the nature of goodness.[14] Yet, due to the processes of modernisation and secularisation, societies became more heterogeneous and plural. This development has led to the coexistence of multiple conceptions of goodness, which cannot always be reconciled. Given this change of circumstances, and despite having been a recurrent theme throughout the history of political thought, the common good has been relegated to a secondary role by contemporary political theorists. At present, the so-called communitarian scholars remain its leading proponents, notably Michael Walzer, Charles Taylor and Amitai Etzioni.[15]

Yet these authors have arguably failed to provide compelling answers as to how the concept of the common good can accommodate the changes wrought by modernisation and secularisation, particularly when it comes to moral and cultural diversity and global interdependence. Indeed, most communitarians still associate the conception of the common good of a given political community with a set of moral beliefs and social and cultural norms widely shared in that community, which they typically take for granted.[16] However, this implausibly replicates the assumptions about cultural homogeneity and broad moral consensus underpinning the works of Aristotle and Aquinas, which no longer hold in contemporary societies. Furthermore, unlike what communitarians seem to assume, self-governing communities such as the nation-state currently lack sufficient means to realise the common good.[17] In fact, given the high level of interdependence that globalisation has brought about, political communities increasingly need each other to pursue the common good. For example, the goal of addressing climate change, which many nation-states consider desirable, can only be fulfilled through close transnational cooperation. As we shall see, the transnational nature of the common good is particularly apparent in the EU case, for which communitarianism has a blind spot.[18] Therefore, a compelling account of the common good for the 21st century will have to accommodate these significant developments.

A few methodological challenges

It is worth noting that the conceptual difficulties underpinning the common good are not only linked to a change in historical circumstances but also to some complex epistemological issues. How can we know, or agree on, what the common good stands for? The so-called epistemic account of democracy advocates "the capacity of 'the many' to make correct decisions and seeks to justify democracy by reference to this ability".[19] In its classical formulation, this view presupposes the existence of independent standards of truth against which competing policy options can be assessed.[20] Thus, on this account, a key challenge is designing procedures through which the "good" options may be effectively selected.

Yet political communities face at least a degree of epistemic uncertainty under which it may be difficult to foresee which course of action will advance the common good.[21] For example, in the face of Russia's threat to invade Ukraine, Western states had to decide whether to adopt bold preventive measures or explore diplomatic channels without knowing which options would be more effective. In addition, "the many" may clearly make bad decisions.[22] Consider, for instance, the victory of the National Socialist Party in the 1933 elections in Germany. Such outcomes have bred "suspicion about the use of independent standards of correctness or truth in the realm of democratic decision making".[23]

Alternatively, it may be plausibly argued that the common good is a socially constructed moral standpoint. According to this view, each polity's understanding of "good" and "bad" collective choices depends on what its citizens have defined as standards of public morality, typically through the mediation of political institutions. Instead of taking the common good as a given, this account equates the latter with *explicit* moral commitments by a community.[24] It thus regards the common good as an "essentially contested concept" in relation to which each community may have more or less plausible *conceptions*.[25] This view is more compelling than the epistemic account, given that it is ready to accommodate the circumstances of moral pluralism and epistemic uncertainty described above.[26] However, it does not automatically circumvent the question of how a common standard of goodness can be found in a morally diverse society in the first place. Indeed, given the high level of moral and political polarisation in many present-day polities, the Rawlsian hypothesis of "overlapping consensus" between competing comprehensive doctrines of the good will hardly hold.[27] If it is reasonable to assume that "individuals have some degree of interpretive competence or authority in the identification and interpretation of common goods", then one will need to identify clearly the putative source of a common moral standpoint that guides collective choices.[28]

Therefore, in order to articulate a conceptual framework of the common good that is suitable for a highly diverse and interdependent EU, we will need to address the following questions: On what philosophical grounds, if any, can a group of states as diverse as Denmark, Italy and Poland speak of their common good? How can we know what specific good(s) are constitutive elements of the conception of the common good of any particular polity, such as the EU? In this chapter, I will claim that these questions can be tackled effectively by analysing the *public values* endorsed by the political institutions of the communities at stake. I will argue that public values provide a common standpoint to normatively assess public choices, irrespective of the multiplicity of private conceptions of the good. As we shall see, these values are outlined in the fundamental sources of any legal order, notably constitutions and international agreements. Subsequently, in Chapter 2, I will apply this theoretical framework to the EU. I will claim that the question of whether a culturally diverse EU where EU citizens are socially detached could share common standards of public morality has to be addressed in light of the international treaties that its member states have *voluntarily entered into* with one another. I will show that EU treaties are morally loaded and provide robust grounds for a shared conception of the common good.

Note that this study of the public values of the EU will have to be complemented by a pragmatic discussion concerning the institutional practices by which these values could be realised.[29] Indeed, the following question will be in order: What types of institutional rules and procedures could facilitate the pursuit of the conception of the common good enshrined in the EU treaties? While in recent years, several proposals to improve the standards of public deliberation have been put forward by the specialised literature, they do not always offer practicable solutions for a transnational polity with nearly 450 million citizens and 24 official languages.[30] Furthermore, a system of multilevel governance, such as the EU, brings about unique challenges that call for tailor-made solutions. Therefore, the question of how to make EU policymaking more oriented towards the common good remains largely unaddressed. As I will argue, the main challenge at the EU level is related to the chronic conflicts of national interests. In a nutshell, even if the member states have agreed, or were to agree, on common values, it may still be hard to mobilise the resources and means to put them into practice. This difficulty is particularly salient given that the institutional architecture of the EU does not comprise a fully-fledged supranational government. I will discuss these issues in detail in Chapters 3 and 4.

What are public values?

Values can be defined as points of reference that provide guidance regarding what is good and bad.[31] In what follows, I will focus on a particular category of values that has been scarcely analysed by moral and political theory – namely, *public* values. Public values are the values endorsed by the political institutions of a polity, notably by explicitly granting them a binding status in the fundamental laws that govern all public policies, state–citizen relations and the relations among citizens.[32] Understood in this way, public values are those values enshrined in the political constitutions of states, as well as in sources with equivalent legal status, such as charters and bills of rights and certain international agreements and conventions.[33] Examples of familiar public values endorsed by most liberal democracies are the rule of law, solidarity, equality (with its many qualifiers, including *social*, *gender* and *intergenerational* equality) and freedom (namely, of expression, association, the press, and so on). As I will claim below, political communities tend to gradually develop the meaning and implications of their values through policymaking processes, landmark judicial decisions and continuous public debates. This interactive process – which I dub the *interpretation of public values* – allows societies to translate such values into particular models of social relations and institutional practices.

What is crucial about public values is that they provide a basic degree of normative consensus that allows citizens to assess social arrangements and patterns of behaviour through common moral lenses despite their different moral outlooks.[34] In contrast to *personal* values, *public* values are not connected to one's particular worldview, ethical convictions or religious beliefs. They provide normative guidance to all public officials and citizens, regardless of their respective backgrounds and perspectives. In doing so, public values create a common viewpoint from which collective choices can be publicly labelled as "good" or "bad" – the *standpoint of the common good*.[35] It should be emphasised that public values do not consist of an all-encompassing code of conduct.[36] As a result, they are compatible with diverse private understandings of the good life. Yet, by the very fact that they have been granted constitutional status, public values have *priority* over private conceptions of the good. For instance, in a political community that has endorsed the value of equality, individuals are expected to make collective choices on the grounds of an egalitarian standpoint, regardless of their ethical convictions and religious beliefs.[37] Admittedly, this expectation presupposes a willingness to compromise for the sake of the community. As I will claim in Chapter 5, this can realistically be achieved in the presence of *civic friendship*.[38]

Now, this conceptual framework raises a few questions that deserve close examination. First, what if a polity has endorsed a set of public values that are morally objectionable? Consider, for instance, a constitution that fails to recognise the value of socioeconomic equality, as in the case of the constitution of Chile.[39] Should constitutions that arguably encompass an undesirable conception of the common good be disregarded? Second, what can be said about cases where public values are one thing on paper and another in practice? For example, the Chinese constitution asserts the equality of all ethnic groups, but the Chinese authorities reportedly persecute the Uyghur minority.[40] What conditions should be fulfilled for a value to be meaningfully endorsed by political institutions? Third, what if the values enshrined in a constitution are not representative of the whole society? Consider, for instance, the 52 (out of 195) world constitutions that fail to sanction gender equality.[41] Can the values of these constitutions still be said to express the standpoint of the common good? Fourth, how exactly does the interpretation of public values work in practice? Can it overcome the fact that certain states do not possess a written constitution? Finally, if public values are crystallised in enduring legal sources such as constitutions and international treaties, how do they accommodate the fact that societies undergo moral change? Can public values also change? I will address each of these issues in turn.

I should begin by explaining why, in most cases, this book takes public values at face value – that is, in how they are phrased in constitutions and other equivalent legal sources. Note that my purpose is not to discuss whether the public values of a given polity are normatively desirable but to investigate whether the values of different political communities may overlap and, if so, to what extent. This exercise calls for empirical sources that allow for meaningful comparisons. By relying on constitutions and international agreements, one can test in a systematic manner the existence of transnational conceptions of the common good.[42] Admittedly, this methodological approach is exposed to the charge that the values endorsed by certain communities translate objectionable conceptions of the common good.

Yet conducting a normative assessment of the values of each political community also comes with distinct risks. To begin with, unless one adopts some form of moral realism, it is difficult to adjudicate categorically which public values are desirable and which are not.[43] Furthermore, a few past attempts to perform similar exercises have simplistically assumed that liberal values are preferable.[44] Therefore, while not every public value is normatively sound, referring to each polity's current inventory of values presents as the most promising strategy.

However, this does not exclude the application of certain basic plausibility criteria. To begin with, it is crucial to ensure a correspondence between the letter of the law and the institutional practices within a political community. Indeed, "[c]onstitutions in authoritarian regimes are often denigrated as meaningless exercises in political theatre".[45] For instance, the Portuguese constitution of 1933 enshrined values such as freedom of expression and association that the authoritarian regime of the Portuguese dictator António de Oliveira Salazar scarcely intended to implement.[46] This variance suggests that an appropriate threshold for a value to qualify as *public* value should incorporate a high level of compliance, not merely explicit adoption through a constitutional text.[47] Furthermore, public values should be reasonably representative of the citizens that they are meant to bind. Note that, in some polities, the values of a particular social group are brutally imposed on other citizens. Consider, for example, the case of the Sunni rule of Iraq under Saddam Hussein, in which a religious minority shaped the values of the whole community. This systemic discrimination of a group of citizens jeopardises the ability of public values to function as a standpoint that can be plausibly regarded as the common good. As we shall see, this suggests that any plausible conception of the common good presupposes the fulfilment of certain fundamental rights.

Let me now turn to the interpretation of public values. Interpreting public values means deliberating about alternative ways of putting them into practice and making corresponding choices. This specification is crucial because, as I have mentioned, values are only points of reference – that is, they are generic and abstract by definition. To illustrate the point, consider the public value of solidarity. Once a political community has endorsed this value, it must decide how it will be realised. For example, solidarity may be translated into universal access to healthcare, a progressive taxation system or access to unemployment benefits. In turn, the healthcare system may be run by the state or the private sector and offer more or less comprehensive coverage. In the specific context of Western democracies, these choices have led to the development of distinctive models of democracy and social welfare that aim at realising similarly democratic public values.[48] It should be added that this process of interpretation takes place through a variety of channels. For instance, at the EU level, the value of solidarity has been interpreted through a wide range of legislation, policy measures, judicial decisions, and public debates.[49] Note that this requirement to interpret public values is not a shortcoming. Rather, it ensures they become a widely internalised moral standpoint. Multiple channels of interpretation also exist in states that, despite not having written constitutions, possess functioning "constitutional orders".[50]

Finally, it is worth addressing briefly the issue of moral change. The fact that societies undergo moral change, at times leading to what have been dubbed "moral revolutions", is undeniable.[51] A constitutional order is able to accommodate such calls in at least two ways. First, the interpretation of the existing public values by judges, policymakers and citizens may evolve as a result of the resetting of the moral compass of society. For instance, many democracies have legalised same-sex marriage by expanding their interpretation of the values of equality and liberty.[52] Second, more radical changes may be institutionalised through effective constitutional amendments or even the redrafting of the constitution. Note that none of these options is merely hypothetical. For example, the Constitution of the United States has been amended 27 times.[53] Similarly, in 1958, France – already a consolidated democracy – elected to rewrite its constitution in the face of profound social and moral change.[54] It should be added that the public values enshrined in constitutions and international agreements may themselves induce moral change, as during the transition from communism to democracy in several former communist states of Central and Eastern Europe. Therefore, public values allow us to capture a community's conception of the common good without prejudice of moral change.

Cultural values versus public values

How does this conceptual framework relate to the uses of values in public discourse? In recent years, values have featured increasingly in European politics. President Emmanuel Macron of France went as far as to say that values are "the most precious feature of a nation, which keeps it alive and makes it great".[55] Yet many public officials do not share the understanding of public values presented above. Instead, they refer to what I dub *cultural values* – that is, points of reference that offer guidance on what is "good" and "bad" based on the social and cultural practices of a specific group. To illustrate the point, consider the EU immigration crisis. In many heated public debates on this matter, the leaders of a few far-right parties conveyed the message that immigrants were undermining "our values", by which they meant cultural categories of values such as "national values", "Christian values" and "Western values". Yet these categories remain underspecified. For example, according to Prime Minister Viktor Orbán, "Hungarian values" can be equated with "Christian values" – even if, as an observer has pointed out, "the policies of Orbán's government don't seem to be particularly Christian".[56] This fluidity suggests that cultural values are poorly codified. In what follows, my goal is not to claim that cultural values are meaningless but rather that they do not offer a consistent basis to approach the common good.

Indeed, cultural values have several shortcomings when it comes to establishing a common moral standpoint in a given society. To begin with, the lack of codification that I have alluded to empowers political actors to shape the meaning of cultural values according to their interests and needs. Consider, for example, the terrorist attack against the headquarters of the French satirical magazine *Charlie Hebdo* in January 2015. In the aftermath of this tragic event, Marine Le Pen of the far-right National Rally contrasted a self-serving understanding of "French values" to those of the Islamic world.[57] While French values were said to be strongly attached to a culture of freedom and toleration, Islamic values were linked to violence and fundamentalism. Paradoxically, the Islamophobia that this recurrent type of public discourse helped generate reportedly caused an increase in anti-Muslim acts in France, thereby further challenging the values that the terrorists had targeted in the first place.[58] Furthermore, cultural values are not usually subject to scrutiny and are not easily contestable. For instance, in oppressive societies, certain discriminated social groups, such as women and LGBTIQ people, may lack a real chance to challenge dominant worldviews and standard cultural practices. This lack of contestability indicates that the cultural values of a large social group should not be directly labelled as public values.

Understanding public values as the values that the political institutions of a nation-state have *explicitly endorsed* has several advantages compared to the alternative of defining them as the cultural values of an "imagined community".[59] First, unlike any unwritten set of cultural values, public values are clearly listed in official documents, and their meaning is interpreted by political institutions in formal proceedings. This publicity provides a clear and widely acknowledged basis for a shared understanding of the common good. Second, as I have shown, public values are contestable and can change. Accordingly, in the presence of representative political institutions, public values will likely not be merely equivalent to the values of a dominant ethnic or religious group. Third, rather than taking a cultural identity for granted, which is a problematic assumption in today's increasingly multicultural societies, public values are the outcome of the social construction of a shared civic identity. This perspective accommodates the fact that in every state, many individuals with different cultural backgrounds abide by the same common moral code.[60] In fact, the large majority of the Islamic community of France, which represents 8.8% of the French population, complies with the French public values, regardless of their cultural background and religious beliefs.[61] Finally, as the following sections will show, understanding national values as publicly endorsed values allows us to investigate the overlaps and disjunctions between "our values" and "the values of others" in a systematic manner.

This line of reasoning suggests that framing the normative diversity across borders in terms of a "clash of civilisations" offers us scant help in making sense of the moral outlook of the international system.[62] Different national communities may uphold diverse values, but this is not *necessarily* a by-product of their contrasting cultures. If this were the case, how would we explain the common list of public values endorsed by the citizens of Switzerland, a country comprised of French, Italian and German-speaking cantons? In fact, the function of explicit and contestable public values as a common standpoint of goodness is what allows highly diverse states to make sound collective choices. Crucially, this argument can be extrapolated: if it is possible to articulate a common standpoint for the nation-state, despite the diversity within it, then nothing should prevent us from thinking that there could be common standpoints beyond borders. While the degree of institutionalisation of values is admittedly lower beyond the nation-state than within, a rich array of international treaties, agreements and conventions provides grounds for (at least minimalistic) regional and global standpoints of the common good. As we shall see, even countries with very different moral outlooks have worked together to fulfil certain basic requirements of the common good.

The common good at the regional and global levels

Public values beyond borders

In the last decades, an extensive institutional framework has emerged through the signing of international agreements. Many of these voluntary agreements are morally loaded, revealing the fact that a few public values are shared across national borders. For instance, the 191 states that have ratified the Treaty on the Non-Proliferation of Nuclear Weapons have jointly endorsed the values of peace, security and cooperation.[63] Note that this treaty is not just a statement of good intentions; indeed, it is subject to regular reviews that recommend follow-up actions.[64] Similarly, the Convention against Torture and Other Cruel, Inhuman or Degrading Treatment or Punishment commits its 173 members to the value of human dignity, establishing a common understanding of this value, particularly by setting certain mandatory requirements concerning the treatment of individuals, which are monitored by the Committee against Torture.[65] In turn, the 182 states that are part of the International Convention on the Elimination of All Forms of Racial Discrimination endorsed jointly the values of equality and non-discrimination.[66] On the grounds of this convention, the Committee on the Elimination of Racial Discrimination has developed a comprehensive jurisprudence on discriminatory practices.[67] By joining these conventions, the signatory states have expressed the view that a good world is one without war, torture and racism. In doing so, they have built a shared – even if minimalistic – understanding of goodness.

Yet the overlap of public values on the international stage goes beyond basic moral standards. Indeed, the so-called "like-minded states" often feature remarkably similar moral outlooks.[68] For example, liberal democracies such as Norway, Australia and Japan endorse analogous public values, including the rule of law, freedom of speech and accountable government. Even if their interpretation of these values may differ, they clearly share a similar "grammar of the common good".[69] Sharing a range of values allows these countries to assess certain international developments from a similar standpoint. For example, a large group of democratic states have jointly condemned human rights violations in China, Russia's invasion of Ukraine and the deforestation of the Amazon rainforest. Similarly, communist states such as Laos, Cuba and Venezuela share a constellation of public values denouncing the wrongdoings of capitalism and imperialism.

Crucially, many like-minded states have joined international organisations that in themselves presuppose certain common values.[70] In fact, some of these organisations have the explicit purpose of advancing a particular set of values. Consider, for instance, the Council of Europe, which aims to promote human rights, democracy and the rule of law.[71]

This moral convergence is nowhere as visible as in the ongoing processes of regional integration. Regional associations, such as the EU, the Association of Southeast Asian Nations (ASEAN) and the Southern Common Market (Mercosur), are grounded on and governed by voluntary international agreements that generate significant normative commitments for their signatories. Indeed, EU membership is conditional on endorsing the values listed in the EU treaties. Building on Ian Manners' research, the next chapter will claim that EU values are sustainable peace, social liberty, consensual democracy, associative human rights, supranational rule of law, inclusive equality, social solidarity, sustainable development and good governance.[72] In turn, the ASEAN Charter advances, among others, the values of the rule of law, good governance, democracy, the promotion and protection of human rights and the promotion of social justice.[73] Along the same lines, Mercosur has enacted protocols regarding the protection and promotion of democracy and human rights, which foresee the possibility of suspending the membership of non-compliant states.[74] Accordingly, as I will argue in Chapter 2, it is plausible to speak of "European" values, "Southeast Asian" values and "South American" values if the latter are equated with the values publicly endorsed within the respective regional frameworks.[75]

This line of argument suggests that it is possible to articulate meaningful conceptions of the common good beyond the nation-state. In the context of the relations between like-minded states, particularly within regional associations, potentially thick shared understandings of the common good may be identified by referring to the values enshrined in the international agreements upon which these organisations are grounded. By applying this strategy, we may speak of the common good of the EU without facing serious charges of conceptual indeterminacy.[76]

In turn, we can consistently speak of the *global common good* by referring to the values explicitly endorsed by a large majority of world states.[77] Despite the diversity of national conceptions of the common good, significant normative overlaps can be found. I have already mentioned the widespread recognition of goods such as non-proliferation, human dignity and non-discrimination, but many other examples of transnational moral consensus could be added. For instance, most states regard environmental protection as a morally desirable goal. This commitment has allowed them to establish common decarbonisation targets, regardless of their disagreements in other domains. The point that a degree of consensus is possible amongst morally diverse states is powerfully illustrated by the fact that the Paris Climate Agreement brought together countries with contrasting moral outlooks, ranging from Israel and Pakistan to Laos and the Holy See.[78]

Of course, this cooperation does not obscure the serious moral disagreements on the international stage. For example, when it comes to the value of human life, states have positioned themselves on different sides of the fence. While 90 countries have endorsed the Protocol to the International Covenant on Civil and Political Rights, which seeks to abolish the death penalty, 110 states have taken no action towards its adoption.[79] More generally, the moral outlooks endorsed by certain states are noticeably in tension with each other. Consider, for example, the case of the United States and Iran. The American public values of religious toleration and freedom of speech seem to be at odds with the values of the "sovereignty of truth" and "Qur'anic justice" prescribed by the Constitution of the Islamic Republic of Iran.[80] Moreover, these contrasting understandings of the common good have generated serious political tensions. For instance, during the Iranian Revolution, the late Ayatollah Ruhollah Khomeini dubbed the United States "the Great Satan". Decades later, President George W. Bush famously labelled Iran as part of an "axis of evil".[81] Such examples raise the following questions: How should countries or regions with different conceptions of the common good interact? To what extent do these disagreements jeopardise the pursuit of the common good at the global level? The following sections will address these questions in detail.

Clashing conceptions of the common good

In this section, I will claim that states have a moral duty to respect each other's conceptions of the common good, provided that the conceptions at stake fulfil a crucial requisite. By respecting a state's conception of the common good, I mean (i) abstaining from any deliberate attempt to interfere in the domestic affairs of another state with the purpose of changing its public values and (ii) maintaining, to the extent possible, certain basic international conditions that allow the conceptions of the common good of other states to be realised. I shall refer to these two moral claims as the *principle of pluralism*. However, I will argue that the duty to comply with this principle is contingent on the fulfilment of a critical requirement – that the conception of the common good of a given state does not bring about the infliction of impermissible harm on its citizens or the citizens of other states. For the purpose of this discussion, I understand impermissible harm as a gross and systemic violation of fundamental rights as codified by international law. For example, the Nazi aspiration of creating an ethnically homogeneous and territorially enlarged German community through the suppression of minorities and the conquest of other nations would not be defensible on pluralistic grounds.[82] I shall dub this requisite as the *principle of respect for fundamental rights*. I will discuss these principles in turn.

Let us begin with the principle of pluralism. Why should states respect each other's conception of the common good? A key reason behind this claim is that a conception of the common good is an important instrument of self-determination. In a broad sense, "self-determination refers to a community's right to govern itself independently".[83] Respecting self-determination means that there are things that we should not do to sovereign states, "even if for their own ostensible good".[84] By coercively imposing its public values on another political community, a given state would undermine that community's ability to define autonomously the key goals that it aims to pursue. This does not mean that *nothing* should be done to promote moral change beyond borders. For example, refraining from "liberal imperialism" does not necessarily imply abstaining from advocating democratic values in the international sphere.[85] To be sure, it is plausible to conceive a world "where democracy spreads through dialogue and incentives, not coercion and war".[86] In particular, non-state actors such as NGOs and think tanks are well positioned to take part in non-hierarchical, non-paternalistic "democratic iterations" because they do not hold coercive power against the states where they would like to promote change.[87] This suggests that respect for moral diversity is compatible with improving the global moral outlook.[88]

What, then, does pluralism entail? At first glance, respecting the diversity of the conceptions of the common good presupposes compliance with the familiar norm of non-interference, according to which states should not meddle in each other's domestic affairs.[89] Yet, abiding by the pluralist principle also requires varying degrees of cooperation between countries with conflicting moral outlooks.[90] Note that if states refuse to engage with each other on the grounds of their moral disagreements, certain basic conditions for realising the common good in their domestic spheres may not be fulfilled.[91] The case of the United States and Cuba is illustrative. Here, two constellations of public values have been in conflict for decades. Given Cuba's geographical location, the functioning of its institutions is highly dependent on its economic relations with the United States. By embargoing trade with its island neighbour, the US government has significantly constrained Cuba's ability to realise the level of social welfare underpinning its public values.[92] A more extreme case is the current overuse of natural resources, which may ultimately leave little room for *any* state to pursue its conception of the common good. Hence, in a highly interdependent world, fulfilling the principle of pluralism presupposes the willingness of morally diverse states to work together.

Yet, the imperative of pluralism should be conditional on the fulfilment of certain fundamental rights, understood as the basic and inviolable rights and freedoms codified in international law.[93] Why is the observance of these rights so important? As has been widely argued, statehood generates duties for political institutions in their relations towards their citizens.[94] Even for a political thinker with authoritarian sympathies, such as Thomas Hobbes, membership in a polity is desirable only if it fosters individuals' chances of self-preservation.[95] These duties suggests that systemic violations of the fundamental rights of citizens are incompatible with any plausible understanding of the common good.[96] For example, authorities in countries that conduct arbitrary arrests, torture and the assassination of minorities on a regular basis cannot reasonably defend these practices by referring to a local understanding of the common good. What is at stake in these cases is not moral diversity but mass violence. While the systemic failure to comply with basic standards of decency does not automatically authorise the use of last-resort means such as humanitarian interventions, it may give grounds for the international community to actively seek a change in the status quo.[97] Therefore, the principle of pluralism should not apply to what John Rawls has referred to as "outlaw states".[98]

This view raises at least two difficult questions: (i) What rights should be regarded as fundamental? (ii) How to set the threshold beyond which fundamental rights violations should no longer be tolerated? Here, I can only provide some general guidelines.[99] Regarding the first question, it should be noted that in the last decades, several international treaties and conventions have codified a number of fundamental rights, including the right to life, bodily integrity and due process.[100] The question remains as to whether a more extensive list of fundamental rights is needed, one that would include, for instance, social rights and democracy.[101] Yet, for the specific purpose of flagging practices that are not worthy of respect under the principle of pluralism, the list of fundamental rights to apply should be relatively parsimonious, or it will risk mirroring the conception of the common good of one particular group of states.[102] Regarding the appropriate threshold to apply, the common denominator across different agencies that monitor compliance with fundamental rights is that violations should be gross and systemic.[103] These international bodies have developed a comprehensive body of case law concerning what counts as a gross and systemic violation. As the multiple international agreements mentioned above illustrate, there is a robust consensus around the list of fundamental rights currently recognised in international law.

Who should bear the burdens of the common good?

Regardless of how thick the moral agreement between a given group of states is, the pursuit of their common good may bring about intricate disputes about who should bear its burdens.[104] On the one hand, there may be grounds to sacrifice the interests of a particular state for the sake of others. To illustrate the point, consider a scarce resource, such as lithium. Assume that the government of Chile – which possesses 55% of the world reserves of this mineral – bans any exports of it to stimulate its national industries.[105] This policy would possibly increase the well-being of Chilean citizens by attracting foreign investment and creating better jobs. Yet, it would also likely retard the development and market uptake of green mobility solutions, which are highly dependent on lithium batteries, thus jeopardising the fight against climate change.[106] This scenario suggests that Chile is morally required to share its lithium reserves with other states.[107] On the other hand, it would seem morally wrong for a given region to seek its common good by means of imposing disproportional sacrifices on a particular state.[108] Yet such an outcome clearly obtains when, for instance, Western states promote high environmental standards in their territories by dispatching decommissioned ships to scrapyards in Bangladesh for polluting and hazardous disassembly. This example suggests that the common good of a given state or region should be pursued only to the extent that doing so does not imply inflicting impermissible harm on others.

Yet, what does *impermissible harm* mean in the context of interstate relations? While discussing this issue in the context of domestic state–citizen relations, I emphasised the moral requirement to respect fundamental rights. Now, if the fundamental rights of citizens are so significant from a normative standpoint, there is no reason to think that those of non-nationals should simply be ignored.[109] This point is particularly relevant for our discussion because the behaviour of a given polity may, in certain cases, dramatically condition the fulfilment of fundamental rights in other polities. An illustrative example is armed conflict. By invading Ukraine, Russia seriously breached the fundamental rights of Ukrainian citizens. This reasoning can duly be extended to several other domains. For instance, the current international division of labour, which has largely been shaped by Western states and multinational firms based in them, has consistently led to the violation of workers' fundamental rights in many developing countries.[110] Consequently, some states are at present able to ensure high levels of welfare for their citizens at the expense of the curtailment of fundamental rights elsewhere. Therefore, the limits to the pursuit of the common good of a state or region can be plausibly formulated in the following way: *the common good of a given state or region should only be pursued to the extent that it does not imply gross and systemic violations of fundamental rights of the citizens of other states or regions.*

A question that follows is how the trade-offs between the common good of different communities could be adjudicated while ensuring high standards of protection of fundamental rights across borders. As we shall see in the following chapters, the EU case offers a promising way forward. Realising the common good of the whole EU often requires sacrificing the interests of a particular member state. For example, ensuring the sustainability of the public finances of most member states required the Irish government to abandon its policy of tax heavens for digital companies, from which the Irish economy has benefited greatly. By the same token, any serious improvement in the working conditions in poor world regions may imply lower profit margins for EU companies and a potentially lower level of economic growth in the common market. Note that the EU possesses a comprehensive institutional framework where these and other trade-offs can be debated democratically, and compromises can be negotiated. Indeed, institutions such as the Council of the European Union and the European Parliament allow for a transnational debate concerning the distribution of the burdens of the common good. Furthermore, the institutional architecture of the EU polity comprises a supranational court which offers legal protection to the fundamental rights of the nearly 450 million individuals who live across the EU. As I shall claim, this form of regional integration facilitates the pursuit of the common good at the global level.

Towards a global common good

As I have argued, most states in the current international system share at least a limited set of public values. This common set allows for a common moral standpoint from which they regard certain conditions and goals as desirable – the standpoint of the *global common good*. Why, then, do they often fail to address challenges such as climate change and global inequality? What seems to be currently missing is not a moral consensus around the undesirable nature of these outcomes but the appropriate institutional setting and incentive structure to address them.[111] This gap has increased since nationalism has become "more prevalent in global politics in recent years".[112] Indeed, we seem to be facing a collective action problem: while at the normative level, most states agree that they should take more decisive action regarding these and other common challenges, they are usually unable to build the coalitions and mobilise the economic resources needed to address them. At the same time, even the most progressive democracies have resisted applying their high standards of respect for fundamental rights beyond their citizenries. Consider, for instance, the inhumane conditions of the Guantanamo prison and a few asylum centres in the EU member states.[113] As I will claim in Chapter 3, this mismatch between the endorsement of common values and the lack of means to realise them suggests that a more consistent pursuit of the common good will imply institutional reforms at the supranational level.

It will be a central contention of the following chapters that the most effective strategy to promote the common good beyond borders is upscaling the ongoing processes of regional integration. Regional organisations such as the EU, ASEAN and the Mercosur facilitate moral convergence, policy coordination and burden-sharing. Indeed, their institutional frameworks host regular political and technical dialogues through which shared understandings of the common good can be developed and put into practice. To the extent regional integration brings about repeated interactions between states, it creates sizeable incentives for taking one another's interests seriously.[114] Since membership in these organisations presupposes state neighbourhood, they are particularly well positioned to address challenges with a strong regional dimension, such as mobility of people, water management and energy supply. Furthermore, regional organisations tend to develop schemes of cooperation based on reciprocity, such as free trade and free movement areas, which typically comprise the recognition and enforcement of at least a few fundamental rights of foreign citizens. Crucially, regional organisations play an important role as aggregators of preferences. This role is critical for the pursuit of the global common good since it is easier to negotiate compromises among a few regional players than among the nearly 200 world states.

The strategy to advance the global common good through regional integration underpinning this book takes the status quo as a starting point but stresses two critical domains for improvement.[115] First, the competences of the existing regional organisations need to be updated and expanded in the face of the multiple challenges raised by globalisation. While comprehensive institutional frameworks already exist at the regional level, these frameworks possess limited means to deal with current challenges such as international tax evasion, water scarcity, social dumping and cyberterrorism.[116] Indeed, the scope of regulatory and enforcement mechanisms required to address these problems effectively is clearly higher than the status quo. Second, the functioning of regional institutions needs to be strongly geared towards the common good. In other words, these institutions should not be held hostage to the struggle of national interests. As we will see in Chapters 3 and 4, this objective could be achieved by (partially) emancipating regions from national governments – that is, by democratising them and creating direct links to citizens – and increasing their capacity to respond to global challenges. This change would legitimise regional organisations to become the main actors in key global frameworks such as the United Nations, thus facilitating the pursuit of the global common good.[117]

Nevertheless, the strategy of advancing the global common good through regional associations will need to be complemented by an upgrade of the global institutional framework. In fact, many states do not belong to any regional block, and some regional associations are too loose or too weak to significantly advance the common good. Accordingly, strengthening the mandate and resources of global institutions such as the United Nations, the World Bank and the World Trade Organisation is key to effectively address many of the challenges mentioned above.[118] Reforming these institutions would certainly not be an easy task, but it could be achieved if citizens increasingly pressed their governments to act upon such challenges.[119] Indeed, as I will claim in Chapter 5, the prospects of ambitious reforms of the global framework depend ultimately on a genuine concern for the global common good by the citizens and their willingness to act upon it. In this regard, regional integration may teach us important lessons on how transnational bonds can be strengthened, which could then be replicated at the global level. Hence, acting at both regional and global levels will be required to advance the common good.

Conclusion

I have argued that the common good is a useful concept for contemporary political theory whenever equated with the public values of a given political community. Public values are enshrined in the fundamental laws of a polity, notably constitutions and international agreements, and are interpreted by public debates, policymaking practices and judicial decisions. I have claimed that public values offer a common moral standpoint from which relevant collective choices can be made despite moral and cultural diversity. Public values need to be endorsed explicitly by the political institutions of a community; they are not equivalent to the values embedded in cultural practices and are not attached to a particular ethnic or religious group. Furthermore, I have claimed that there may be overlapping public values across borders, particularly between states that have concluded international agreements. I have argued that the international diversity of the conceptions of the common good should be respected, provided that the governments comply with the fundamental rights recognised in international law. Finally, I claimed that in a pluralist international system grounded on respect for fundamental rights, the chances of achieving the global common good could be maximised through regional integration.

Notes

1 Patrick Riordan, *A Grammar of the Common Good: Speaking of Globalisation* (London, 2008).
2 As I will claim, realising the common good of a group of individuals may require certain sacrifices by one or more of its members. Consider the cases in which the common good is achieved through certain risky professions,

such as firefighters, nurses and police officers. For this reason, I refrain from equating the common good with *equal* benefits for all citizens. However, it should be noted that this assumption is not consensual. For example, John Rawls has defined the common good as "maintaining conditions and achieving objectives that are similarly to everyone's advantage". For the quote, see John Rawls, *A Theory of Justice: Revised Edition* (Cambridge MA, 1999), p. 205. For a detailed discussion about the role of the common good in the works of John Rawls, see Roberto Luppi (ed.), *John Rawls and the Common Good* (New York, 2021).

3 See Charles Taylor, "Irreducibly Social Goods", *Philosophical Arguments* (Cambridge MA, 1997).

4 George Duke, "The Distinctive Common Good", *The Review of Politics* 78 (2016), pp. 227–250.

5 This claim has forcefully been made by the so-called "responsive communitarians", who attempt to balance the pursuit of the common good with the protection of certain key individual rights. See notably Amitai Etzioni, *The Common Good* (Cambridge, 2007).

6 For an influential formulation of this argument, see Kate Pickett and Richard Wilkinson, *The Spirit Level: Why More Equal Societies Almost Always Do Better* (New York, 2009). I shall discuss this issue in depth in Chapter 5.

7 Peter Singer, "Famine, Affluence and Morality", *Philosophy & Public Affairs* 1 (1972), pp. 229–243. The criticism that redistribution jeopardises individual rights has notably been put forward by Robert Nozick, *Anarchy, State and Utopia* (Malden, 1974).

8 Gross violations of fundamental rights are a reasonable proxy for impermissible harm because they cover particularly objectionable forms of behaviour that are jointly regarded as impermissible by rival moral accounts of harm. For instance, murder is morally wrong according to both deontological and utilitarian accounts of harm.

9 Contractarian accounts share the fundamental insight that political obligation is best understood in terms of a voluntary agreement concluded between a group of individuals with the purpose of ensuring that life in organised society is both possible and desirable. However, contractarian approaches diverge regarding the nature of the consent to the common rules. For an overview, see Ann Cudd and Seena Eftekhari, "Contractarianism", *The Stanford Encyclopedia of Philosophy* (Winter 2021 Edition), Edward N. Zalta (ed.), https://plato.stanford.edu/archives/win2021/entries/contractarianism/ (accessed 15 February 2024).

10 Rawls, *A Theory of Justice: Revised Edition*, p. 205.

11 See, for instance, Justin Greenwood, *Interest Representation in the European Union* (London, 2017); and Christine Mahoney, *Brussels versus the Beltway: Advocacy in the United States and the European Union* (Washington, 2008)

12 For a similar conclusion, see Michael J. Sandel, *The Tyranny of Merit: What's Become of the Common Good?* (London, 2021); and Robert B. Reich, *The Common Good* (New York, 2018).

13 See Aristotle, *Politics*, ed. R.F. Stalley (Oxford, 2009); and Jean-Jacques Rousseau, *The Social Contract*, ed. Christopher Betts (Oxford, 1999).
14 See Aquinas, *Political Writings*, ed. R.W. Dyson (Cambridge, 2002). For a helpful discussion of Aquinas' account of the common good, see Mary M. Keys, *Aquinas, Aristotle, and the Promise of the Common Good* (Cambridge, 2008)
15 See, for example, Michael Walzer, *Spheres of Justice: A Defence of Pluralism and Equality* (New York, 1983); Charles Taylor, "Atomism", in Shlomo Avineri and Avner de-Shalit (eds), *Communitarianism and Individualism* (Oxford, 1992); Amitai Etzioni, *The Common Good* (Cambridge, 2007).
16 For instance, the authors of a classic work within the communitarian movement have claimed that a "real community" is a community of memory and tradition. According to them, "the stories that make up a tradition contain conceptions of character, of what a good person is like, and of the virtues that define such character". See Robert N. Bellah, Richard Madsen, William M. Sullivan, Ann Swidler and Steven M. Tipton, *Habits of the Heart: Individualism and Commitment in American Life* (Berkeley, 1985), p. 153.
17 For example, in his influential discussion of what the United States should do to protect the public interest from powerful interest groups, Amitai Etzioni strikingly fails to consider the effects of globalisation. See Amitai Etzioni, *The Spirit of Community* (New York, 1993).
18 As discussed in the introduction, it is striking that communitarian authors have neglected the emergence of the EU polity. It bears noting that ongoing processes of regional integration pose a serious challenge to their case.
19 Melissa Schwartzberg, "Epistemic Democracy and Its Challenges" *Annual Review of Political Science* 18 (2015), p. 187.
20 See Joshua Cohen, "An Epistemic Conception of Democracy", *Ethics* 97 (1986), pp. 26–38.
21 This applies not only to decision-makers and citizens, but also to policy experts. See Philip E. Tetlock, *Expert Political Judgment: How Good Is It? How Can We Know?* (Princeton, 2017).
22 On this point, see, for example, Douglas Murray, *The Madness of Crowds: Gender, Race and Identity* (London, 2019).
23 Schwartzberg, "Epistemic Democracy and Its Challenges", p. 187.
24 This claim is key for the contractarian approach presented above. For an influential contemporary statement, see David Gauthier, *Morals by Agreement* (Oxford, 1987).
25 See W.B. Gallie, "Essentially Contested Concepts", *Proceedings of the Aristotelian Society* 56 (1956), pp. 167–198.
26 Accordingly, by employing expressions such as "pursuing the common good", "realising the common good" and "advancing the common good" in this book I mean, respectively, pursuing, realising, and advancing the *conception* of the common good of a given polity, be it a national or a supranational polity, such as the EU. In other words, I do not assume that there is a single or objective understanding of the common good.
27 John Rawls, "The Idea of an Overlapping Consensus", *Oxford Journal of Legal Studies* 7 (1987), pp. 1–25.

28 William Rehg, "Solidarity and the Common Good: An Analytic Framework", *Journal of Social Philosophy* 38 (2007), p. 7.
29 These two complementary tasks have been referred to as the "substantive" and the "procedural" dimensions of the common good. See Christopher Thomas, "Globalising Sovereignty? Pettit's Neo-Republicanism, International Law, and International Institutions", *The Cambridge Law Journal* 74 (2015), pp. 568–591.
30 For instance, the so-called deliberative accounts of democracy have made several valuable proposals for new decision-making methods involving citizens. A key insight behind this approach is that, if citizens are well-informed and deliberate through appropriate channels, they are likely to make good collective choices. However, this approach has neglected the question of how to make representative institutions, which are subject to electoral incentives, more oriented towards the common good. As we shall see, this question is crucial for the EU institutional apparatus. For an overview of the "deliberative turn", see Ian O'Flynn, *Deliberative Democracy* (Medford MA, 2022).
31 Adapted from François Foret and Oriane Calligaro, "Analysing European Values", in *European Values: Challenges and Opportunities for EU Governance* (New York, 2018), pp. 3–4. Note that Foret and Calligaro also emphasise the role of values as cultural representations, which, as I will claim in the next section, should be distinguished from their role as moral guidelines for public life.
32 The preliminary question of why citizens are morally required to comply with the fundamental laws endorsed by political institutions is directly linked to the problem of political obligation, which I cannot discuss here. In what follows, I assume that citizens have certain associative obligations by virtue of their membership of a given political community, which include the duty to comply with the law. For a discussion, see Samuel Scheffler, "Membership and Political Obligation", *Journal of Political Philosophy* 26 (2018), pp. 3–23.
33 The claim that the values endorsed via international agreements and conventions are a constitutive part of the conception of public morality of a given polity is the reason that leads me to rely on the concept of *public* values, instead of the narrower notion of *constitutional* values. Note that, in the context of EU membership the principle of the supremacy of EU law establishes that it has precedence over national law. This means that all national policies and legislation should be consistent not only with the constitutional values of member states, but also with EU values. For a discussion on the concept of constitutional values, see Gary Jeffrey Jacobsohn, "Constitutional Values and Principles", in Michel Rosenfeld and András Sajó (eds), *The Oxford Handbook of Comparative Constitutional Law* (Oxford, 2012).
34 Barry Bozeman, *Public Values and Public Interest: Counterbalancing Economic Individualism* (Washington, 2007), p. 13.
35 In the field of legal theory, the point that fundamental laws express the standpoint of the common good has recently been made by Adrian Vermeule, *Common Good Constitutionalism: Recovering the Classic Legal Tradition* (Cambridge, 2022).
36 Note that, unlike most accounts of the common good, which focus on certain socially relevant choices, comprehensive doctrines of the good provide moral

prescriptions that cover potentially every domain of life. For instance, utilitarianism considers that utility is intrinsically good and should *always* be maximised. For a classical statement, see John Stuart Mill, *On Liberty, Utilitarianism and Other Essays*, ed. Mark Philp (Oxford, 2015).

37 In certain cases, there may be strong tensions between the religious beliefs of some citizens, on the one hand, and the public values endorsed by the political institutions, on the other. Consider, for example, the current cleavages in the United States regarding the application of the value of freedom of choice to abortion. While, as I claim below, citizens are allowed to call for changes in the public values of their societies, they are required to comply with the existing set of public values without cherry-picking based on their beliefs. For a discussion, see Kent Greenawalt, *Private Consciences and Public Reasons* (Oxford, 1995).

38 My account has an affinity with the doctrine of constitutional patriotism, which "designates the idea that political attachment ought to centre on the norms, the values, and, more indirectly, the procedures of a liberal democratic constitution". In Chapter 5, I will address the criticism raised recurrently against constitutional patriotism according to which, in the absence of certain common sociological features, such as culture and ethnicity, an attachment by citizens to an abstract set of values will be difficult to obtain. See Jan-Werner Müller and Kim Lane Scheppele, "Constitutional Patriotism: An Introduction", *International Journal of Constitutional Law* 6 (2008), pp. 67–71.

39 See Domingo Lovera-Parmo, "Protests, Riots, Inequality and a New Constitution for Chile", *Oxford Human Rights Hub* (15 December 2019), https://ohrh.law.ox.ac.uk/protests-riots-inequality-and-a-new-constitution-for-chile/ (accessed 14 December 2022).

40 *Constitution of the People's Republic of China*, article 4.

41 United Nations, "Gender Equality: Women and the Sustainable Development Goals", www.un.org/en/global-issues/gender-equality (accessed 14 December 2022).

42 This methodology is typically applied by studies in the field of comparative constitutional law. For an overview of the available approaches in this discipline, see Oliver Brand, "Conceptual Comparisons: Towards a Coherent Methodology of Comparative Legal Studies", *Brooklyn Journal of International Law* 32 (2007), pp. 405–466. Note that the alternative – relying on empirical sources regarding the values of *individuals*, such as the World Values Survey – points us towards *personal* values, rather than public ones. See World Values Survey, www.worldvaluessurvey.org/wvs.jsp (accessed 26 July 2023).

43 Note that moral realism asserts the existence of certain moral facts. For an influential statement, see Thomas Scanlon, *What We Owe to Each Other* (Cambridge MA, 1998).

44 On this point, see Uday Singh Mehta, *Liberalism and Empire: A Study in Nineteenth-Century British Liberal Thought* (Chicago, 1999).

45 Tom Ginsburg and Alberto Simpser (eds), *Constitutions in Authoritarian Regimes* (Cambridge, 2013).

46 See *Constituição Política da República Portuguesa* (1933), article 8. This phenomenon has been labelled "constitutions without constitutionalism". See, for

instance, Augusto Zimmermann, "Constitutions without Constitutionalism: The Failure of Constitutionalism in Brazil", in Mortimer Sellers and Tadeusz Tomaszewski (eds), *The Rule of Law in Comparative Perspective* (Dordrecht, 2010).
47 This is often ensured through dedicated bodies that enforce the constitution and its values, such as the Federal Constitutional Court of Germany, the Constitutional Council of France, and the Supreme Court of the United States.
48 See, respectively, David Held, *Models of Democracy* (Cambridge, 2006) and Gøsta Esping-Anderson, *The Three Worlds of Welfare Capitalism* (Cambridge, 2004).
49 Consider, for instance, the *European Social Charter* (1961, revised in 1996); the European Commission's *White Paper on Social Policy* (1994); the Directive 2004/38/EC (also known as the "Citizens Rights Directive"), the *European Pillar of Social Rights* (2017); the *European Pillar of Social Rights Action Plan* (2021); and landmark decisions by the Court of Justice of the European Union (CJEU), such as *Elisabeta Dano and Florin Dano v. Jobcenter Leipzig*.
50 A number of legal theorists have argued that legal orders that do not possess a codified constitution may nonetheless be grounded on a set of fundamental principles and values that guide the actions of public authorities and social relations. Even if these normative commitments have not been consolidated in a single document, they deserve the status of "constitutional order". For a discussion regarding the paradigmatic case of the United Kingdom, see Colin Turpin and Adam Tomkins, *British Government and the Constitution* (Cambridge, 2007).
51 Kwame Anthony Appiah, *The Honor Code: How Moral Revolutions Happen* (New York, 2010).
52 For the so-called theory of "constitutional momentums", which explains how constitutional change can happen without formally changing the constitution, see Bruce Ackerman's, *We the People, Volume 2: Transformations* (Cambridge MA, 2000).
53 *The Constitution of the United States*, 1st to 27th amendments.
54 See, for instance, Serge Berstein, *The Republic of de Gaulle 1958–1969* (Cambridge, 2006).
55 Emmanuel Macron, *Discours du Président de la République lors de la Commémoration du Centenaire de L'Armistice* (11 November 2018), www.elysee.fr/emmanuel-macron/2018/11/12/discours-du-president-de-la-republique-emmanuel-macron-a-la-ceremonie-internationale-du-centenaire-de-larmistice-du-11-novembre-1918-a-larc-de-triomphe (accessed 5 October 2022).
56 Shaun Walker, "Orbán Deploys Christianity with a Twist to Tighten Grip in Hungary" *The Guardian* (14 July 2019), www.theguardian.com/world/2019/jul/14/viktor-orban-budapest-hungary-christianity-with-a-twist (accessed 21 September 2022). Note that most Christian confessions endorse the values of tolerance and solidarity, particularly towards those most vulnerable, namely refugees.

57 Reuters, "Marine Le Pen Blames Radical Islamism for Charlie Hebdo Attack – Video", *The Guardian* (8 January 2015), www.theguardian.com/world/video/2015/jan/08/marine-le-pen-radical-islamism-charlie-hebdo-attack-video (accessed 21 September 2022).
58 TellMAMA: Measuring Anti-Muslim Attacks, "Anti-Muslim Incidents in France after the Charlie Hebdo Massacre", https://tellmamauk.org/project/anti-muslim-incidents-in-france-after-the-charlie-hebdo-massacre/ (accessed 26 July 2023).
59 See Benedict Anderson, *Imagined Communities: Reflections on the Origin and Spread of Nationalism* (London, 2016).
60 This raises the question of whether a civic identity presupposes some degree of cultural homogeneity. This seems to be the case only to a limited extent. For instance, to allow for a meaningful public debate and to be able to exercise their rights, citizens should be able to speak a common language. Yet the existence of, say, a common ethnicity, religion and food habits do not seem to be necessary conditions to develop a shared civic identity.
61 Conrad Hackett, "5 Facts about the Muslim Population in Europe", *Pew Research Center* (29 November 2017), www.pewresearch.org/fact-tank/2017/11/29/5-facts-about-the-muslim-population-in-europe/ (accessed 22 September 2022).
62 Samuel P. Huntington, *The Clash of Civilizations and the Remaking of World Order* (London, 2002).
63 United Nations, "Treaty on the Non-Proliferation of Nuclear Weapons", www.un.org/disarmament/wmd/nuclear/npt/ (accessed 22 September 2022). The figures in this paragraph refer to ratification and accession, rather than the mere signature of international agreements as the former express unequivocally the endorsement of the agreements at stake.
64 It could be argued that the values enshrined in international treaties (such as peace, security, and cooperation) are "empty signifiers" (in the sense coined by Ernesto Laclau) that do not commit states to anything in practice. Accordingly, so the argument will go, they cannot be regarded as indicators of a transnational moral agreement. See Ernesto Laclau, *On Populist Reason* (London, 2005). However, as I have suggested above, the fact that abstract values (such as peace, security, and cooperation) must be interpreted by shared international bodies (such as the regular review conferences of the parties to the Treaty on the Non-Proliferation of Nuclear Weapons) to be translated into concrete policy actions does not mean that they are irrelevant. This is corroborated by the empirical finding that compliance with international agreements is "relatively good in general". See George W. Downs and Michael A. Jones, "Reputation, Compliance, and International Law", *Journal of Legal Studies* 31 (2002), p. S96.
65 For the figures, see Office of the High Commissioner for Human Rights, "Status of Ratification Interactive Dashboard", https://indicators.ohchr.org/ (accessed 22 September 2022).
66 Office of the High Commissioner for Human Rights, "Status of Ratification Interactive Dashboard".
67 Office of the High Commissioner for Human Rights, Selected Decisions of the Committee on the Elimination of Racial Discrimination (Geneva, 2012).

68 See, for instance, Mark G. Rolls, "Like-Minded States: New Zealand–ASEAN Relations in the Changing Asia-Pacific Strategic Environment", in Anne-Marie Brady (ed.), *Small States and the Changing Global Order: New Zealand faces the Future* (Cham, 2019).
69 Riordan, *A Grammar of the Common Good: Speaking of Globalization*.
70 See James D. Fry, Bryane Michael and Natasha Pushkarna, *The Values of International Organizations* (Manchester, 2021).
71 *Statute of the Council of Europe* (1949).
72 Ian Manners, "The Constitutive Nature of Values, Images and Principles in the European Union", in Sonia Lucarelli and Ian Manners (eds), *Values and Principles in European Union Foreign Policy* (New York, 2006).
73 *ASEAN Charter*, article 2.
74 *Protocolo de Asunción sobre compromiso con la promoción y protección de los Derechos Humanos en el MERCOSUR* and *Protocolo de Ushuaia sobre Compromiso Democrático en el MERCOSUR, La Republica de Bolivia e la Republica de Chile*.
75 This view is in tension with the cultural approach to European values. As I will argue in Chapter 2, the cultural approach is of limited interest for the questions addressed by this book.
76 Note that, as I have suggested, addressing the question "what does the common good of the EU mean?" presupposes the identification of a substantive source of a common standpoint within the EU polity (such as EU values). In the absence of such source, any account of the common good of the EU will suffer from a lack of specification.
77 Of course, some states may endorse a particular value but systematically fail to comply with it. More to the point, there may be *no value* that all world states have equally endorsed. However, these cases do not jeopardise the debate about the global common good. Indeed, it would be implausible to think that the concept of global common good is only useful if *all* world states endorsed a set of common values and complied with them. For example, if all states bar North Korea and Iran agreed that the non-proliferation of nuclear weapons was desirable, the abstention of these two should not prevent us from acknowledging a widely shared understanding of this good at the global level.
78 United Nations, "Status of the Paris Agreement", https://treaties.un.org/Pages/ViewDetails.aspx?src=TREATY&mtdsg_no=XXVII-7-d&chapter=27&clang=_en#1 (accessed 23 September 2022). A similar point is made by A.C. Grayling, *For the Good of the World: Is Global Agreement on Global Challenges Possible?* (London, 2022), p. 180.
79 Office of the High Commissioner for Human Rights, "Status of Ratification Interactive Dashboard".
80 *Constitution of the Islamic Republic of Iran*, article 1.
81 Ruhollah Khomeini, *American Plots against Iran Speech* (1979), http://emam.com/posts/view/15718/Speech (accessed 6 October 2022); George W. Bush, *State of the Union Address* (2002), https://georgewbush-whitehouse.archives.gov/news/releases/2002/01/20020129-11.html (accessed 6 October 2022).

82 For the normative conception of the community in Nazi Germany, see Martina Steber and Bernhard Gotto (eds), *Visions of Community in Nazi Germany: Social Engineering and Private Lives* (Oxford, 2014).
83 Anna Stilz, "The Value of Self-Determination", in David Sobel, Peter Vallentyne and Steven Wall (eds), *Oxford Studies in Political Philosophy*, volume 2 (Oxford, 2016), p. 98.
84 Michael Walzer, *Just and Unjust Wars: A Moral Argument with Historical Illustrations* (New York, 2015), p. 89.
85 See Stephen M. Walt, "Top 10 Warning Signs of Liberal Imperialism", *Foreign Policy* (10 May 2013), https://foreignpolicy.com/2013/05/20/top-10-warning-signs-of-liberal-imperialism/ (accessed 30 September 2022).
86 Daniele Archibugi, *The Global Commonwealth of Citizens: Toward Cosmopolitan Democracy* (Princeton, 2008).
87 On this point, see Seyla Benhabib, *Another Cosmopolitanism* (Oxford, 2006).
88 Note that global moral progress does not necessarily presuppose the recognition of universal moral truths. For instance, according to the influential view of Peter Singer, moral progress takes place when the moral agents expand their circle of moral concern – that is, from family to friends to fellow citizens and to the individuals in the rest of the world. See Peter Singer, *The Expanding Circle: Ethics and Sociobiology* (New York, 1981).
89 This norm is notably enshrined in the *United Nations Charter*.
90 See Michael Walzer, "Governing the Globe: What Is the Best We Can Do?", *Dissent* (Fall edition, 2000).
91 Bruce M. Russett and John D. Sullivan, "Collective Goods and International Organization", *International Organization* 25 (1971).
92 Note that the US embargo has made the export of Cuban products more difficult and it lowered the degree of access to certain basic goods, such as food and medical supplies by its population. For an overview of the relations between the United States and Cuba, see Arne Westad, *The Cold War: A World History* (London, 2018).
93 Note that this focus on the rights presently codified in international law does not substitute for the existence of additional *moral* rights that have not yet been granted legal recognition. My goal here is to refer to standards that are widely accepted and can serve effectively as a reference point for all states. For a discussion on the need to expand the prevailing understanding of fundamental rights, see Charles Beitz and Robert Goodin (eds), *Global Basic Rights* (Oxford, 2011).
94 See, for instance, James Crawford, "The Criteria for Statehood in International Law", *British Yearbook of International Law* 48 (1977), pp. 93–182.
95 For instance, Hobbes claims that citizens have a moral right to run away from the authorities if they have been sentenced to death. See Thomas Hobbes, *Leviathan*, ed. Noel Malcolm. More generally, the right to self-preservation has played a key role in the structure of the arguments of most natural rights theories. For an overview, see Richard Tuck, *Natural Rights Theories: Their Origin and Development* (Cambridge, 1981).
96 Note that the duty to respect fundamental rights is justifiable on the grounds of most available moral theories, ranging from natural law theory to deontology to virtue ethics to moderate versions of utilitarianism.

97 Consider, for instance, the use of the so-called "smart sanctions" against ruling elites and trade of weapons. On this point, see Joy Gordon, "Smart Sanctions Revisited", *Ethics & International Affairs* 25 (2011), pp. 315–335.
 98 John Rawls, *The Law of Peoples* (Cambridge MA, 2001).
 99 Note that this book focuses on the EU polity, where the track record of compliance with fundamental rights is generally high. The recent cases of gross and systemic violations of EU values in a limited number of member states will be discussed in detail in Chapter 2.
100 Consider, for instance, the following sources: the *Convention on the Prevention and Punishment of the Crime of Genocide* (1948); the *International Covenant on Civil and Political Rights* (1966); the *Convention on the Rights of the Child* (1989); the *International Convention on the Suppression and Punishment of the Crime of Apartheid* (1973); the *International Convention for the Protection of All Persons from Enforced Disappearance* (2006); the *Convention on the Rights of Persons with Disabilities* (2006).
101 This question has been a matter of an extensive debate in the specialised literature and cannot be addressed here. See, for instance, Henry Shue, *Basic Rights: Subsistence, Affluence, and U.S. Foreign Policy* (Princeton, 1996); and Joshua Cohen, "Is there a Human Right to Democracy?", in Christine Sypnowich (ed.), *The Egalitarian Conscience: Essays in Honour of G. A. Cohen* (Oxford, 2006).
102 This is the reason why I abstain from directly equating fundamental rights with a comprehensive list of *human* rights. Indeed, the contemporary human rights regime has been criticised on the grounds of being "Eurocentric in character and hegemonic in practice". See Hakimeh Saghaye-Biria, "Decolonizing the 'Universal' Human Rights Regime: Questioning American Exceptionalism and Orientalism", *ReOrient* 4 (2018), pp. 59–77. However, it should be noted the fact that the *history* of human rights has been Eurocentric does not mean that the *idea* of global human rights is unsound. For this view, see Fernando Suárez Müller, "Eurocentrism, Human Rights, and Humanism", *International Journal of Applied Philosophy* 26 (2012), pp. 279–293.
103 Indeed, it would be implausible to think that occasional violations of the fundamental rights of some individuals would justify interference. Even states deeply committed to respecting fundamental rights cannot ensure compliance levels of 100%. For instance, the public authorities of France and the Netherlands have occasionally been condemned by the CJEU and the European Court of Human Rights for infractions against some of their citizens.
104 In the domestic sphere, the tension between the enhancement of the common good and of individual rights has generated an intense debate opposing communitarian to liberal scholars. For an overview, see Daniel Bell, *Communitarianism and its Critics* (Oxford, 1993).
105 Robert Rapier, "The World's Top Lithium Producers", *Forbes* (13 December 2020), www.forbes.com/sites/rrapier/2020/12/13/the-worlds-top-lithium-producers/ (accessed 2 August 2023).
106 On the role of lithium in the green transition, see, for instance, World Bank, *Minerals for Climate Action: The Mineral Intensity of the Clean Energy Transition* (Washington, 2020).

107 Of course, there may be additional grounds to share natural resources, notably related to justice claims. For a discussion, see Leif Wenar, "Natural Resources", in David Held and Pietro Maffettone (eds), *Global Political Theory* (Cambridge, 2016).
108 The question of whether a given sacrifice is proportional should be assessed in light of the *necessity* and the *magnitude* of the sacrifice at stake vis-à-vis the goal to be achieved. For a comprehensive discussion, see Aharon Barak, *Proportionality: Constitutional Rights and their Limitations* (Cambridge, 2012).
109 On this point, see Seyla Benhabib, *The Rights of Others: Aliens, Residents and Citizens* (Cambridge, 2004).
110 See, for instance, Joseph H. Chung, "Human Rights Violations by Multinational Corporations: Corruption, Lawlessness and the 'Global Value Chain'", *Centre for Research on Globalisation*, www.globalresearch.ca/human-rights-violation-multinational-corporations-global-value-chain-corruption-lawlessness/5779160 (accessed 26 July 2023).
111 The need for a more comprehensive institutional framework at the supranational level has been advocated by several authors, notably Jürgen Habermas, *The Postnational Constellation: Political Essays* (Cambridge, 2001).
112 Florian Bieber, "Is Nationalism on the Rise? Assessing Global Trends", *Ethnopolitics* 17 (2018), p. 519.
113 See, for instance, Human Rights Watch, *Locked Up Alone: Detention Conditions and Mental Health at Guantanamo* (New York, 2008); and Anthony Deutsch, "Dutch Refugee Council Sues State over 'Inhumane' Asylum Centres", *Reuters* (18 August 2022), www.reuters.com/world/europe/dutch-refugee-council-sues-state-over-inhumane-asylum-centres-2022-08-18/ (accessed 1 January 2023).
114 See, for instance, Stephen J. Majeski, "Generating and Maintaining Cooperation in International Relations: A Model of Repeated Interaction Among Groups in Complex and Uncertain Situations", *International Interactions* 21 (1996), pp. 265–289.
115 This is line with the so-called practice-dependence approach in the fields of moral and political theory. As I mentioned in the introduction, the main reasons to prefer this approach are that it offers clear practical guidance and it has better feasibility prospects than idealistic approaches that would attempt to redesign the international system from scratch. For a discussion, see Eva Erman and Niklas Möller, "What Distinguishes the Practice-Dependent Approach to Justice?", *Philosophy & Social Criticism* 42 (2016), pp. 3–23.
116 In addition to already mentioned cases such as the EU, ASEAN, Mercosur and the African Union, consider the Economic Community of West African States, the Gulf Cooperation Council, the European Free Trade Association and the Nordic Council.
117 Note that this already applies to the EU to a certain extent. For instance, the EU has competence to negotiate and conclude international agreements in certain areas on behalf of its member states, such as customs. See Council of the European Union, "The Role of the Council in International Agreements", www.consilium.europa.eu/en/council-eu/international-agreements/ (accessed 25 October 2022).

118 A number of valuable proposals to improve the problem-solving capacity of these institutions are currently available in the literature. See, for example, Jussi M. Hanhimäki, "Reform and Challenges: the Future of the United Nations", *The United Nations: A Very Short Introduction* (Oxford, 2008); Pedro Alba, Patricia Bliss-Guest and Laura Tuck, "Reforming the World Bank to Play a Critical Role in Addressing Climate Change", *Center for Global Development Policy Paper* 288 (2023); Marianne Schneider-Petsinger, *Reforming the World Trade Organization: Prospects for Transatlantic Cooperation and the Global Trade System* (2020).

119 Philip Kotler, *Advancing the Common Good: Strategies for Businesses, Governments and Nonprofits* (Santa Barbara, 2019), p. 93.

2

Understanding EU values

Introduction

This chapter addresses the following questions: In what sense can we speak of EU values? What is the link between EU values and the common good? What consequences should apply if a member state does not comply with EU values? How can EU institutions enable a systemic realisation of EU values? I argue that EU values are the public values jointly endorsed by the EU institutions and the political institutions of the member states by means of adopting EU treaties. I claim that EU values allow for the mapping of conditions and goals that member states jointly consider desirable, thus translating a shared understanding of the common good. I argue that this conception of the common good is distinctive because it comprises a particular model of liberal democracy, social welfare and environmental protection. However, I stress that the list of EU values is not European by definition; like-minded polities beyond Europe have also endorsed several of these values.

In view of the normative relevance of EU values, I claim that EU institutions should act as their guardians and enablers. First, I claim that the EU should put in place effective safeguards against internal breaches of EU values, including enforcing the provision of the TEU for the suspension of the voting rights of non-compliant member states and the creation of a procedure through which chronically non-compliant member states could be ejected from the Union. Second, I argue that the best way to empower national governments to address challenges against EU values is to further unite efforts at the EU level. In a globalised world, only regional blocks have the capacity to pursue the basic conditions that enable the public values of their members to be realised. Accordingly, I claim that EU member states could jointly launch a set of bodies with the critical mass to address the threats against EU values posed by non-state actors. I discuss three examples of such institutions: (i) a European Transnational Tax Authority; (ii) a European Credit Rating Agency; and (iii) a European Agency for Fair Trade.

I begin by discussing the notion of EU values and claim they are a meaningful concept in the EU political lexicon. Subsequently, I introduce the "thin" and "thick" conceptions of EU values, explaining why the latter is preferable. I then outline a list of EU values and identify the main distinguishing features of the European Model. Next, I elaborate on the role of the EU institutions as guardians and enablers of EU values in the current political and economic landscape. First, I present the problem of systemic noncompliance with EU values by the governments of two member states and discuss possible institutional solutions. Second, I explain how a wide range of non-state actors has gradually undermined the European Model. Focusing on its social dimension, I discuss three examples of new institutions that could re-empower the European public authorities to realise the goals of the European Model.

EU values: a meaningful concept?

What are EU values?

Recall that, in Chapter 1, I defined public values as the values endorsed by the political institutions of a given polity. By endorsing a particular set of public values, I meant the fulfilment of two complementary conditions: (i) granting them recognition in fundamental laws, notably constitutions and international treaties, and (ii) ensuring that public authorities act consistently in accordance with these values. I have argued that, unlike other categories of values, such as cultural values, public values should not be taken as given; they ought to be adopted explicitly by the relevant public authorities, and they bind all citizens equally, irrespective of their personal beliefs and worldviews. I have also claimed that, insofar as public values capture the fundamental conditions and goals that a given society considers desirable, they translate a substantive understanding of the common good. Accordingly, the public values of a given polity can be regarded as the pillars of its standpoint of the common good. As I have argued, these values are actionable through appropriate legislation, public policies and judicial decisions. Thus, the institutional framework within a given polity, as well as its public reasoning procedures and decision-making rules, should be set up in a way that fosters the realisation of its public values.

Now, this conceptual framework can be applied to the EU polity. Thus, EU values can be defined as the public values jointly endorsed by the EU institutions and the political institutions of the member states. In what sense have these institutions endorsed EU values? As far as EU institutions and policies are concerned, the TEU states plainly that they should be guided by EU values. Indeed, article 13 requires that "[t]he Union shall have an institutional framework which shall aim to promote its values".[1] Furthermore, article 21 asserts that "[t]he Union shall define and pursue common policies and actions, and shall work for a high degree of cooperation in all fields of international relations, in order to safeguard its values".[2] Hence, EU values govern the functioning of EU institutions. Regarding the political institutions of the member states, the voluntary ratification of the TEU indicates their endorsement of EU values. Indeed, the TEU states that one of the primary purposes of the EU is to advance EU values: "[t]he Union's aim is to promote peace, *its values* and the well-being of its peoples".[3] Thus, by ratifying the TEU, member states have agreed to abide by EU values. Furthermore, compliance with EU values is a fundamental precondition for accession to the EU. In fact, only a state "which respects the values referred to in article 2 and is committed to promoting them may apply to become a member of the Union".[4]

Against what has been argued by a few authors, EU values are not merely "a broad and flexible symbolic repertoire".[5] In fact, EU values are widely present in the primary institutional practices of the EU, including Council conclusions, decisions of the CJEU, resolutions of the European Parliament, trade agreements with third-party states, public justifications for adopting EU policies, and so on. The impact of EU values on policymaking is particularly notorious when it comes to policy areas that are, by definition, value-based. Consider, for instance, a wide range of EU policy actions in the fields of gender equality, the rights of minorities and artificial intelligence.[6] In these areas, EU values have not been mere statements of intentions but an effective instrument to achieve social change. Thus, EU values have played a significant role in structuring certain transnational debates and in justifying collective action at the EU level. It should be acknowledged that "EU treaties and official documents do not refer to values in a fully coherent way". However, this may have more to do with the ambiguous character of values such as liberty and equality than with the lack of substantive meaning of EU values.[7] While, as we shall see, not all political actors comply with EU values, the "normative power" of those values in the current political landscape of the Union seems hard to deny.[8]

My understanding of EU values as an explicit agreement regarding public morality between the political institutions of the member states contrasts with the cultural approach to European values, which has been discussed in Chapter 1. Central to this view is the idea of an emerging European identity, which is arguably grounded on a transnational collective memory comprising points of reference such as the Roman Empire, Christianity and the struggle against totalitarianism, as well as shared symbols and meanings, including Mediterranean food and the Eurovision music festival.[9] As I have suggested in Chapter 1, a key distinctive feature between these two accounts of values is the role assigned to human agency. While in my account, EU values are *voluntary* – that is, they might *not* have been endorsed by the political actors in Europe – the cultural account presupposes that European values are deeply attached to the cultural practices of Europeans and are somewhat inescapable. This assumption is problematic for at least two reasons. First, it neglects the role played by the citizens who, as free moral agents, should be in a position to decide which public values they wish to endorse (even if through the mediation of political institutions). Second, it fails to acknowledge the fact that a variety of cultures can be found within Europe and that many EU citizens do not regard themselves as Europeans.[10]

Unlike what one is often led to believe, the link between EU values and the European continent is not logically necessary but merely contingent. Admittedly, culture and history are part of the extensive list of explanatory variables that can tell us why a particular constellation of public values has been endorsed by a given polity.[11] For example, given that many member states have experienced the horrors of Nazism and communism, they may be intensely concerned about promoting pluralism and preventing discrimination. However, it is not necessarily the case that all European states that share, to a certain degree, a common history and cultural practices will adopt EU values. In fact, certain non-EU states have a "European" background, and yet their public values seem to be at odds with those of the EU. Consider, for instance, the case of Serbia.[12] At the same time, a few EU values have been adopted by non-European states or are arguably universal values, as the TEU itself claims.[13] Therefore, EU values are normatively relevant because they have been endorsed by the political institutions of the EU member states and not because they were invented by ancient Greek philosophers or French revolutionaries.[14] This view is consistent with Dario Castiglione's compelling claim that the European identity is primarily a *political* identity (rather than a *cultural* one), which is grounded on the fact that EU citizens share common public values and take part in shared political institutions.[15]

Towards a list of EU values

So far, I have been referring to EU values as an abstract concept. Yet what specific ideals do EU values bring about? There are at least two possible approaches to this question. To begin with, what I dub the "thin" conception of EU values regards the latter as a loose and underspecified constellation of democratic values that are nonetheless useful as a public discourse that may serve a variety of purposes. In other words, EU values are mainly a *rhetorical device* lacking substantive meaning and may be called to justify contradictory political goals.[16] On this account, the values listed in the TEU are too generic to provide a clear moral blueprint for the EU. Note that, according to the TEU, these values include "respect for human dignity, freedom, democracy, equality, the rule of law and respect for human rights, including the rights of persons belonging to minorities".[17] According to this view, the fact that the TEU establishes a direct correspondence between EU values and the member states' values warrants the former limited added value. Indeed, the TEU states that EU values "are common to the member states in a society in which pluralism, non-discrimination, tolerance, justice, solidarity and equality between women and men prevail".[18] For these reasons, the "thin" account claims that EU values should be regarded as an open and flexible repertoire of the values of the member states.

Conversely, the "thick" account of EU values claims that EU values have *robust substantive content* and bring about a distinctive model of society. According to this view, the charge that the values listed in the TEU are too generic also applies to the constitutions of most world states, in which the exact meaning of values such as tolerance, justice and liberty is typically not expanded. Thus, the concrete implications of EU values should be derived from political statements and legal sources in which EU values have been interpreted by the EU institutions and member states, including Council conclusions and key decisions of the CJEU. Furthermore, the fact that EU values are derived to a certain extent from the values of the member states does not mean that they are irrelevant. On the contrary, the "thick" account argues that since many member states have projected their normative frameworks onto the EU, they expect the latter to take bold measures to realise these values. For example, in response to the conservative views of the so-called Visegrad Group regarding the admittance of refugees in Europe, President Macron stated that EU membership "is no menu *à la carte*".[19] Therefore, the main challenge faced by the "thick" account is to elaborate the values presented in the TEU by complementing them with a wider range of normative sources at the EU level.

A remarkable proponent of this view is Ian Manners, who builds on a broad range of official sources to substantiate the distinctive nature of the so-called "European Model".[20] He outlines the shape of this model by analysing what he dubs "European perspectives" on five key dimensions of the social order: (i) economics; (ii) society; (iii) conflict; (iv) the environment; and (v) politics. The result is a list of nine TEU values that are coupled with qualifiers, namely *sustainable* peace, *social* liberty, *consensual* democracy, *associative* human rights, *supranational* rule of law, *inclusive* equality, *social* solidarity, *sustainable* development and *good* governance.[21] What is compelling in Manners's approach is not only his carefully argued list of EU values but also his ability to translate the latter into a concrete model of political, social and economic organisation.[22] Indeed, he forcefully describes the model implicit in EU values as a *liberal democracy* backed by a *robust welfare system* and a commitment to a *sustainable environment*. According to Manners, this model is the outcome of a combination of liberal democratic values (such as peace, liberty and democracy) and social democratic ones (such as equality, solidarity and sustainable development). While he warns that these values "are not uniquely European", he stresses that they play "a constitutive role in shaping the EU".[23]

Manners's conception of the European Model is consistent with the insight that EU values differ not only from the public values of non-democratic states but also from those of other democracies, such as the United States. For instance, the fact that many materially deprived US citizens do not have access to basic healthcare coverage despite the country's manifest affluence would be hard to justify within the European Model. Similarly, the fact that gun possession is permitted in the United States and publicly justified on the grounds of individual liberty is puzzling from the standpoint of the European Model. This reflection suggests that EU values are not just a set of dry institutional commitments without any practical expression. To be sure, empirical research has demonstrated that EU values are widely shared by EU citizens. Drawing on European Values Study data from 1990 to 2020, a recent study has concluded that EU citizens support EU values "strongly and increasingly over time".[24] Yet, one might ask: if EU values are widely shared, why are they so contentious in the political arena? As we shall see in Chapter 3, the basic moral consensus within the EU is, at times, obscured by conflicting interests regarding the distribution of the burdens of realising EU values. However, the European Model's distinctive nature is particularly apparent when contrasted with alternative models.

If Manners's view is to be accepted, two important conclusions should be drawn. First, to the extent they consist of a substantive set of public values shared by all member states, EU values provide grounds for a transnational conception of the common good. Even if the member states' national identities and political cultures are diverse, their political institutions have agreed upon a common value-based framework they wish to advance together. This framework provides them with a common moral standpoint from which they can assess policy choices in areas as diverse as international security, gender inequality and climate change. Second, adopting Manners's view suggests that the "thin" account of EU values is unsatisfactory. While it is true that a few political actors have used EU values to serve diverse ends and that certain governments have avoided the burdens of realising the European Model, this does not per se eliminate the substantive content of EU values nor the responsibilities to realise the European Model. If anything, the fact that EU values are not always respected and that the

How should EU values be realised?

If there is, indeed, a distinctive list of EU values, how should EU institutions realise them? An episode that followed the appointment of Ursula von der Leyen as President of the European Commission in 2019 illustrates some of the tensions in play. Shortly after being appointed, President Von der Leyen announced the creation of a portfolio dubbed "protecting our European way of life". While her stated intention was to address challenges to democracy, it was striking that the portfolio covered immigration policies. Her choice was strongly criticised by a wide range of actors who claimed that the EU should not seek to defend its values by searching for scapegoats.[25] Furthermore, the ambiguous notion of the "European way of life" lacks widespread agreement and anyway seems unsuitable for the EU polity.[26] Facing intense criticism, President Von der Leyen decided to rebrand this portfolio, which came to be known as "promoting our European way of life". Yet this alternative branding raised additional doubts, particularly regarding the extent to which the EU should actively promote its model of social and political organisation. Regardless of a recent cross-party statement that "European values are not for sale", it is not clear what this axiom would mean in terms of policymaking.[27] Hence, the following questions are in order: Should EU values be protected? If so, from whom? Should they be promoted? If so, among whom?

The answers to these questions are not as straightforward as one might think. On the one hand, there is an understandable distrust in portraying EU institutions as advocates of a set of values on the world stage. European states have a history of imposing violently their values on other countries, often under the guise of promoting desirable ends. Consider, for instance, the medieval Crusades, which claimed to defend Christian values, and the "civilisational mission" of the colonial period, which aimed at advancing the values of the European Enlightenment in the New World.[28] This record of using public values as a justification for oppressive practices has led a few authors to speak of the dark side of European values.[29] On the other hand, it is reasonable to think that political institutions should actively engage with the values they have endorsed, ensuring high levels of compliance and enacting policies that foster their fulfilment. For example, it may be plausibly argued that EU member states should teach the value of social equality in their schools and should create appropriate legal sanctions for those who engage in discriminatory behaviour. Similarly, they may soundly adopt public policies that put the value of social solidarity into practice, such as creating a universal healthcare system. This suggests that it may be not only desirable but morally required for EU institutions to advance EU values.

With a view to reconciling these perspectives, I shall claim that EU institutions should act as *guardians of EU values* and as *enablers of the European Model*, provided that the two principles for interstate relations discussed in Chapter 1 are met. By being a guardian of EU values, I mean preventing or responding to policies that are starkly at odds with EU values. For example, as I will claim, EU institutions should take action to address the systemic breach of freedom of speech by the government of Hungary. As we shall see, this could be achieved by creating effective mechanisms to enforce EU values. In turn, by enabling the European Model, I mean promoting certain basic conditions without which this model cannot subsist. More specifically, EU institutions should seek to build, in cooperation with other polities, an international order where the goals of realising liberal democracy, social welfare and environmental protection remain feasible. For instance, I shall claim that they should adopt bold measures to prevent international tax evasion, which jeopardises the functioning of the welfare systems of a few member states.[30] However, in line with what I have argued in Chapter 1, moral limits for the actions undertaken by EU institutions while performing their roles of enablers and guardians of EU values should be drawn by applying the principles of pluralism and respect for fundamental rights.[31]

Note that respecting the diversity of the conceptions of the common good does not imply that any EU action to advance its values should only produce effects within the political boundaries of the Union. This requirement would seem unfeasible in an interdependent world where many of the challenges faced by EU values do, in fact, originate beyond its borders. Consider, for instance, the recurrent cyberattacks and disinformation campaigns led reportedly by non-EU actors.[32] As I have suggested in Chapter 1, the feasibility of the European Model – and likely of any other model – seems to require certain basic conditions to be fulfilled by the international order. For example, realising the value of sustainable peace within the EU is only possible if its neighbouring states maintain non-aggressive behaviour. Similarly, the EU depends critically on other polities to realise the goal of environmental protection. Given this high degree of interdependence, the EU has reasonable grounds to seek, within the limits of non-interference drawn by the principle of pluralism, an international order that enables the fulfilment of its public values.[33] Incidentally, as Chapter 1 has claimed, several likeminded polities beyond Europe have also endorsed a few EU values. As a result, polities in the EU and beyond can work together to create a socioeconomic environment that allows for the fulfilment of their overlapping values. Later in this chapter, I will offer a few examples of institutional reforms that might allow this goal to be achieved.

In the following sections, I will discuss in detail the role of EU institutions as guardians of EU values and enablers of the European Model in the face of the current political and socioeconomic landscape. I will focus my attention on two particularly complex and pressing challenges against EU values: (i) the systemic *noncompliance* with EU values by two member states and (ii) the *disempowerment* of several member states to pursue the European Model as a result of the constraints imposed by a variety of non-state actors. Why do these aspects deserve special attention? First, despite being particularly critical for the future of the EU, the ways forward in the existing literature are relatively scarce. Second, as will become apparent, each of these challenges triggers collective action problems, which can only be dealt with effectively at the supranational level. Therefore, I will present concrete EU policies and institutional reforms through which they could be overcome. While the following sections will focus on the *substantive* dimension of the common good, which, as Chapter 1 has argued, refers to the normative content of EU values, Chapters 3 and 4 will focus on its *procedural* dimension, discussing how decision-making in EU institutions could be more oriented towards the common good, regardless of the specific policy field at stake.

The EU as guardian of EU values

Why the EU should act on breaches of EU values

In recent years, EU values have been systemically breached within the EU, notably by the governments of Hungary and Poland under the Fidesz and the Law and Justice party (PIS) rule, respectively.[34] In Hungary, the public authorities have reportedly discriminated against certain minorities, have limited the freedom of the press, and have interfered in the functioning of schools and universities. For instance, in 2018, Hungary adopted legislation clearly aimed at preventing the Central European University – a renowned private institution funded by the American investor and philanthropist George Soros – from operating further in the country. Similarly, in 2021, the Hungarian Parliament passed a law that banned the dissemination in schools of contents regarding homosexuality and gender change. Similarly, the government of Poland has allegedly politicised the functioning of the judiciary, thereby challenging the rule of law. For example, in recent years, Polish authorities have arbitrarily changed the procedures for appointing judges to the Supreme Court and created a new disciplinary system that made judges of ordinary courts liable for the content of their judicial decisions, thus jeopardising their independence. As has often been stressed by the European Commission, the European Parliament and the CJEU, these actions are sharply at odds with the EU values presented above.[35]

A question that has been raised in the specialised literature is whether and the extent to which the EU should take measures against these breaches.[36] The first reason to support such measures is that, as we have seen, the pursuit of EU values constitutes one of the fundamental goals of the EU.[37] Being a member of the EU presupposes upholding its values, and indeed, all member states have voluntarily agreed to comply with these values through the accession process. More specifically, they were required to fulfil the so-called Copenhagen criteria, which, among other things, assess the candidate's performance in terms of democracy, the rule of law, and human rights.[38] Hence, "[t]he EU's moral appeal as well as the backbone of its legal system collapse when its member states no longer honour EU values".[39] Furthermore, it would be unfair to leave the non-compliant governments in a position where they can use their unwillingness to comply as grounds for paralysing the functioning of the Union. In fact, the governments of Hungary and Poland have recurrently blocked or delayed crucial EU legislation to obtain concessions concerning EU values. Consider, for instance, their veto of a critical EU plan to address the socioeconomic effects of COVID-19 on the grounds of a rule-of-law clause.[40] All this calls for the creation of mechanisms that can deal effectively with systemic breaches of EU values.

Against this view, it may be argued that insofar as they translate the collective will of democratic peoples, the policies of the non-compliant states should be respected.[41] While many national citizens and activists have openly criticised the choices made by the governments of Hungary and Poland, they seem to have recruited significant support from their electorates. For example, Hungary's Viktor Orbán has consistently obtained significant parliamentary majorities in general elections. Accordingly, so the argument will go, any attempt by the EU to enforce EU values will paradoxically lead to a "tyranny of values".[42] However, this argument misses the point that "[i]f it ceases to be a union of rule-of-law-abiding democracies, the EU is unthinkable".[43] As I have mentioned, EU values are a crucial precondition for EU membership. One cannot plausibly be said to be a member of an association and then fail to comply with the most basic rules of that association. It should be added that the conception of democracy attached to EU values – namely, *liberal* democracy – does not hold that democracy should be *directly* equated with the collective will. This claim holds particularly when respect for human rights is at stake.[44] Even if, as we will see in Chapter 4, there are compelling reasons to think that the citizens' views should play a more prominent role in EU politics, they do not obliterate the responsibility of the national governments to comply with EU values.[45]

Beyond the normative reasons presented above, there are strong pragmatic arguments as to why systemic noncompliance with EU values should be tackled through the creation of effective mechanisms. A particularly significant one is linked to the capacity to respond to a scenario in which defiance of EU values spreads out. Consider the following questions: what if not just two but four or five member states were to be ruled by political parties and leaders that systemically breached EU values? Furthermore, what if a large and powerful member state, such as France, which can influence EU policy on its own, were to follow a similar path? Under the current institutional configuration, any of these scenarios would likely jeopardise the EU institutions' ability to uphold EU values and promote the common good of the EU polity. Indeed, one could anticipate that in a strongly divided European Council, national governments would increasingly fail to stand behind common values and seek balanced compromises regarding the distribution of the burdens of the common good. Similarly, a European Parliament increasingly dominated by nationalist and extremist political parties would likely fail to denounce breaches of EU values perpetrated by the national authorities. This conjecture suggests that the EU polity needs to be well-equipped to deal with such a scenario, should it ever come to light.

It would be a mistake to quickly dismiss these scenarios as unlikely. Since the landmark electoral result of the Freedom Party in Austria in the early 2000s, the position of the nationalist parties in the EU political system has steadily strengthened. Indeed, by the end of 2019, these parties had won more than 20% of the votes in elections in five EU member states and more than 10% in 14 of them.[46] In a few member states, these parties have become key political actors. For example, the extreme right party Sweden Democrats became the second largest political force in Sweden in 2022, providing parliamentary support to the governing coalition. This trend has not only been observed in small member states but also in some of the most influential ones. Indeed, the nationalist party Brothers of Italy was the most voted party in the 2022 Italian general election, which allowed its leader, Giorgia Meloni, to become Italy's Prime Minister. In turn, the far-right Marine Le Pen has twice reached the final round of the French Presidential election, attracting 41% of the votes in 2022.[47] In Germany, the nationalist platform Alliance for Germany has performed well in several national and regional elections since its foundation in 2013 and became the third largest political force in the country in the 2017 general election. We therefore have good reason to think that, under favourable political and socioeconomic circumstances, nationalist platforms could take an even more prominent role in Europe, putting EU values seriously at risk.

A development that may make this landscape even more challenging is the future EU accession of countries with a poor track record of compliance with democratic values. For example, Albania, North Macedonia, and Serbia – which all possess full candidate status – are still "transitional or hybrid regimes", according to the Freedom House index of democracy.[48] In turn, Bosnia-Herzegovina, Kosovo, and Ukraine, which are also on their way to accession, are ranked similarly or even more poorly.[49] This prospect reinforces the need for the EU to create effective response mechanisms.

Despite having recurrently expressed grave misgivings about the non-compliance trend, the instruments that the EU has set in place to address this problem have so far been ineffective.[50] As we shall see, the Commission has made several (albeit unsuccessful) attempts to launch an instrument to enforce the provisions of the TEU related to EU values.[51] Similarly, a wide range of statements and resolutions by the European Parliament, notably the so-called "Tavares report", have fallen short of an appropriate follow-up.[52] Other "soft" EU instruments, including the European Semester and the annual rule-of-law dialogue, have been equally ineffective.[53] Similarly, strategies within the domain of interstate relations, such as isolating non-compliant governments – along the lines of the cordon sanitaire created by several member states when the leader of the Austrian Freedom Party was about to become chancellor in 1999 – have become politically unfeasible in a context in which the constituencies of most EU states feature well-represented nationalist parties. While some progress has been made concerning setting financial penalties for the backsliding states, "pretty much all the discussion of the enforcement of EU law has until very recently been ignoring a crucially important element of the puzzle of the effectiveness of EU law: values".[54] For these reasons, "the enforcement of values should occupy a key place in the story of the enforcement of EU law".[55] Yet how can this be achieved?

Making article 7 of the TEU work

In 2010, the Treaty of Lisbon introduced a new provision aimed at enforcing EU values, which relies on the powerful threat of suspending the voting rights of non-compliant member states in the Council of the European Union. More specifically, article 7 of the TEU states that the Council, "acting by a majority of four fifths or its members after obtaining the consent of the European Parliament, may determine that there is *a clear risk* of a serious breach by a Member State of the values referred to in Article 2" – that is, EU values.[56] Then, acting by unanimity, the European Council "may determine the *existence of* a serious and persistent breach" by that member state.[57] If this is the case, then the Council, "acting by a qualified majority, may decide to suspend certain of the rights deriving from the application of the Treaties to the member state in question, including the voting rights of the representative of that member state in the Council".[58] This sanction could be revoked "in response to changes in the situation which led to their being imposed".[59] Despite its apparently serious consequences for the backsliding states, article 7 has hardly contributed to higher compliance with EU values. In fact, this provision has only been activated once by the Commission, without any follow-up at the Council level.[60] Why, then, does article 7 not work?

One of the reasons is linked to the practical difficulties in setting up a functioning and credible mechanism to identify serious breaches of EU values. What should the criteria for a serious breach of EU values be? What agents should decide on whether this threshold has been crossed? In this regard, article 7 is admittedly vague.[61] To address these shortcomings, in 2014, the Commission launched a three-step procedure to trigger article 7, in which the former would play a major role.[62] However, this methodology has received sharp criticism from the Council Legal Service, which considers that the framework set out by the Commission "is not compatible with the principle of conferral which governs the competences of the institutions of the Union".[63] In turn, national governments do not seem to be in a position to assess one another's compliance, both because they could use this opportunity to serve their own political purposes and because their fear of future retaliation could prevent them from ever censoring their peers. Finally, the party politics underpinning the functioning of the European Parliament seem to make it unfit to objectively assess any infringement of EU values, as the European People's Party's reluctance to expel Viktor Orbán has shown.[64] These observed difficulties suggest a lack of *criteria* and *agency* to apply article 7 of the TEU.

Another reason is that the sanctions foreseen by article 7 may be too extreme to deal with certain types of infringement. For this reason, former European Commission President José Manuel Barroso has described invoking article 7 as "the nuclear option".[65] This description not only reflects the dramatic nature of the sanctions at stake – namely, curtailing member states' voting rights in the Council – but also the fact that all the players would be forced to take sides in a procedure against a particular member state. Such a requirement might deepen the already pronounced divisions within the Union, strengthening the role of alliances such as the Visegrad Group. In the absence of a widely trusted mechanism that could issue early warnings regarding noncompliance, which would then be followed by proportional sanctions, EU institutions are faced with a difficult choice: they can either seek to use the "nuclear option", thereby risking antagonising some member states and jeopardising the credibility of the mechanism, or they can abstain from acting, thus tolerating the systemic infringements of EU values mentioned above. A less polarised setting in which intermediate steps were taken could produce a faster and more effective response to breaches of EU values, particularly given that the activation of article 7 seems to imply a rather lengthy process.

Jan-Werner Müller has put forward a promising proposal to address these concerns.[66] Müller argues that the EU should launch an independent watchdog to monitor compliance with EU values – which he tentatively dubs the "Copenhagen Commission" in reference to the Copenhagen criteria for EU accession. This independent body would develop sound criteria to assess compliance with values such as the rule of law and freedom of speech, as institutions such as the Council of Europe and Transparency International have successfully done. According to Müller, this new entity would require an autonomous apparatus, which would be empowered to investigate relevant developments in the member states. More specifically, the Copenhagen Commission "should be composed of legal experts (such as judges seconded from national systems, or retired judges, or also academics) as well as statesmen and stateswomen with a proven track record of political judgment".[67] Regarding the opening of investigations, this body "should be able to take the initiative in cases of possible threats".[68] This independent structure would allow this commission to operate impartially. As Müller rightly concludes, this body could then aspire to be "an agent of credible legal-political judgment as to whether a country is systematically departing from what one could call the European Union's normative acquis".[69]

Yet, unlike what Müller seems to suggest, the proposed Copenhagen Commission should be a complement rather than a substitute for article 7. Müller argues that this new entity should not only have a monitoring role but also the power to enact sanctions against the member states. Yet this would bring the EU from one extreme scenario in which EU values can be politicised to another in which the actions of the guardians of EU values are not subject to any form of democratic scrutiny. Alternatively, it is plausible to conceive a scenario in which the Copenhagen Commission would regularly produce country reports that could function as an early warning system and give credible grounds for activating article 7. For example, it would be possible that a certain number of consecutive reports of a particular country scoring very poorly would automatically trigger a debate under article 7. However, in order for a suspension of the voting (or other) rights of a given member state to take place, there would still be the need for a vote by the European Council under the qualified majority rule. This combination of independent and democratic procedures would arguably strike a desirable balance between impartiality and legitimacy, ensuring that legal and political evidence could be reliably collected while avoiding the complete outsourcing of the process to an unelected agency. This option also has the advantage of likely being more feasible than a fully-fledged independent body.[70]

Beyond article 7 of the TEU

Yet the question remains: what if, despite the warnings of the Copenhagen Commission, the activation of article 7 of the TEU, and even the suspension of its voting rights in the Council, a given member state insists on not complying with EU values? In such a case, the suspension or withdrawal of its membership should be considered. As we have seen, the TEU states that one of the main goals of the EU is to realise a particular set of public values.[71] If a state consistently refuses to be aligned with the aim of the Union and to comply with its basic functioning rules, then its membership may be inappropriate. In fact, the Copenhagen accession criteria should not be regarded as a one-off list of conditions for membership but as a stable set of requirements that apply as long as a state remains a member. Accordingly, "the same conditions which need to be met when it accedes to the EU can logically become a reason to eject such a Member State from the EU".[72] While the TEU comprises a legal procedure for the voluntary withdrawal of a member state, it does not include any provision regarding the suspension nor termination of EU membership at the request of the other member states.[73] Note that this sort of mechanism already exists in other international organisations. For example, articles 7 and 8 of the Statute of the Council of Europe provide the legal basis for the suspension and expulsion of its members.[74]

As Carlos Closa has argued, the current state of affairs could be improved by creating a procedure in the TEU through which chronically non-compliant member states could be ejected from the Union.[75] The advantages of creating this type of provision would clearly outweigh the shortcomings. To begin with, the new mechanism could have a deterrence effect, creating higher incentives for compliance. Yet why should we think that the threat of expulsion would be sufficiently compelling to persuade backsliding member states to change their behaviour? At the very least, the high political and economic costs of a withdrawal, illustrated so vividly by Brexit, would give national governments much food for thought. Second, the ejection procedure could "potentially reinforce the effectiveness of other sanctions".[76] This potential reflects "[t]he huge effects of such a procedure's eventual deployment probably make the threat itself unusable, while making less harmful penalties more credible at the same time".[77] While the objection that by expelling a backsliding member state, the EU would abandon its citizens to their own luck is compelling, it could be partially avoided if the suspension of membership was also possible. In turn, using this instrument for political purposes could be avoided by setting up a rigorous inter-institutional procedure. Finally, the objection that it would be unfeasible to make this change in the treaty does not necessarily hold since, after all, the Lisbon Treaty broke the withdrawal taboo.

A new package including a Copenhagen Commission, a fully functioning article 7 and an ejection mechanism would offer a coherent institutional framework to ensure compliance.[78] It may be argued that by adopting sharper mechanisms to enforce EU values, EU institutions would fuel nationalist narratives by boosting the perceptions of supranational interference in domestic politics. This move, so the argument would go, could ultimately prompt a few member states to leave the EU. However, it should be emphasised that the EU should not seek to avoid fragmentation by forfeiting its public values. From the standpoint of the common good, the scenario of a shrinking EU, while certainly undesirable, is possibly not the worst outcome. In fact, an arguably more damaging scenario would be one in which the goals and competences of the EU would be gradually downgraded due to pervasive internal conflicts, leading to a thinner form of intergovernmental organisation. Such a circumstance would undoubtedly limit the EU's ability to seek the common good. Yet, this does not mean that the concerns regarding the top-down governing of the Union should simply be ignored. As I will claim in Chapter 5, EU institutions' enhanced role as guardians of EU values should go hand in hand with wider opportunities for citizens to participate in the political processes that translate these values into policies.

The EU as enabler of the European Model

A few challenges facing the European Model

As I have argued earlier, the EU institutions' tasks regarding EU values should go beyond addressing the issue of noncompliance. Indeed, they should also promote certain enabling conditions that empower the member states to successfully put this normative framework into practice. The role of EU institutions as enablers of the European Model has become particularly important in the face of the emergence of a wide range of non-state actors, which no state can effectively control. This trend linked to globalisation has put public institutions "under siege".[79] This is both because it subjected many national political systems to powerful minority interests and because it undermined certain tools and resources that were traditionally at the disposal of national authorities to advance the public interest.[80] As I shall explain below, the steady disempowerment of the national actors that were traditionally able to implement policies for the common good has translated into a lack of means to realise fully the three dimensions of the European Model – namely, liberal democracy, social welfare, and environmental protection. These problematic developments have only been worsened by the neoliberal agenda implemented across the EU, which is clearly incompatible with certain aspects of the European Model.[81] As a result, the EU and its member states find themselves in a position where they lack the political agency and the economic resources to realise their shared conception of the common good.

These constraints imposed by non-state actors have affected each dimension of the European Model in its own way. Regarding liberal democracy, a few examples are worth mentioning. For instance, a wide range of disinformation campaigns hosted by social media platforms has discredited science in the public debate, leading to a "post-truth politics in Europe".[82] Consider, for instance, the widespread scepticism regarding the effects on human health of the COVID-19 vaccines.[83] While misinformation is also recurrent in political campaigns that shape the future of the Union, such as that of the Brexit referendum, private platforms such as YouTube retain the power to decide what content to allow and what to ban.[84] At the same time, hacking critical information systems can potentially undermine democratic institutions, as illustrated by the 2021 cyberattack on an Italian COVID-19 vaccination booking system. Despite the progress achieved through the adoption of the General Data Protection Regulation (GDPR) by the EU, the personal data of EU citizens is exposed to constant harassment for commercial and surveillance purposes.[85] While the opportunities for citizens' participation in EU policymaking are regarded as scarce, the lobbying by well-organised interest groups in Brussels is reportedly flourishing due to a "lack of comprehensive regulation".[86] These examples indicate that democratic values are facing multiple challenges in the EU.

In turn, the social dimension of the European Model is also under pressure. Under the current regulatory framework, multinational companies can easily relocate their production to states without robust welfare systems. They can also easily change their fiscal headquarters to ensure tax optimisation. As I have argued elsewhere, this state of affairs jeopardises the fiscal capacity of several member states that do not have the resources to play the game of tax competition.[87] In addition, multinational companies have led most member states to lower the protection level of their workers to prevent further delocalisation of private investment, thus leading to so-called social dumping.[88] At the same time, global business giants – particularly in the digital sector – recurrently avoid paying taxes on profits earned in most countries where they operate.[89] In turn, the private rating agencies have acquired the power to decide the fate of the member states' social welfare models by rating their public debt. Indeed, if they classify the treasury bonds of a given country below a critical threshold, its borrowing rates will skyrocket, forcing it to undertake swingeing cuts in its public expenditure to secure much-needed access to the financial markets.[90] Note that this rating process is hardly scrutinised. In the face of these and other constraints, the public authorities within the EU seem hard-pressed to counteract the rise of socioeconomic inequalities.

Finally, the environmental dimension of the European Model has also suffered from the constraints that the EU and national institutions face to pursue their values. A case in order is climate change. A recent United Nations report has concluded that, even if all countries were to comply with their current climate targets, the global temperature would rise by 2.7 degrees Celsius by the end of the century, with catastrophic consequences.[91] Despite the efforts made by EU institutions, notably through the European Green Deal policy package and the European Climate Law enshrining it into law, well-organised interest groups have recurrently lowered the ambition of EU regulation. As an illustration, consider the pressure successfully made by the automobile industry to downgrade the EU's CO_2 fleet targets.[92] Similarly, the EU has been compelled to postpone more ambitious climate targets in the face of threats that multinational firms will relocate offshore, presumably in search of alternative locations where environmental protection costs are lower. While this risk can be contained through a "carbon tariff" restricting EU imports from states that do not comply with high environmental standards, such a measure was only recently introduced on a very limited set of goods.[93] This state of affairs has led several environmental groups to assess EU climate policy as "not enough".[94]

These are just a few examples of the ways in which non-state actors undermine the feasibility of the European Model, to which many others could be added. Altogether, these developments have put the EU at a crossroads. On the one hand, bold measures to re-empower political institutions in relation to non-state actors are not easy to set in place since they presuppose a willingness to counteract well-organised interests and the ability to recruit broad domestic support to further regional integration and new supranational bodies. Pressed by the rise of nationalist parties and urged to deliver results in the short term, national governments have often been unable to seek more structural solutions at the EU and global levels. On the other hand, a failure to deliver on the EU's promise of boosting democracy and social welfare within Europe will likely only increase Euroscepticism and fuel nationalist discourses. As Michael Sandel has argued, if citizens' urge to regain control of their collective future is not addressed by the mainstream political parties, it may well be picked up by nationalist platforms, as has happened in the United States and the United Kingdom.[95] This possibility indicates that there are not only normative but also pragmatic grounds to reform the political and economic configuration of the EU.[96] For these reasons, the EU should act promptly to rescue the European Model.

How to rescue the European Model?

While a variety of social and political actors have called on the EU to address these challenges, a consensual political vision to achieve this goal seems to be missing. In the scholarly literature, arguments in favour of the prioritisation of the public interest vis-à-vis private agendas have notably been advanced by republican political theorists.[97] Republican theories address multiple forms of domination undermining freedom in contemporary societies, thereby re-empowering citizens to shape their collective future. Yet, many republican theorists regard the EU institutional apparatus as an additional source of disempowerment rather than a channel through which that predicament can be overcome.[98] Indeed, they tend to regard sovereignty as instrumental to realising the common good. By delegating many core competences to Brussels, so their argument goes, national governments have alienated the means to pursue this goal. Accordingly, the solution consists in recovering the state powers that were once outsourced, thus re-establishing the sovereign status of the nation-state. While a limited number of republican accounts acknowledge the irreversible character of globalisation, they remain sceptical of large-scale international organisations, seeking ways to recalibrate the state in the face of expanding competences.[99]

However, this strategy of returning to the Westphalian world would hardly be effective. Indeed, as I have suggested, individual member states are currently too weak to impose high social and environmental protection standards on a wide range of non-state actors. In view of this, the republican scholar Philip Pettit has recognised that "free peoples" need to be "entrenched against domination by other states and from the various non-state actors".[100] Yet, a united front of like-minded states presupposes hard choices, which, unlike what Pettit seems to suggest, are unlikely to be made only through ad hoc consensual agreements. As Chapter 3 will show, this becomes apparent by comparing the outcomes of two main decision-making methods in the EU. For example, in the field of tax policy, the *unanimity rule* typically brings about suboptimal policy outcomes, which consist of the minimum common denominator between the positions of the member states.[101] For this reason, unfair practices such as tax competition and tax avoidance are widely disseminated and have never been properly addressed. By contrast, in the domain of consumer protection, where the *qualified majority rule* applies, an extensive body of regulation promoting the safety and health of EU consumers has been enacted. This state of affairs suggests that a stronger emphasis on supranationalism is needed to enable the European Model.

In fact, the most effective way for the member states to address the challenges presented in the previous section is not to reclaim sovereign control but to join forces to transform the international environment in which they are embedded. Indeed, the scope of its political institutions and the size of its common market empower the EU to pursue the common good beyond borders in at least three ways. First, democratic institutions such as the European Parliament and the Council of the European Union can host a pan-European debate about certain interdependencies linked to the fulfilment of the European Model and which cannot be satisfactorily addressed by the national democracies. Consider, for instance, the cases of international tax avoidance and climate change. Second, the EU institutional framework comprises effective supranational enforcement mechanisms that can be used to implement ambitious agendas for the common good. Consider, for example, the binding decisions of the CJEU. Finally, economic integration gives EU member states significantly higher leverage to defeat private actors that jeopardise the public interest, notably through the threat of exclusion from operating in the world's largest internal market. Hence, the member states could seek to achieve together the political and economic conditions that the European Model presupposes.

What would this mean in practice? In the next section, I will illustrate how certain institutional reforms could create the enabling conditions to realise the European Model. Given the limitations of space, I will focus on the social dimension of the European Model, presenting proposals for new EU bodies that could address some of the challenges mentioned above. More specifically, I will claim that the three following supranational bodies should be launched: (i) a European Transnational Tax Authority (ii) a European Credit Rating Agency and (iii) a European Agency for Fair Trade. By at least partially shielding the national welfare systems from the pressure exerted by tax avoidance, financial speculation and fierce trade competition, these proposals could create an economic environment more consistent with the social dimension of the European Model. While this package does not aim to be exhaustive, it would be sufficiently ambitious to produce a significant transformation of the international order and to allow the governments of the member states to ensure a decent level of social welfare for their citizens.[102] The following chapters will expand this argument by outlining a broader institutional apparatus that would be equipped to interpret and realise EU values in the face of multiple and evolving challenges.

Three proposals for EU institutional reform

Let us begin with the proposal to create a European Transnational Tax Authority. This new EU body would have a clear purpose: preventing and tackling tax evasion. More specifically, it would have a mandate to ensure compliance with tax regulation by transnational economic players. To begin with, it could scale up the member states' efforts to enforce the national tax laws by cross-checking critical sources of information, including tax declarations and financial statements in the multiple locations where a given agent operates.[103] Furthermore, this new authority could effectively enforce supranational tax regulation, notably the two-pillar strategy to address the fiscal challenges underpinning digitalisation, which aims at ensuring "that multinational enterprises will be subject to a minimum tax rate of 15%, and will re-allocate profit of the largest and most profitable multinational enterprises to countries worldwide".[104] Thus, this EU body would then ensure that the minimum rate is duly applied and the reallocation of profits takes place. If cross-border inconsistencies were detected, the agency could refer the case to the national authorities, which could then press legal charges.[105] In addition, the tax authority could make recommendations for EU legislation on transnational taxation and disseminate best practices. By containing tax evasion, this agency could reduce the budgetary pressure, which has led to the shrinking of several national welfare systems.

Another institution that could add to these efforts would be a European Credit Rating Agency. Set up as an independent public agency, this body would bring about more transparency and fairness to the credit rating process. The purpose would be to provide a sound and credible analysis of the member states' public debt, which investors and policymakers could then use as a reference. In fact, the existing private agencies "may have incentives to be lax in its ratings when a bubble is about to burst and severe after a shock that has hit its reputation and the economy".[106] While these agencies are subject to the supervision of the European Securities and Markets Authority, it is usually impossible to fix any damage caused by inadequate credit rating. Consider, for example, the US subprime crisis and the EU sovereign debt crisis, which were at least partially the outcome of a failure to assess the credit risk accurately.[107] An independent public body could solve the problematic conflict of interests stemming from the fact that the "big three" rating agencies belong to firms with their own investment agendas.[108] The objection that an EU agency would be exposed to political interference by the national governments could be avoided by replicating the governance structure of the European Central Bank (ECB), whose independence is trusted by the markets.[109] By creating a more reliable rating system, this agency could reduce the speculation on the possible default of treasury bonds, partially shielding the European standards of social welfare from the aggressive dynamics of the financial markets.

Finally, the European Agency for Fair Trade would seek decent standards of social rights for all EU and non-EU workers involved in the production and distribution of goods and services exchanged in the common market. While many trade and investment agreements between the EU and other regional blocks and states contain dispositions regarding working conditions, they are insufficient and poorly enforced.[110] As a result, the EU imports goods from companies whose labour standards would not meet basic standards inside the European Union. This circumstance has an obvious impact on the welfare and well-being of the local workers who suffer from poor working conditions, but also on the EU workers who are exposed to fierce competition by exploitative companies. To improve the position of workers in the EU and beyond, the Agency for Fair Trade could create a scorecard to monitor the working conditions in countries with which the EU has sizeable economic relations.[111] For those trade partners below a given threshold of decency, a social tariff would be applied to their exports to the EU.[112] While it may be argued that this system would affect the economies of some poor countries, mitigating measures could be foreseen, such as upscaling the resources available for capacity-building and granting temporary exceptions to countries below a given level of development.[113] This policy would protect EU workers from the competitive pressure of global trade and incentivise other regions of the world to offer better conditions to their workers.

These examples illustrate the point that the renewal of the EU institutional setting could enhance the feasibility of the European Model. This strategy could be replicated in other dimensions, namely by creating supranational institutions that could support liberal democracy and environmental protection. It should be emphasised that this enhanced EU institutional framework should be democratically responsive. Depending on the level of ambition of the mandates of the new EU bodies, a revision of the EU treaties might be required to launch them. In any case, the operation of these agencies – and, for what matters, of several other EU agencies – should be subject to regular democratic scrutiny. In Chapter 4, I will explain ways in which the EU institutional setting could become more democratic, and the opportunities for citizens' participation could be expanded. More specifically, I will claim that the interdependencies underpinning the EU membership should be subject to the scrutiny of an EU Citizens' Assembly, which would have meaningful agenda-setting powers. Combined with the internal reforms of the EU decision-making processes presented in the following chapters, this renewed institutional framework would give the EU the firepower to uphold its public values in a complex global scene.

Conclusion

I have argued that EU values are a substantive conception of the common good, which all the member states have endorsed. More than just a statement of intentions, they have shaped concrete EU policies in multiple areas and been translated into a distinctive model of social organisation – the European Model. I have observed that EU values face difficult challenges from within the EU and beyond and argued that the EU should put in place an effective mechanism to enforce article 7 of the TEU, namely by relying on a new "Copenhagen Commission" that would monitor member states' compliance with EU values. Furthermore, a provision to expel chronically non-compliant states should be added to the treaties. In the face of the multiple threats posed by non-state actors, I argued that the member states should join efforts to create an international environment in which the European Model can flourish. In practice, this would imply upgrading the EU supranational framework to develop the means to shield the three dimensions of the European Model. With a view to ensuring the feasibility of a decent level of social welfare provision in particular, the EU should create a European Transnational Tax Authority, a European Credit Rating Agency and a European Agency for Fair Trade.

Notes

1 *Treaty on European Union*, article 13.
2 *Treaty on European Union*, article 21.
3 *Treaty on European Union*, article 3. Italics added.
4 *Treaty on European Union*, article 49.
5 François Foret and Oriane Calligaro (eds), *European Values: Challenges and Opportunities for EU Governance* (New York, 2018).
6 Consider, for instance, the EU gender equality strategy, the LGBTIQ equality strategy and the plan of an initiative in the field of artificial intelligence. See European Commission, *Communication to the European Parliament, the Council, the European Council, the European Economic and Social Committee and the Committee of the Regions: A Union of Equality – Gender Equality Strategy 2020–2025* (2020); European Commission, *Communication to the European Parliament, the Council, the European Council, the European Economic and Social Committee and the Committee of the Regions: Artificial Intelligence for Europe* (2018); and European Commission, *Communication to the European Parliament, the Council, the European Council, the European Economic and Social Committee and the Committee of the Regions: Union of Equality – LGBTIQ Equality Strategy 2020–2025* (2020).
7 François Foret and Oriane Calligaro, "Analysing European Values: An Introduction", in François Foret and Oriane Calligaro (eds), *European Values: Challenges and Opportunities for EU Governance* (New York, 2018), p. 4.
8 See Ian Manners, "The Normative Ethics of the European Union", *International Affairs* 84 (2008), pp. 45–60.

9 For an overview of this account, see Étienne François and Thomas Serrier (eds), *Europa: Notre Histoire* (Paris, 2019).
10 For a discussion, see Erich Striessnig and Wolfgang Lutz, "Demographic Strengthening of European Identity", *Population and Development Review* 42 (2016), pp. 305–311.
11 The formulation of the TEU is telling: public values developed "drawing inspiration from the cultural, religious and humanist inheritance of Europe". See *Treaty on European Union*, Preamble.
12 See Ola Listhaug, Sabrina P. Ramet and Dragana Dulić (eds), *Civic and Uncivic Values: Serbia in the Post-Milošević Era* (Budapest, 2011).
13 Indeed, the TEU asserts "the *universal* values of the inviolable and inalienable rights of the human person, freedom, democracy, equality and the rule of law". See *Treaty on European Union*, Preamble. Italics added.
14 In fact, democratic practices have been present in non-European regions of the world since antiquity. See David Stasavage, *The Decline and Rise of Democracy: A Global History from Antiquity to Today* (Princeton, 2020).
15 See Dario Castiglione, "Political Identity in a Community of Strangers", in Jeffrey T. Checkel and Peter J. Katzenstein (eds), *European Identity* (Cambridge, 2009).
16 For example, while several EU leaders have argued that compliance with EU values should be a precondition for accessing EU funding, the Portuguese Prime Minister António Costa has claimed that "we cannot and should not use European values, democracy and the rule of law as a bargaining chip in negotiations about money". See Caroline de Gruyter, "European Values Are Non-Negotiable", *EUObserver* (22 July 2020), https://euobserver.com/opinion/148998 (accessed 28 October 2022).
17 *Treaty on European Union*, article 2.
18 *Treaty on European Union*, article 2.
19 Emmanuel Macron in Claire Stam, "Europe Is no 'Menu à la Carte', Macron Tells Visegrad Four and Salvini", *Euroactiv* (20 September 2019), www.euractiv.com/section/uk-europe/news/europe-is-no-menu-a-la-carte-macron-tells-visagrad-four-and-salvini/ (accessed 30 March 2022).
20 Ian Manners, "The Constitutive Nature of Values, Images and Principles in the European Union", in Sonia Lucarelli and Ian Manners (eds), *Values and Principles in European Union Foreign Policy* (New York, 2006).
21 Manners elaborates carefully the meaning of each of these qualifiers in the article mentioned in the previous footnote.
22 In what follows, I shall refer to a "model" as a set of political, economic and social institutions which aims to realise the public values of a given polity. Accordingly, I regard the European Model as the institutional framework that sets EU values in place.
23 Manners, "The Constitutive Nature of Values, Images and Principles in the European Union", p. 41.
24 Plamen Akaliyski, Christian Welzel and Josef Hien, "A Community of Shared Values? Dimensions and Dynamics of Cultural Integration in the European Union", *Journal of European Integration* 44 (2022), pp. 569–590.

25 See, for instance, Daniel Trilling, "Protecting the European Way of Life from Migrants is a Gift to the Far Right", *The Guardian* (13 September 2019), www.theguardian.com/commentisfree/2019/sep/13/protecting-europe-migrants-far-right-eu-nationalism (accessed 7 April 2022).

26 The concept of a "way of life" is unsuitable for the EU because it refers not so much to common values agreed by the member states, but rather to a common cultural identity, which is absent in the EU context. Note that the use of this concept at the nation-state level is also questionable. For example, it is true that there are many references to an "American way of life" and to a "British way of life" in the public discourses of the United States and the United Kingdom, respectively. But even in these national contexts, which arguably exhibit more cultural homogeneity than the EU as a whole, the concept of a "way of life" remains ambiguous. For instance, what precisely constitutes the American way of life? Is it Sunday barbecues, participation in Fourth of July parades or the right to armed self-defence of private property? Importantly, do morally questionable but prevalent behaviours, such as the discrimination or stigmatisation of certain groups, fall under the umbrella of a "way of life"?

27 In October 2020, the leaders of the four main political parties in the European Parliament – the European People's Party, the Social Democrats, Renew Europe and the Greens/European Free Aliance – co-authored an article in defence of EU values. See Manfred Weber, Iratxe García Pérez, Dacian Cioloş, Ska Keller and Philippe Lamberts, "European Values Are not for Sale", *Politico* (6 October 2020), www.politico.eu/article/european-values-not-for-sale-rule-of-law-eu-budget-and-recovery-plan/ (accessed 27 October 2022).

28 It is noteworthy that the project of expanding the values of Europe has been signed off not only by certain conservative social groups, but also by progressive intellectuals such as John Stuart Mill, for whom colonialism was justified as long as it delivered substantial improvements for the colonised populations. See John Stuart Mill, *On Liberty, Utilitarianism and Other Essays*, ed. Mark Philp (Oxford, 2015).

29 See, for instance, Dipesh Chakrabarty, *Provincializing Europe: Postcolonial Thought and Historical Difference* (Princeton, 2008).

30 Note that the roles of guardian and enabler are different in character. As a guardian of EU values, the EU seeks to ensure compliance with the moral and legal blueprint of those values by those who have endorsed it (i.e., the member states). However, the absence of explicit actions against EU values does not automatically mean that the European Model is realised. For instance, in an EU where member states are genuinely committed to EU values and generally compliant there may be a lack of capacity and resources to ensure, say, universal access to healthcare by all EU citizens. The EU's role as enabler of the European Model will precisely be addressing these gaps.

31 This means that, while seeking to realise EU values, the EU should abstain from attempting to change the public values of other polities, provided that they comply with the fundamental rights of the individuals under their jurisdictions.

32 See Michael Birnbaum and Craig Timberg, "EU: Russians Interfered in Our Elections, Too", *The Washington Post* (14 June 2019), www.washingtonpost.com/technology/2019/06/14/eu-russians-interfered-our-elections-too/ (accessed 6 April 2022).

33 Note that between the extreme cases of interference and isolationism lies a continuum of possibilities that are potentially normatively sound. This point is forcefully made by Seyla Benhabib, *Another Cosmopolitanism* (Oxford, 2006).

34 In what follows, I focus on systemic, rather than episodic breaches of EU values, due to their greater normative relevance and higher impact on the functioning of the Union. However, it should be acknowledged that there are a few cases in which member states which have a generally compliant outlook may disrespect a specific value for a limited period. Consider, for instance, France's discriminatory deportations of Roma people under the presidency of Nicolas Sarkozy. For the contrasting nature of the breaches by Hungary and Poland in relation to those perpetrated by other member states, see Gráinne De Búrca, "Poland and Hungary's EU Membership: On Not Confronting Authoritarian Governments", *International Journal of Constitutional Law* 20 (2022), pp. 13–34.

35 See, for instance, European Commission, *Proposal for a Council Decision on the Determination of a Clear Risk of a Serious Breach by the Republic of Poland of the Rule of Law* (2017); European Parliament, *Resolution of 12 September 2018 on a Proposal Calling on the Council to Determine, pursuant to Article 7(1) of the Treaty on European Union, the Existence of a Clear Risk of a Serious Breach by Hungary of the Values on which the Union is Founded* (2017); Court of Justice of the European Union, "The Conditions Introduced by Hungary to Enable Foreign Higher Education Institutions to Carry Out their Activities in its Territory are Incompatible with EU Law", Press Release 125/20 (2020).

36 See, for instance, Armin von Bogdandy and Pál Sonnevend (eds), *Constitutional Crisis in the European Constitutional Area: Theory, Law and Politics in Hungary and Romania* (Oxford, 2015); Carlos Closa and Dimitri Kochenov (eds), *Reinforcing Rule of Law Oversight in the European Union* (Cambridge, 2016); Theodore Konstadinides, *The Rule of Law in the European Union: The Internal Dimension* (Oxford, 2017); Kim Lane Scheppele and R. Daniel Kelemen, "Defending Democracy in EU Member States", in Francesca Bignami (ed.), *EU Law in Populist Times: Crises and Prospects* (Cambridge, 2020); Werner Schroeder (ed.), *Strengthening the Rule of Law in Europe: from a Common Concept to Mechanisms of Implementation* (Oxford, 2016); and Tom Theuns, "Is the European Union a Militant Democracy? Democratic Backsliding and EU Disintegration", *Global Constitutionalism* (2023), pp. 1–22.

37 See *Treaty on European Union*, article 3.

38 The Copenhagen criteria are a set of rules of eligibility for EU membership, crystallised at the meeting of the European Council in Copenhagen in 1993. They include political criteria, economic criteria, and administrative and institutional capacity criteria.

39 Kim Lane Scheppele, Dimitry Vladimirovich Kochenov and Barbara Grabowska-Moroz, "EU Values Are Law, after All: Enforcing EU Values through Systemic

Infringement Actions by the European Commission and the Member States of the European Union", *Yearbook of European Law* 39 (2020), p. 5.
40 This plan to support the economic recovery of the EU in the aftermath of the COVID-19 pandemics came to be known as "Recovery and Resilience Facility" (RFF). The veto by the governments of Poland and Hungary was a response to the incorporation of the so-called "rule-of-law clause" in the rules of access to funding under the RFF, which would make any financial assistance conditional on compliance with EU values. The RFF was eventually adopted by unanimity, as the other member states threatened to launch it on the grounds of an intergovernmental agreement between 25 member states, thus excluding Hungary and Poland.
41 For this line of argument, see Margaret Canovan, *The People* (Cambridge, 2005); and Roger Eatwell and Matthew Goodwin, *National Populism: The Revolt Against Liberal Democracy* (London, 2020).
42 Armin von Bogdandy, "Principles and Challenges of a European Doctrine of Systemic Deficiencies", *Common Market Law Review* 57 (2020), p. 705.
43 Kim Lane Scheppele, Dimitry Vladimirovich Kochenov and Barbara Grabowska-Moroz, "EU Values Are Law, after All: Enforcing EU Values through Systemic Infringement Actions by the European Commission and the Member States of the European Union", p. 5.
44 As has been argued, whenever certain basic rights fail to be respected, there is the serious risk of turning democracy into a "tyranny of the majority". For an influential discussion, see Alexis de Tocqueville, *Democracy in America* (Chicago, 2000).
45 Here I cannot analyse the social, political and cultural conditions that have led the governments of Hungary and Poland to challenge EU values in the first place. For a comprehensive discussion, see Stephen Holmes and Ivan Krastev, *The Light That Failed: Why the West Is Losing the Fight for Democracy* (London, 2020).
46 BBC, "Europe and Right-Wing Nationalism: A Country-by-Country Guide" (13 November 2019), www.bbc.com/news/world-europe-36130006 (accessed 26 April 2022).
47 Franceinfo, "Résultats de l'Élection Présidentielle 2022", www.francetvinfo.fr/elections/resultats/#xtor=SEC-799-BIN[FTVI_Election_Presidentielle_Resultats_Metropole_search_2022_2nd_tour]-[Election_Presidentielle_Resultats_Nationaux]-S-[1143493031073414] (accessed 26 April 2022).
48 This index measures, in a scale from 0 to 100, the quality of democracy. In 2021, Albania scored 46/100, North Macedonia 47/100 and Serbia 46/100, far below the threshold of consolidated democracies (68/100). See Freedom House, "Democracy Status" (2021), https://freedomhouse.org/explore-the-map?type=nit&year=2022 (accessed 18 May 2022).
49 Bosnia-Herzegovina, Kosovo and Ukraine scored 38/100, 38/100 and 39/100, respectively.
50 For this conclusion, see Laurent Pech and Kim Lane Scheppele, "Illiberalism Within: Rule of Law Backsliding in the EU", *Cambridge Yearbook of European Legal Studies* 19 (2017), pp. 3–47.

51 See, for instance, European Commission, *Communication to the European Parliament and the Council: A new EU Framework to Strengthen the Rule of Law* (2014); European Commission, *Communication to the European Parliament, the European Council and the Council: Further Strengthening the Rule of Law within the Union – State of Play and Possible Next Steps* (2019); European Commission, *Communication to the European Parliament, the European Council, the Council, the European and Social Committee and the Committee of Regions: Strengthening the Rule of Law within the Union – A Blueprint for Action* (2019).

52 For the report on the situation in Hungary by the Committee on Civil Liberties, Justice and Home Affairs of the European Parliament led by the Member of the European Parliament Rui Tavares, see European Parliament, *Report on the Situation of Fundamental Rights: Standards and Practices in Hungary* (2013). See also European Parliament, *Resolution of 25 October 2016 with Recommendations to the Commission on the Establishment of an EU mechanism on Democracy, the Rule of Law and Fundamental Rights* (2016); and European Parliament, *Resolution of 14 November 2018 on the Need for a Comprehensive Democracy, Rule of Law and Fundamental Rights Mechanism* (2018).

53 The European Semester covers areas related to EU values, such as the functioning of the justice system, social rights and corruption. However, the recommendations presented under this tool are not binding. Furthermore, they are typically made from the standpoint of a well-functioning common market, rather than that of a multilevel EU democracy committed to EU values.

54 Dimitry Kochenov, "The Acquis and Its Principles: The Enforcement of the 'Law' versus the Enforcement of 'Values' in the EU", in András Jakab and Dimitry Kochenov (eds), *The Enforcement of EU Law and Values: Ensuring Member States' Compliance* (Oxford, 2017), p. 11.

55 Kochenov, "The Acquis and Its Principles: The Enforcement of the 'Law' versus the Enforcement of 'Values' in the EU", p. 12.

56 *Treaty on European Union*, article 7. Italics added.

57 *Treaty on European Union*, article 7. Italics added. Note that, in the context of this procedure, unanimity does not include the member state at stake, as specified by article 354 of the Treaty on the Functioning of the European Union.

58 *Treaty on European Union*, article 7.

59 *Treaty on European Union*, article 7.

60 This was a response to the contentious judiciary reform adopted by the government of Poland. See European Commission, *Proposal for a Council Decision on the Determination of a Clear Risk of a Serious Breach by the Republic of Poland of the Rule of Law* (2017).

61 This point has recurrently been made by scholars of EU law. See, for instance, Leonard Besselink, "The Bite, the Bark and the Howl: Article 7 TEU and the Rule of Law Initiatives", in András Jakab and Dimitry Kochenov (eds), *The Enforcement of EU Law and Values: Ensuring Member States' Compliance* (Oxford, 2017).

62 European Commission, *Communication to the European Parliament and the Council: A New EU Framework to Strengthen the Rule of Law* (2014).

63 Council of the European Union, "Commission's Communication on a New EU Framework to Strengthen the Rule of Law: Compatibility with the Treaties", *Opinion of the Legal Service* 10296/14 (2014), nr. 28.
64 In fact, the European People's Party (EPP) tolerated Orbán's behaviour for several years and refused to expel or to suspend his party Fidesz from EPP membership until 2021. See Jennifer Rankin and Shaun Walker Orban, "EU Centre-Right Bloc Accused of Sheltering Hungary's Orbán", *The Guardian* (5 April 2018), www.theguardian.com/world/2018/apr/05/eu-centre-right-bloc-accused-of-sheltering-hungarys-orban (accessed 19 May 2022).
65 José Manuel Barroso, *State of the Union Speech* (2013).
66 Jan-Werner Müller, "Why the EU Needs a Democracy and Rule of Law Watchdog", *Aspen Review* (15 March 2017), www.aspen.review/article/2017/why-the-eu-needs-a-democracy-and-rule-of-law-watchdog/ (accessed 19 May 2022).
67 Müller, "Why the EU Needs a Democracy and Rule of Law Watchdog". Note that the objection that the national allegiances of these experts could prevent them from being impartial in their judgements could also be raised in relation to the judges of the CJEU who arbitrate interstate disputes. Therefore, the critical challenge is to ensure that, similarly to what happens in the CJEU, the process through which these experts are appointed is credible.
68 Müller, "Why the EU Needs a Democracy and Rule of Law Watchdog".
69 Müller, "Why the EU Needs a Democracy and Rule of Law Watchdog".
70 Both modalities (i.e., the original Copenhagen Commission proposal and my reformulated one) would admittedly require a treaty change. Yet the extension of the change is lower in my account, which would maintain the logic of article 7 by maintaining the last word regarding sanctions in the European Council. This would certainly increase the likelihood of member states endorsing this change.
71 *Treaty on European Union*, article 3.
72 Carlos Closa, Dimitry Kochenov and J.H.H. Weiler, "Reinforcing Rule of Law Oversight in the European Union", *RSCAS Working Papers* (2014), p. 20.
73 This provision is the article 50 of the TEU, which was invoked in 2017 by the United Kingdom, triggering the Brexit process.
74 See Kanstantsin Dzehtsiarou and Donal K. Coffey, "Suspension and Expulsion of Members of the Council of Europe: Difficult Decisions in Troubled Times", *International and Comparative Law Quarterly* 68 (2019), pp. 443–476.
75 Closa, Kochenov and Weiler, "Reinforcing Rule of Law Oversight in the European Union", p. 20.
76 Closa, Kochenov and Weiler, "Reinforcing Rule of Law Oversight in the European Union", p. 20.
77 Closa, Kochenov and Weiler, "Reinforcing Rule of Law Oversight in the European Union", p. 20.
78 It should be acknowledged that additional proposals to address noncompliance have been put forward, notably linked to the so-called "reverse Solange" doctrine. These proposals could potentially be combined with those discussed above. While my main purpose in this section was to offer a systemic view

of how to articulate different, yet complementary instruments, I do not claim that the list of proposals that I have presented is exhaustive. For a discussion, see Armin von Bogdandy, Carlino Antpöhler, and Michael Ioannidis, "Protecting EU Values: Reverse Solange and the Rule of Law Framework", in András Jakab, Dimitry Kochenov (eds), *The Enforcement of EU Law and Values, Ensuring Member States' Compliance*.

79 Daphné Josselin and William Wallace (eds), *Non-State Actors in World Politics* (New York, 2001).
80 This point is forcefully made by Colin Crouch, *Post-Democracy* (Cambridge, 2004).
81 For example, Fritz Scharpf has highlighted the tension between the liberalising agenda of the Union and the high level of social protection underpinning the European Model. See Fritz W. Scharpf, "The European Social Model: Coping with the Challenge of Diversity", *Journal of Common Market Studies* 40 (2002), pp. 645–670.
82 Maximilian Conrad, Guðmundur Hálfdanarson, Asimina Michailidou, Charlotte Galpin and Niko Pyrhönen (eds), *Europe in the Age of Post-Truth Politics: Populism, Disinformation, and the Public Sphere* (Cham, 2023).
83 See European External Action Service, *Special Report Update: Short Assessment of Narratives and Disinformation around the Covid-19/Coronavirus Pandemic* (27 April 2020), www.eeas.europa.eu/delegations/un-geneva/eeas-special-report-update-short-assessment-narratives-and-disinformation_en (accessed 31 July 2023).
84 On the "post-truth politics" of the Brexit referendum campaign, see Hannah Marshall and Alena Drieschova, "Post-Truth Politics in the UK's Brexit Referendum", *New Perspectives* 26 (2018), pp. 89–106.
85 See, in particular, Shoshana Zuboff, *The Age of Surveillance Capitalism: The Fight for a Human Future at the New Frontier of Power* (London, 2019).
86 Transparency International, "About Lobbying", https://transparency.eu/priority/eu-money-politics/#lobbying (accessed 15 June 2022).
87 João Labareda, *Towards a Just Europe: A Theory of Distributive Justice for the European Union* (Manchester, 2021).
88 See Dorothee Bohle, "Race to the Bottom? Transnational Companies and Reinforced Competition in the Enlarged European Union", in B. van Apeldoorn, J. Drahokoupil and L. Horn (eds), *Contradictions and Limits of Neoliberal European Governance* (London, 2009).
89 For a comprehensive discussion on the moral problems raised by tax competition, see Peter Dietsch, *Catching Capital: The Ethics of Tax Competition* (Oxford, 2015).
90 This threshold corresponds to the downgrading of a country's sovereign debt from "investment" to "speculative" grade, meaning banks can no longer use its treasury bonds as collateral for their borrowings from the European Central Bank. The interest rates needed to attract sales of sovereign debt subsequently spike sharply.
91 United Nations Environment Programme, *Emissions Gap Report 2021: The Heat Is On – A World of Climate Promises Not Yet Delivered* (Nairobi, 2021).

92 CO_2 fleet limits "set an upper limit on the average emissions of new vehicles sold by a car manufacturer". For an overview of the impact of the automobile industry on the EU's CO_2 fleet limits, see Tobias Haas and Hendrik Sander, *The European Car Lobby: A Critical Analysis of the Impact of the Automobile Industry* (Brussels, 2019).

93 For a critical analysis, see Kira Taylor, "EU Countries Agree World's First Carbon Tariff, but Leave Out Controversial Issues", *Euractiv* (16 March 2022), www.euractiv.com/section/energy-environment/news/eu-countries-agree-worlds-first-carbon-tariff-but-leave-out-controversial-issues/ (accessed 14 June 2022).

94 Jessica Corbett, "'Not Enough!' Climate Activists Disappointed with New EU Emissions Deal on Eve of Biden Summit", *Common Dreams* (21 April 2021), www.commondreams.org/news/2021/04/21/not-enough-climate-activists-disappointed-new-eu-emissions-deal-eve-biden-summit (accessed 14 June 2022).

95 Michael Sandel, "The Energy of the Brexiteers and Trump is Born of the Failure of Elites", *The New Statesman* (13 June 2016), www.newstatesman.com/politics/2016/06/michael-sandel-the-energy-of-the-brexiteers-and-trump-is-born-of-the-failure-of-elites (accessed 16 June 2022).

96 See William E. Scheuerman, *The Realist Case for Global Reform* (Cambridge, 2011).

97 For the so-called neo-republican revival, see notably Philip Pettit, *Republicanism: A Theory of Freedom and Government* (Oxford, 1997); Michael Sandel, *Democracy's Discontent: America in Search of a Public Philosophy* (Cambridge MA, 1996); Quentin Skinner, "The Republican Ideal of Political Liberty", in Gisela Bock, Quentin Skinner and Maurizio Viroli (eds), *Machiavelli and Republicanism* (Cambridge, 1991).

98 See Justine Lacroix, "French Republicanism and the European Union", in Samantha Besson and José Luis Martí (eds), *Legal Republicanism: National and International Perspectives* (Oxford, 2009).

99 See, for instance, Philip Pettit, *Just Freedom: A Moral Compass for a Complex World* (New York, 2014). An exception to this intellectual landscape is Richard Bellamy, *A Republican Europe of States: Cosmopolitanism, Intergovernmentalism, and Democracy in the EU* (Cambridge, 2019).

100 Pettit, *Just Freedom: A Moral Compass for a Complex World*, p. 153.

101 This is the so-called "joint-decision trap". For a discussion, see Fritz W. Scharpf, "The Joint-Decision Trap: Lessons from German Federalism and European Integration", *Public Administration* 66 (1988), pp. 239–278. Note that the criticism according to which this concept became outdated in the aftermath of the Treaty of Lisbon is inaccurate. It is true that the Lisbon Treaty extended qualified majority to a number of areas which were previously subject to the unanimity requirement. However, while the qualified majority rule now applies to most policy areas *within* the EU's competences, unanimity is required to pass proposals in domains which are *beyond* such competences. These domains include, among others, fiscal policy, social policy, health policy and education policy. For a reassessment, see Fritz W. Scharpf, "The Joint-Decision Trap Revisited", *Journal of Common Market Studies* 44 (2006), pp. 845–864.

102 It should be noted that these institutions would not replace the member states' role in, for instance, modernising their welfare states. For a comprehensive discussion, see Anton Hemerijck, *Changing Welfare States* (Oxford, 2012).
103 Note that at present the national tax authorities have limited means to investigate the gains of companies beyond their national borders. While cooperation mechanisms do exist, they have a limited scope and degree of effectiveness.
104 OECD, *Two-Pillar Solution to Address the Tax Challenges Arising from the Digitalisation of the Economy* (2021), p. 3, www.oecd.org/tax/beps/brochure-two-pillar-solution-to-address-the-tax-challenges-arising-from-the-digitalisation-of-the-economy-october-2021.pdf#:~:text=Pillar%20Two%20puts%20a%20floor%20on%20tax%20competition,it%20does%20set%20multilaterally%20agreed%20limitations%20on%20it (accessed 20 June 2022).
105 This system would be predicated on the principle of applicability of EU law and international agreements in the national courts, which is key in the EU legal order. Note that there would be different possible criteria to decide to which country the case should be referred, including the state which was most affected by the infraction at stake and the state in which the company is based. For reasons of manageability, the new European body would only investigate multinational companies with profits above a certain threshold.
106 Julien Trouillet, "Credit Rating Agencies, Shock and Public Expectations", *AFSE 2015 64th Congress* (2015).
107 See, for instance, Lawrence J. White, "A Brief History of Credit Rating Agencies: How Financial Regulation Entrenched this Industry's Role in the Subprime Mortgage Debacle of 2007–2008", *Mercatus on Policy* 59 (2009).
108 The "big three" are S&P Global Ratings, Moody's and Fitch.
109 Note that the agency would not replace the private rating agencies, but work in parallel, thus offering an alternative source of information.
110 Indeed, many of the states with which the EU has signed preferential trade agreements have not endorsed key conventions of the International Labour Organization (ILO). Nonetheless, the dispute settlement mechanisms set up by these agreements do not foresee the imposition of trade sanctions as a result of a failure to enforce basic labour standards. This state of affairs is even more worrying in certain states with which the EU does not have preferential agreements. Indeed, these countries export their goods to the common market under the regulatory framework of the World Trade Organization (WTO), which is rather minimalistic in terms of workers' rights. For an overview, see European Parliamentary Research Service, *Labour Rights in EU Trade Agreements: Towards Stronger Enforcement* (2022).
111 For instance, this scorecard could comprise an analysis of which conventions under the ILO framework have been ratified and are generally enforced by a given state or region.
112 In the case of the countries with which the EU has preferential trade agreements, the implementation of this system would require a revision of the chapters on trade and sustainable development. Note that calls for such a review have been increasingly made in recent years. On this point, see James Harrison, Mirela Barbu, Liam Campling, Franz Christian Ebert, Deborah Martens, Axel Marx,

Jan Orbie, Ben Richardson and Adrian Smith, "Labour Standards Provisions in EU Free Trade Agreements: Reflections on the European Commission's Reform Agenda", *World Trade Review* 18 (2019), pp. 635–657. It should be added that the efforts to prevent the exploitation of workers should be coordinated at the global level, particularly through a reformed WTO. For well-argued proposals, see Mathias Risse and Gabriel Wollner, *On Trade Justice: A Philosophical Plea for a New Global Deal* (Oxford, 2019).

113 For instance, countries below a very low level of GDP could be temporarily exempted on the grounds of their lack of resources to provide social welfare to their citizens, under a formal commitment to improve the labour standards as their economic outlook improves. The upgrading of the resources for capacity-building could be funded by the gains obtained through the social tariff.

3

National interests versus the common good: A way forward for the European Union

Introduction

This chapter addresses the following questions: What is a "national interest"? In what sense do national interests pose a challenge to EU values? How can EU institutions effectively prevent, or overcome, internal divisions and political deadlocks with a view to achieving the common good? I argue that adopting ambitious EU policies for the common good requires not only endorsing common values and principles but also coming to a pragmatic agreement regarding what resources are to be employed and what interests are to be sacrificed to advance them. I claim that two complementary strategies should be pursued: (i) promoting the convergence of the national interests of the 27 member states by means of better representing the standpoint of the common good in the domestic public spheres and (ii) overcoming conflicts of interests through more effective supranational institutions. First, building on Robert Putnam's two-level game theory, I argue that EU actors should play a more active role in the processes of national interest formation at the domestic level. I claim that an effective avenue to achieve this goal would be rethinking the role of the Representations of the European Commission in the EU capitals. Instead of being limited to a ceremonial role, these institutions could actively participate in the public debate, bringing issues that concern the common good of the whole EU to the attention of national authorities and citizens. Second, I claim that EU institutions should be reformed to allow for a more consistent supranational debate on the common good. I argue that, in the context of the decision-making procedures of the Council of the European Union (the Council), the unanimity rule is normatively undesirable and should be abolished. I further claim that the reform of the Brussels institutional apparatus should have two main aims: (i) increasing the means at the disposal of EU supranational institutions to realise the common good; and (ii) making EU institutions more representative of the EU demos as a whole, as opposed to separate national demoi. I argue that abusive uses of majoritarian decision-making could be prevented by a few already existing features of the EU legal order, such as the Charter of Fundamental Rights of the European Union and the principles of proportionality and subsidiarity.

I begin by discussing the concept of national interest and explaining why national interests pose a challenge to the pursuit of the common good. I then introduce two complementary strategies to advance the common good in the EU. To understand the logic behind the first strategy, I examine the processes through which national interests are formed, and I investigate the structure of international negotiations in the context of EU membership. Subsequently, I put forward a proposal for a new role of the Representations of the Commission in the member states. I then turn to the second strategy to advance the common good in the EU. I begin by comparing two modes of public reasoning in the EU as a function of the decision-making method at stake, namely, qualified majority and unanimity. Then, I introduce a few proposals for institutional reform to overcome pervasive political deadlocks and refocus EU debates on what ought to be done from the standpoint of the common good. I conclude by discussing a few safeguard mechanisms that protect member states from impermissible sacrifices for the common good.

Beyond national interests

In the previous chapter, I argued that EU values face a variety of challenges linked to the emergence of non-state actors, such as big data operators, rating agencies and multinational companies, which pursue agendas that often jeopardise the common good. The behaviour of these agents, I claimed, has put liberal democracy, the European standards of social welfare and environmental protection at risk, both by directly undermining the conditions that make them possible and by disempowering national governments from maintaining these conditions. I claimed that the most effective and desirable way for EU member states to address these challenges is not to isolate themselves, as many nationalist platforms have suggested, but to articulate their efforts to reform the international environment in which they are embedded. Given its unique position in the global order, I argued that the EU should establish several bodies with the critical mass to address certain consequences of globalisation, including an independent credit rating agency, a transnational tax authority and an agency to enforce fair international trade standards. I further argued that the EU should put in place more effective safeguards against internal breaches of EU values, including a robust monitoring system that could lead to the suspension of the voting rights of systemically non-compliant member states and an ejection mechanism to be used as a last resort.

Yet, a powerful objection to this agenda is that it may remain a mere statement of good intentions, given that values and interests do not always overlap.[1] Indeed, recent years have shown that, even if member states have endorsed common values, they may have divergent views regarding the appropriate strategies, resources, and timings to realise them. Consider, for instance, the failure to agree on regulations to contain tax competition in the EU, which would have helped ensure the sustainability of the European Model.[2]

Why is it difficult to put EU values into practice? A preliminary answer is that realising EU values may require sacrifices that jeopardise the interests of some states. In the words of former Chancellor Angela Merkel, "speaking in one voice is often difficult given our different interests".[3] Note that for the regulation on tax competition to be adopted, the winners of this practice would have to weigh its negative impacts on the whole EU against their own national gains. As we shall see, this may be particularly difficult to achieve given the political system of the EU. Since the leaders of EU member states are accountable to domestic electorates only, it may be politically unfeasible for them to endorse common policies with wide-ranging support abroad but little support in their constituencies. This circumstance leads the EU to recurrent political deadlocks. Therefore, the following questions are in order: How can the common good be realised in an EU where national interests are so diverse? How can the conflicting positions of some member states be more effectively bridged?[4]

The national interest defined

Before addressing these questions, I should clarify what I mean by "national interest". The constructivist school of international relations has rightly emphasised that national interests are not independent of our social constructions of reality. A constellation of values, norms and ideas shape the identities of states, as well as their understandings of their national interests.[5] In turn, national interests translate into particular sets of policy preferences. For example, after the traumatic inflationary experience of the interwar period (1918–1939), achieving price stability has become a recognisable national interest for Germany. In terms of policy implications, this goal has shaped Germany's positions regarding a few critical files in EU politics, including the design of the Eurozone, the conditionality underpinning the EU bailouts during the 2008–2012 crisis and the mandate of the ECB.[6] Similarly, in an influential collection of essays, Peter Katzenstein and his collaborators showed how different cultures of national security in the

United States, the Soviet Union, and China have shaped the way national interests are defined in areas as varied as nuclear weapons and humanitarian intervention.[7] Hence, are there national interests in any straightforward sense, or is the national interest "what states make of it"?[8]

This question becomes even more relevant when certain private interests are labelled as national interests. For instance, in 2016, when President François Hollande travelled to India to close a deal on the sale of 36 combat aircraft worth €5 billion, many wondered whose interests he was actually serving.[9] Was the French president advancing the national interest of France or the interests of the French arms industry? One may argue that these two are interrelated since the contract at stake would increase national exports and create jobs. However, the extent to which the interests of small groups should be equated with the *national* interest remains a matter of controversy.[10] At the same time, the interests of large groups of citizens may fail to be taken into account in the definition of national interest. Consider Iceland's unilateral decision to increase its mackerel fishing quotas, backing away from previous international commitments.[11] In so doing, "Icelandic authorities have been accused of putting the valuable mackerel stock at risk in order to solve their financial problems in the short term".[12] Since future generations will need to pay the price of today's unsustainable fishing practices, it is not clear whether this policy serves the *national* interest. These examples suggest that claims of national interest are not scientific statements; rather, they are used as rhetorical devices in the political arena.[13]

Therefore, by saying in this chapter that member state X has a national interest Y or Z, I do not assume that it is *objectively* in the best interest of X to pursue goal Y or Z. Rather, I mean that *the authorities* of member state X have expressed interest in pursuing goals Y or Z. At the EU level, the expression of national interests takes place notably in the form of *national positions presented to the Council of the European Union*, which constitutes a tangible operational definition of national interest. This definition does not substitute for the fact that claims of national interest should be subject to normative scrutiny, for instance, via testing against criteria of *public* interest.[14] As we shall see, the definition presented above is consistent with the constructivist insight that any understanding of national interest is formed through complex social interactions and is therefore amenable to change. Indeed, national interests are not rigidly linked to material forces; ideational aspects also play a role in their formation. Accordingly, they should not simply be equated with sources of hard power, such as the size of a country, its population, and its resources.[15] Since national interests, *as expressed by the authorities of states*, remain the main currency of international negotiation, they deserve careful treatment.

National interests and the common good: a difficult relation

Despite sharing a set of common values, member states often struggle against each other to advance their national interests and to obtain advantages for their citizens or certain groups. How, then, can an agenda for the common good be implemented? One could deconstruct this puzzle by arguing that, in the context of EU membership, national interests are, to a great extent, convergent. For instance, all member states seem to have a common interest in a functioning internal market, which in turn requires a wide range of common policies regarding state aid control, consumer protection and the removal of trade barriers. This overlap led Heiko Maas, Germany's foreign minister between 2018 and 2021, to state: "There is a name for our national interest in Germany – Europe".[16] However, in areas such as social policy, environmental protection and external relations, the interests expressed by member states repeatedly clash. Consider, for instance, the cacophony of interests regarding the enlargement of the EU in the Balkans. It should be added that even when the interests of the member states overlap, a common interest is not necessarily equivalent to the common good.[17]

The diversity of national interests in the EU suggests that if member states intend to achieve the common good, they will need to negotiate with each other. However, this raises the normative question of whether the common good *should* be negotiated at all.[18] What if the outcome of interstate negotiation is simply a minimum common denominator of the different positions or a second-best solution, as the Multiannual Financial Framework 2021–2027 has been described?[19] Does this mean that the purpose of achieving the common good has been entirely compromised? Alternatively, the pursuit of the common good can be thought of as a continuum, where the actions to achieve this end may vary in degree of ambition. For example, reducing greenhouse emissions by 10% is clearly worse than cutting them by 20%. Yet, the former policy can still be said to serve the common good, at least if the baseline scenario is that no reductions would be secured.[20] Note that, in this example, it is not the common good in itself (i.e., addressing climate change) that is being negotiated but the political actions to realise it. Even if negotiation is regarded as a legitimate instrument for the common good, it may be insufficient when the intensity of national interests is very high, and a compromise is beyond reach. Consider, for instance, the field of taxation, where many EU regulatory efforts have failed.

A question that follows is whether any measures could be adopted to address the most difficult conflicts of national interests in the EU or to prevent them from emerging in the first place. According to the neorealist school of international relations, the *structure* of the international system determines how states act.[21] In this account, competition for power and scarce resources limits the scope of international cooperation because "a state cannot be sure that today's friend will not be tomorrow's enemy".[22] While the EU has rightly been presented as a case against realist assumptions, the recurrent tensions among member states should not be understated. One reason is that the different geopolitical realities and socioeconomic profiles of member states cannot easily be changed.[23] For instance, while Greece and Italy have been overwhelmed by an influx of undocumented migrants, Ireland and Denmark can hardly be reached by asylum seekers due to their geography. Similarly, the southern EU economies are financially distressed, but the northern ones are generally wealthy. Another reason is that the distribution of power among member states is clearly asymmetrical, which means that the ability of a "giant" such as Germany to advance its interests is much greater than that of other member states.[24] Does this leave EU institutions hopeless in the face of the "tragedy of great power politics"?[25]

The gradual development of resilient mechanisms to address political conflict in the EU seems to suggest otherwise. A case in point is the delegation of competences to the European Commission. By constituting an arbitrator for their disputes, member states significantly reduced the likelihood of political deadlocks in the EU. Yet why did member states accept putting themselves in a position where their interests could be thwarted? A possible explanation is that delegating competences to a supranational body ultimately served their national interests. Indeed, it has been argued that the incentives to cooperate in contexts of repeated interaction are very high.[26] For example, the functioning of the internal market clearly requires the effective enforcement of a set of common rules. An alternative explanation is that governments are sometimes ready to sacrifice certain interests for the sake of their values. In fact, the delegation of competencies to the Commission extended to areas where "the transfer was not really required by the functional needs of the single European market".[27] Thus, national public authorities may have agreed to delegate competences because they regard European integration as a normatively desirable project.[28] More generally, altruistic behaviour seems to be present in international relations in formats as diverse as the intake of refugees and humanitarian assistance.[29]

Irrespective of self-interested or altruistic motives on the member states' side, the scale of cooperative behaviour in the EU suggests that the existence of strong national interests is not *necessarily* incompatible with the pursuit of the common good. What conclusions can we draw regarding possible strategies to advance the common good in the EU? On the one hand, if states always consider their national interest first, it should be possible to advance a given EU policy by strengthening the perception that endorsing such policy would be in the best interest of the member states. On the other hand, if member states are willing to forgo some of their interests because they are committed to EU values, there is a reason to believe that the combination of a more robust supranational debate and sharper decision-making procedures could lead to broader compromises. These hypotheses point towards two complementary lines of enquiry: (i) How can the common good of the EU be taken into account in the process of national interest formation? (ii) How can conflicts over competing interests among member states be more effectively solved? I will discuss these questions in turn.

Two strategies to pursue the common good

This chapter introduces two complementary strategies to advance ambitious policies for the common good in the EU. The first strategy consists of giving a stronger voice to EU representatives in the national public spheres, allowing them to participate in the process of national interest formation. The goal is to bring the perspective of the common good of the EU to the public debate *before* national positions are crystallised. This strategy is grounded on two key insights. First, if understandings of national interest are, indeed, socially constructed, then social agents can actively participate in their construction, potentially influencing their ultimate configuration. This possibility applies particularly to democratic regimes where public authorities are expected to be responsive, taking into account a wide variety of legitimate interests. A second insight is that, in a multilevel polity, democratic representation should be a two-way street. In other words, if national interests ought to be represented at the supranational level, then supranational interests also deserve to be represented at the national level. As I shall claim, the reason is that, in the context of EU membership, the choices made by a single member state have the potential to affect the democratic life and the welfare of the EU as a whole. Accordingly, these impacts should be subject to public debate in the national capitals and not only in Brussels.

The second strategy aims at addressing pervasive conflicts over competing interests among member states in an effective manner. Even if the goals of the Union are better incorporated within national debates, one should expect that a few fundamental disagreements will remain. At this point, a distinction should be made between cases where the national positions are very diverse or polarised, such as in matters related to social justice, and those cases in which there is broad support for taking a given action, but one state or a small group of states blocks the reform, as with the CAP.[30] The first type of case is more difficult to solve and will be dealt with in greater depth in Chapter 4. However, the second type of case should not be neglected. Indeed, the list of critical EU proposals that have been blocked by a small minority of states is by no means short.[31] Note that many of the policy areas where such deadlocks occur are those where the majority rule does not apply in the Council. I shall claim that this state of affairs is normatively undesirable. While the political autonomy of member states should be respected, their responsibilities as members of an interdependent union should not be forgotten. As I shall claim, the right to veto should not be regarded as absolute; it needs to be balanced against the duty not to paralyse the EU. As I shall argue, the implication is that the burden of justification in the EU should lie with those member states that intend to block large consensus.

What are the similarities and differences of these strategies? Both strategies aim to create conditions to advance the common good by rethinking the role of national interests in EU policymaking. However, two main differences between the strategies are worth stressing. To begin with, the goals of the strategies differ. While the first strategy intends to *prevent* or *minimise* conflicts of national interests, the second strategy aims to solve conflicts that cannot be prevented. Whereas the second strategy explores pathways through which EU institutions could address difficult political deadlocks, the first strategy acknowledges that it may be difficult to build consensus when the member states' positions are already too far apart. Thus, the first strategy seeks to bridge different points of view in the EU before national authorities have crystallised their positions. Another important difference between the two strategies is linked to the level of government at stake. While the first strategy aims to bring EU politics to European capitals and expand the public debate about EU issues at the member-state level, the second strategy focuses on the Brussels-based institutional apparatus, investigating ways to improve EU decision-making. In the following sections, I will discuss these strategies in depth.

Strategy one: closing the gap between national interests

The formation of national interests

I have claimed that national interests are socially constructed. Yet *how exactly* are they formed? To understand the dynamics of national interest formation, consider a government's decision on whether to intervene militarily in another state. How does a *particular* view on this matter end up being regarded as *the* national interest? Take, for example, the United States' decision to intervene in Vietnam. When President Lyndon Johnson faced a choice on whether to escalate American operations in this country, a few alternative courses of action were available. The putative national interest to intervene in Vietnam was not defined *a priori* in any government manual; it was formed through complex exchanges among stakeholders, including politicians, military staff, academics, journalists, businesspeople, and the like. Each of these groups' goals and preferences may have played a role in the process. For instance, Yuen Foong Khong shows that the use of historical analogies by senior US officials, notably regarding the failure to intervene preventively in Germany before World War II, helped frame the Vietnam debate.[32] This recounting suggests that social interactions brought about the *perception* that it would be in the American interest to intervene in Vietnam.[33] Yet, how did the option of intervening overcome competing interpretations of the national interest of the United States?

As has been argued, *ideational background* plays a key role in the process of "constructing national interests".[34] Consider, for instance, the following dimensions: (i) the ideological landscape, (ii) policy orthodoxies and (iii) media coverage. First, ideology provides a framework within which national goals are defined and against which different scenarios are tested. Returning to our previous example, we can see how the Vietnam intervention was deeply rooted in the ideological context of the Cold War. In fact, "[h]ad it not been for the Cold War, the US, China and the Soviet Union would not have intervened in what would likely have remained a localised anticolonial struggle in French Indochina".[35] Second, the most popular policy doctrines at a given moment of time influence calculations of the national interest. In our example, domino theory created the perception among top American decision-makers that failing to act in Vietnam would mean the communist block would gain the upper hand over the United States.[36] Third, the content of the messages conveyed by the media influences public opinion, thus shaping the range of possibilities available to public authorities. Indeed, it has been argued that the endorsement by the media of official government views helped support the case that an American engagement in Vietnam would serve the national interest.[37] Therefore, "ideas are often important determinants of government policy".[38]

Another key variable that explains why a particular understanding of national interest prevails over alternative ones is the configuration of *public representation* in a given polity.[39] Indeed, goals and preferences that are "made present" in the public sphere have a much better chance of influencing national positions than those without a voice.[40] For example, trade unions have typically been effective in shaping national positions regarding the protection of wages of national workers. Yet, how do these groups achieve such impact? On the one hand, well-represented groups may *directly* shape the process of national interest formation by relying on economic or political leverage. For instance, a trade union's public engagement in favour of policy X may be backed by the threat of calling for a strike if this policy is not adopted.

On the other hand, a few groups may *indirectly* achieve policy impact by influencing public opinion. Consider the case of the environmental movement. By voicing its concerns forcefully in the public space, the green platform steadily cultivated public support. This support, in turn, changed the electoral calculations of governments and opposition parties, leading many EU member states to incorporate the green agenda in their definitions of the national interest.[41] Therefore, the pattern of public representation may determine which goals and preferences are ultimately equated with the national interest.

This point is of much relevance to our discussion. If public representation plays a role in the process of constructing the national interest, then those ideas, goals and preferences that lack a voice may fail to be taken into account. As we shall see, a voice that expresses the impacts of national policy choices on the whole EU is clearly missing in the *domestic public spheres*. In the EU political system, influence is exercised by the European Commission "through the front and the back doors" of member states, but there is no agent in a position to directly represent the common good from within.[42] For instance, when the Irish government proposed a radical tax reform to attract the biggest companies from other member states, very few actors made the case that the dramatic effects of the move on the whole EU should be taken into account.[43] Since national governments and oppositions are not accountable to electorates beyond their borders, it would be ill-considered to assume they will *always* be willing to represent the common good of the EU in domestic public spheres. In many cases, the electoral gains of pursuing "selfish" policies outweigh any complaints coming from Brussels or other European capitals. As we shall see, giving a voice to EU institutions in national public debates could have a transformational impact on these political dynamics. This transformation, in turn, could create political conditions that would enable necessary sacrifices for the common good.

Robert Putnam's two-level model revisited

Let me now turn to the question of how the national interests of the different member states interact with each other at the EU level. Robert Putnam has influentially conceptualised the politics of international negotiations as two-level games.[44] According to Putnam, the first level consists of a complex process of social interaction along the lines described in the previous section. Governments define national goals through an exchange of ideas and bargaining of preferences and goals of different groups. In turn, on the second level, governments negotiate on the international stage, where they "seek to maximize their own ability to satisfy domestic pressures, while minimizing the adverse consequences of foreign developments".[45] Putnam's model seeks to analyse the interaction across the two levels and the possible outcomes of the game. He claims that the structure of the two-level game leads to a difficult equilibrium in international negotiations. As Putnam puts it, "[a]ny key player at the international table who is dissatisfied with the outcome may upset the game board, and conversely, any leader who fails to satisfy his fellow players at the domestic table risks being evicted from his seat".[46] Therefore, the success of the game is critically dependent on clever players who "spot a move on one board that will trigger realignments on other boards, enabling them to achieve otherwise unattainable objectives".[47]

Putnam's explanatory model leads us to an empirical conclusion and a normative question regarding EU policymaking. Concerning the former, if international politics can be plausibly conceived as a two-level game, then many attempts to advance the common good at the second level may be doomed to fail. Reaching consensus at the second level may be very difficult given the very different goals and preferences already crystallised in the first level. This challenge applies notably to policies that generate an uneven pattern of costs and benefits across borders. Recall the case of the Irish tax breaks mentioned above. While Ireland would benefit enormously from this policy, all other member states could lose. As Putnam rightly observes, national leaders are accountable to domestic electorates only. Such accountability means that if they prioritise the common good of the whole EU over domestic preferences, national leaders risk losing office.[48] As Putnam suggests, skillful leaders may build resourceful coalitions and achieve unexpected breakthroughs. Yet, this coalition-building does not happen so easily. For example, it took more than ten years for the EU to approve legislation to contain the Irish tax exemptions. Hence, as a result of the two-level nature of the game, a *vacuum of agency* may arise in which there is no agent with the political leverage to advance the common good of the EU.[49] This type of deadlock is recurrent in the EU political system, which suggests that, if the common good is to be pursued consistently, EU actors will need to play a role on the first level.

A question that follows is whether granting EU representatives a stronger voice in national debates is normatively desirable. To begin with, we might argue that allowing EU institutions to intervene in domestic public spheres would ultimately undermine self-government. For those who already regard the EU as a "regulatory state", extending the Union's voice to public debates at the national level could undermine the last vestige of sovereignty left to European states.[50] In addition, intervening in the process of preference formation with the intention to nudge its outcome may be regarded as "anti-democratic and anti-political".[51] However, as I shall explain, giving voice to the standpoint of the common good of the whole EU is neither less democratic nor less political than representing any other legitimate interest with the purpose of influencing policy outcomes. Indeed, the proposal that I will present in the next section implies that EU representatives would participate in the process of national interest formation *alongside a variety of actors*. If, instead, one claims that giving voice to the EU would be undemocratic because foreign citizens are not part of the *demos*, then one should be ready to exclude foreign embassies, foreign companies, and foreign think tanks from any meaningful participation in domestic policymaking. Such an exclusion would seem implausible.

Incidentally, there is a compelling normative justification for why representing EU institutions at the domestic level is not only permissible but morally required. To understand the point, we might find it useful to invert the puzzle: Why should EU member states and their citizens be represented at the *supranational* level? In a variety of ways, the most plausible answers will refer to the *effects* of EU decision-making on the member states. Since member states are subject to EU directives, regulations and decisions, the argument would go, they should have a say in the process through which these measures are adopted. Now, the same argument applies to the relations among member states. Indeed, in the context of EU membership, the domestic decisions of a state as small as Luxembourg have the potential to affect all the others. By virtue of the high degree of economic and political integration in the EU, member states are able to impose significant negative externalities on the Union as a whole. For instance, by indebting themselves beyond sustainable levels, member states may put the financial stability of the whole Eurozone at risk.[52] This possibility suggests that the policies of a member state should, at least to a certain degree, take their impacts on the rest of the Union into account. As I shall claim, this does not call for additional controls from Brussels but instead entails bringing the EU perspective into national debates.

A new role for the Representations of the Commission

I have suggested that it is possible to enhance cooperation on the second level of the game by creating the appropriate political conditions on the first level. How might this be accomplished? A promising avenue to achieve this goal would be rethinking the role of the Representations of the European Commission in the EU capitals. Instead of being limited to a purely ceremonial role, these institutions could actively participate in public debates, bringing issues that concern the common good of the whole EU to the attention of national authorities and citizens. The Representations could be involved, for instance, in high-level meetings, public consultations, interviews in the media, and via social media to create awareness of the impacts of national policies on the other member states. At the same time, the Representations could present rationales for certain EU policy proposals by detailing the conditions prevailing in other member states that justify the adoption of those policies. Of course, the national authorities would be free to endorse or refute the points raised by the Representations, which would be one actor among many in the public debate. However, by giving a voice to EU institutions on the first level of the game, the common good could be made more visible, and greater public support for it could be recruited. Public justification would be available for certain pro-EU sacrifices. Doing so would give national governments more room to manoeuvre in adjusting their choices on the second level.

A question arises as to whether the European Commission and its Representations would be able to perform the difficult task of representing the common good of the EU. Sceptics may raise at least three types of concerns. To begin with, the Commission is not an elected body, which may cast doubt on its ability to represent the common good of European citizens at large. This concern is particularly relevant given that, as has been argued, a few member states have a disproportional capacity to influence the Commission's views on certain policy matters.[53] Second, similar to what we have seen regarding domestic actors, the Commission operates within a given ideational background, which can bring about certain biases. Consider, for instance, the Commission's reluctance to reform its competition law despite the recurrent charges of "inadequacy" and "obsolescence" presented against the latter.[54] Third, it may be added that the EU is not a unitary actor. Different EU institutions, including the European Parliament, the European External Action Service, the ECB and the several Directorates-General of the Commission, may have different views on what the common good entails. As a result, it is unclear how the Representations could convey a consolidated EU perspective on concrete policy matters.

These objections are important, but they do not defeat my proposal. In Chapter 4, I will claim that, as long as its bureaucratic apparatus functions impartially, the Commission will be in a privileged position to advance the common good. By impartial decision-making, I mean that "official judgements and reports should be based on objective and relevant criteria, without bias or prejudice, and not take sides".[55] At the same time, I will argue that the Commission's choices should be more clearly linked to the will of the European citizens. Among other measures, this could be achieved by launching direct elections for the Commission presidency. Note that these two claims are not incompatible. Indeed, I will argue that an *elected political leadership* for the Commission and an *impartial bureaucratic apparatus* can co-exist if the former focuses on establishing political priorities and common rules and the latter deals with implementing and overseeing such priorities and rules. Finally, it should be noted that the need to articulate contrasting views within the EU institutional framework is not new. Indeed, the Commission recurrently negotiates its positions with those of other EU institutions through, for instance, inter-institutional consultations and the so-called "trialogues".[56] These practices are, in fact, inescapable, given that the Commission has the power to propose, but not to adopt, new directives.

Upgrading the role of the Representations of the Commission could have significant advantages. To begin with, it could generate a more inclusive and better-informed debate about EU affairs in the member states' domestic public spheres. Since the 2008–2012 financial crisis, "the politicisation of European affairs at both the EU level and in the domestic politics of member states is inevitable and here to stay".[57] Thus, the participation of EU actors in national debates would bring a European perspective to the discussion, broadening the scope of the debate. Furthermore, enhanced Representations could answer for the policy decisions taken in Brussels, which would no longer be perceived as external impositions that cannot be contested. This arrangement would make it harder for national governments to make EU institutions political scapegoats for national problems or policy challenges. At the same time, my proposal would create the political conditions for national governments to make difficult choices for the common good. By voicing the impacts of national policies on other member states, the Commission would make public justification for certain sacrifices readily available in the domestic spheres. Publishing such information could fundamentally change the dynamics of the two-level game, contributing to reducing the tensions among member states.

Strategy two: addressing conflicts of interests effectively

Public reasoning in the European Union

So far, I have discussed how to promote the convergence of national interests, allowing the pursuit of the common good in the EU. However, it is obviously not always possible to prevent conflicts over competing interests from emerging. In some cases, the positions presented by EU leaders in Brussels are visibly far apart and seemingly irreconcilable, due either to a lack of political will to make concessions and search for reasonable compromises or to a genuine disagreement on what the common good entails.[58] While this and the following sections address the former case, Chapter 4 will deal with the latter.

To understand the problem addressed in this section, recall the case of tax competition. In this example, a small group of member states has blocked the adoption of a minimum corporate tax rate in the Union. These states seek to avoid losing the sizeable benefits gained by attracting the headquarters of companies of other member states to their territories. Strikingly, they have been able to achieve this goal without having to justify themselves.

Under the current EU institutional framework, they have been able to exercise a veto over the proposal, disregarding the harmful impacts of tax competition on the member states that cannot afford to enter the fiscal race to the bottom. How could the standards of public reasoning be improved in the EU? How could EU debates be more consistently conducive to the common good?

To address these questions, it is worth asking how the Council typically seeks to reconcile the different interests of the member states.[59] The answer fundamentally depends on which decision-making method applies to a given policy area. If the decision-making method at stake is qualified majority, the Council's primary role can be described as *negotiating national interests*.[60] How does this work in practice? Once member states have formulated their positions domestically, they seek to advance them on the EU stage. Whenever their goals are unattainable, they search for multilateral compromises with other member states. In so doing, they exchange arguments and make concessions to each other. This exchange creates a norm of compromise and mutual justification. However, when the unanimity rule applies, the Council's primary role should instead be described as *avoiding vetoes*. In this case, each member state can rely on its veto right to block policy proposals unilaterally. This leads to a peculiar setting of political bargaining. Indeed, in a scenario where only one or a small group of member states is opposing a given proposal, the unanimity requirement puts the burdens of justification on the large majority that intends to approve it. In fact, vetoing states are not required to provide any justification when exercising their veto; it is the majority that is expected to provide the minority with convincing reasons as to why they should not veto a proposal.

Accordingly, the puzzle faced by the Council presidency, which act as brokers of the diverse interests of member states, changes significantly depending on whether qualified majority or unanimity apply. When qualified majority applies, the key question for the presidency is: "How can we best accommodate the interests of everyone?". In turn, under the unanimity rule, the question becomes: "How can we avoid a veto by member state X or Y?" As I have suggested, these alternative settings may lead to contrasting policy outcomes. Even when the bargaining process underpinning majoritarian decision-making leads to non-ideal policies, they will likely benefit the EU at large. The reasons are twofold: (i) a high threshold of representing 65% of the EU population has to be met, and (ii) none of the individual member states is in a position strong enough to impose its preferences on others. In contrast, when the unanimity rule applies, member states can act unilaterally on the EU political stage. National positions can be upheld inflexibly, however harmful their impacts on other member states may be. Thus, each member state can block important reforms for the common good on the grounds of their national interests only. Qualified majority does not guarantee that the common good will be achieved, but it sets the EU in this direction more reliably than unanimity.

Therefore, extending qualified majority to *all* policy areas of EU policymaking could facilitate the pursuit of the common good in the Union. By extinguishing the unanimity rule, the EU would *shift the burdens of justification* from large majorities of member states to small minorities. In practice, it would then be for the opponents of widely endorsed reforms to explain the merits of their case. To achieve their particular goals, individual states or small groups of nations would need to provide compelling justifications to persuade other member states or put forward balanced compromises. Accordingly, they would no longer be in a position to advance their national interests at any cost nor to shield benefits that they gain unfairly at the expense of other member states. Note that the impact of this proposal would by no means be marginal. Despite applying to a limited number of policy areas, unanimity is required in critical domains, such as taxation and social policy.[61] Moreover, as I shall claim, this proposal would not expose member states to the risk of a "tyranny of the majority", given the robust set of rights and guarantees of the EU legal order. Therefore, abolishing the unanimity rule would allow the common good not to remain hostage to the national interests of one or a few member states.

Towards a European debate on the common good

As Chapter 1 argued, the common good of a group of states may require sacrifices, understood as courses of action that do not maximise the individual utility of each of them. Indeed, a few key common policies can be very costly, and they may generate unequal payoffs across national borders. For instance, a large-scale EU policy aimed at addressing coastal erosion would have significant benefits for coastal states but minimal benefits for the inland states. Similarly, an EU policy to reduce material deprivation in the Union would mainly benefit the relatively disadvantaged member states. As I have claimed, these policy proposals may recruit limited support in the constituencies of the states that would expect to become net contributors to such schemes. Since the 27 national demoi are represented in the Council as separate units and each leader is accountable to their national electorate only, the required sacrifices for the common good may become politically unfeasible. Abolishing the majority rule will partially address this problem, but it may not be enough given that the Council is designed to negotiate win–win compromises among national leaders. This setup is particularly problematic with regard to much-needed common policies where the distribution of costs and benefits is highly uneven.[62]

How could the political system of the EU be better equipped to adopt crucial reforms that imply considerable costs for some member states but overall serve the common good of the Union? There are at least two types of possible answers (which are complementary). A first approach consists of increasing the means at the disposal of EU supranational institutions to realise the common good beyond the constraints imposed by national governments. Note that this approach would not necessarily reduce the Council to a secondary role, nor would it automatically lead to a very high degree of centralisation. A minimalist version of this approach would propose an increase in the Union's own financial resources while mostly maintaining the current distribution of competences across the different levels of government in the EU polity. This increase could be achieved, for instance, by launching an EU corporate tax.[63] In this case, the Commission would no longer depend on the goodwill of the Council to obtain funds for new common policies. The necessary funds would be readily available through an autonomous common budget, which would not be contingent on the willingness of member states to increase national transfers. However, the Council would continue to have the last word on how these funds are allocated. With an enlarged common budget ready to be spent, debates on whether particular member states would be willing to pay the costs of certain EU policies would lose their political appeal. This approach is promising because it would give more firepower to EU institutions without jeopardising a meaningful role for national governments.

A second (and complementary) approach consists of making EU institutions more representative of the EU demos as a whole, as opposed to separate national demoi.[64] This step would be instrumental to reframe the debates at the EU level, leading to a greater focus on what the EU should do *from the standpoint of the common good*. An example can help illustrate the point. At the peak of the last global financial crisis, the Commission proposed an EU tax on financial transactions. This tax aimed at "making the financial sector pay its fair share", taking into account its responsibilities for the origin of the crisis and the need to use public funds to rescue several financial institutions.[65] After years of discussions in the Council, the Commission's proposal failed to be translated into an EU policy due to a complex puzzle of national interests. However, note that this proposal did recruit widespread public support: 61% of EU citizens were in favour of its adoption, and only 25% were against it.[66] Had this proposal reflected the will of the *whole* EU demos, it would have been adopted. The same applies to other areas where it has proved very difficult for the EU to adopt common policies. For example, 88% of EU citizens support tougher rules on tax avoidance and tax havens despite the inability of national governments to agree on this matter.[67] This example suggests that a stronger link between

EU citizens and EU institutions could empower the latter to act for the common good, at least in a few crucial fields.

Yet, how could a stronger link between EU institutions and EU citizens be built? As Chapter 4 will claim, this could be achieved through reforming the EU institutional framework. One of the proposals presented in the next chapter is adopting transnational lists to elect Members of the European Parliament (MEPs), thereby creating a pan-European constituency. This move would lead the political parties of the different member states to articulate common agendas and make each MEP representative of all European citizens unambiguously.[68] At the same time, as I will argue, directly electing the presidents of the Commission and the European Council would make both institutions accountable to all EU citizens, and it could prompt EU leadership to think more in terms of European goals and solutions rather than in terms of interstate negotiations. As I shall argue, creating a Citizens Assembly where EU citizens could jointly deliberate over what the common good entails beyond narrow definitions of national interest would be an additional step forward. The proposals to be discussed in Chapter 4 would change the configuration of the two-level game, making it possible to address disputes among national governments more effectively.

Critics of my proposals may argue that the EU currently lacks a common demos.[69] They may point to the sharp social and cultural differences within the EU and the arguably weak civic bonds among EU citizens, claiming that the idea of an EU demos is hard to conceive. Accordingly, so the argument would go, bypassing the will of sovereign national demoi would be both undemocratic and unfeasible.[70] However, the current model of political representation in the EU polity, which relies heavily on mediation by national governments, leads to outcomes that seem far less democratic than my proposals. Consider the case of the CAP, which for decades consumed the lion's share of the Union budget. This common policy was purportedly designed to serve the interests of French farmers, who have successfully shaped the positions of the French government.[71] Governing the resources of the Union according to the interests of French farmers can hardly be considered democratic. Therefore, even if no such demos exists, a question arises as to whether "there *should* be a common demos".[72] Would this common demos be feasible? As I will claim in Chapter 5, any demos should be regarded as a dynamic outcome of political choices rather than as a stable social entity that is either present or absent. As we shall see, the feasibility of an EU demos is largely contingent on a set of political and socioeconomic conditions that are shaped by EU institutions and national governments.

The limits of the common good

I have argued that member states, as members of the EU polity, should be ready to accept certain sacrifices for the common good of the whole EU. Yet, how far should they be ready to go? Consider a policy proposal that would improve the average welfare of EU citizens but impose disproportionate costs on limited groups. For example, consider a relaxation of the regulation that restrains the use of the label "Port" to wines produced in the Douro Valley in Portugal. Under this proposal, "Port" wine could be produced in every member state, thus creating new business opportunities and jobs. Furthermore, this policy would reduce the price to be paid by consumers, given the increase of competition in the market of Port wine. However, this measure could have a devastating effect in Portugal, leading to heavy job losses. Is this policy compatible with the common good? What costs can be legitimately imposed on a member state for the sake of the common good of the whole EU? Furthermore, assume that the proposals presented above regarding extending majoritarian decision-making and better representing EU citizens were in place. Would this not leave, say, Portuguese citizens too exposed to the will of the EU majority? What safeguards, if any, would they have against a "tyranny of the majority"?[73]

To address these questions, we might find it useful to recall the definition of the common good presented in the introductory chapter of this book. I defined common good in the context of EU membership as the conditions and goals that benefit the EU as a whole *without imposing impermissible harm on some EU citizens or member states*. This definition suggests that the common good is not an ultimate good – that is, it should not be sought at all costs. As I have mentioned, an illustrative example is the carrying out of promising but unethical medical experiments on patients. As I have argued, this type of harm would be impermissible, even if inflicted to achieve the common good. However, in this chapter, I have also claimed that realising the common good of the whole EU may require *certain* sacrifices by one or more member states or by groups of their citizens. The question is, then, how to set the boundary between permissible and impermissible harm. What kinds of sacrifices should *not* be imposed on the citizens of a given member state? In Chapter 1, I argued that the concept of fundamental rights draws clear limits to what should be asked from individuals for the sake of the common good and constitutes a useful proxy for impermissible harm. Now, I shall argue that the existing EU institutional framework already offers robust safeguards against a wide range of impermissible policy outcomes.

There are at least three types of safeguards. The first is the Charter of Fundamental Rights of the European Union. The Charter sets out a vast array of rights and liberties that all EU policies should not contravene. The latter include, for instance, a right to bodily integrity, non-discrimination, fair and just working conditions, and a high level of consumer protection.[74] In our previous example, relaxing the rules concerning the labelling of Port wine without replicating this policy to other intellectual property rights in other member states would be a discriminatory measure.

The second safeguard is the well-established EU legal principles of conferral, subsidiarity and proportionality. In particular, the principle of proportionality establishes that "the content and form of Union action shall not exceed what is necessary to achieve the objectives of the Treaties".[75] Thus, the proposal mentioned above would most likely violate this principle insofar as extinguishing intellectual property rights does not seem necessary for the construction of a single market. The third safeguard is the Court of Justice of the European Union (CJEU), which is responsible for enforcing the Charter and the three legal principles mentioned above. In addition, the CJEU has built extensive case law which protects the rights of EU citizens. These three safeguards set clear limits to the pursuit of the common good in the EU.

Conclusion

In this chapter, I have argued that a more consistent pursuit of the common good in the Union requires rethinking EU politics. I introduced two strategies to this end. The first strategy consists of promoting the convergence of national interests. I claimed that by giving the EU a stronger voice in national debates, where the broader European picture often remains underrepresented, the perspective of the common good of the whole EU might be more smoothly incorporated into national positions, and it might recruit greater public support. In practice, this would mean that the Representations of the Commission in the member states would act as the face of the EU at the national level. In turn, the second strategy entails addressing conflicts of national interests more effectively. I argued that this could be achieved by withdrawing the unanimity rule in the Council, increasing the means at the disposal of EU supranational institutions to realise the common good, and making EU institutions more representative of the EU demos as a whole, as opposed to separate national demoi. Altogether, these proposals could change the dynamics of the two-level game in the EU, creating the political conditions for the common good to be realised.

Notes

1 Along the lines of the previous chapter, I understand values as normative frameworks to guide human action. In turn, by interests I mean the courses of action that agents pursue in maximising their utility. In this account, values belong to the normative realm, while interests consist of descriptive claims. For instance, I may endorse the *value* of solidarity and not have an *interest* in giving all my money to charities. Note that, by arguing that this distinction is meaningful, I do not claim that values and interests are unrelated. As I shall claim, values can influence our perception of interests, while interests may shape how far we are ready to go for our values.
2 There have been a few attempts to establish a minimum corporate tax rate in the EU with the purpose of avoiding a race to lower taxes. Tax competition is particularly harmful for the public finances of member states that can neither afford to lower their tax rates, nor to lose the tax revenue linked to the companies that operate in their territories. Under fierce tax competition, it will likely become impossible for a number of member states to maintain the levels of social provision underpinning the European Model.
3 Angela Merkel, "Merkel: Europe Must Unite to Stand Up to China, Russia and U.S.", *The Guardian* (15 May 2019), www.theguardian.com/world/2019/may/15/angela-merkel-interview-europe-eu-unite-challenge-us-russia-china (accessed 28 February 2021).
4 Note that my purpose is not to investigate how political conflict can be eliminated in the EU, but to search for institutions and processes by which it may more likely be conducive to the common good. Political conflict is a constitutive part of politics and cannot be suppressed, particularly in a democratic context. However, as has been argued, well-designed institutions and decision-making processes may facilitate the creation of consensus. On this point, see Jane J. Mansbridge, *Beyond Adversarial Democracy* (Chicago, 1983).
5 Nicolas Onuf, "Constructivism: A User's Manual", in Vendulka Kubálková, Paul Kowert and Nicholas Onuf (eds), *International Relations in a Constructed World* (New York, 1998).
6 See Markus K. Brunnermeier, Harold James and Jean-Pierre Landau, *The Euro and the Battle of Ideas* (Princeton, 2018).
7 Peter J. Katzenstein (ed.), *The Culture of National Security: Norms and Identity in World Politics* (New York, 1996).
8 Alexander Wendt, "Anarchy is What States Make of It: The Social Construction of Power Politics", *International Organization* 46 (1992), pp. 391–425.
9 Franceinfo, "En visite en Inde, François Hollande Réussira-t-il à Conclure la Vente de 36 Rafale?" (24 January 2016), www.francetvinfo.fr/economie/aeronautique/rafale/francois-hollande-reussira-t-il-a-vendre-des-rafale-a-l-inde_1283507.html (accessed 7 March 2021).
10 For instance, for Miroslav Nincic, "our ability to judge whether a policy does serve the national interest is intimately connected to how democratic the decision behind the policy is". This would likely exclude President Hollande's sales

trip from the scope of the national interest. See Miroslav Nincic, "The National Interest and its Interpretation", *The Review of Politics* 61 (1999), pp. 29–55.

11 The decision has been justified on the grounds of advancing Iceland's national interest vis-à-vis other nations. For instance, in the words of the Icelandic Minister for Fisheries and Agriculture, Kristján Þór Júlíusson, "Iceland won't be left out while other nations fish from the mackerel stock they share". See Gréta Sigríður Einarsdóttir, "EU to Threaten Sanctions Against Iceland and Greenland Over Mackerel Dispute" (26 August 2019), *Iceland Review*, www.icelandreview.com/news/eu-to-threaten-sanctions-against-iceland-and-greenland-over-mackerel/ (accessed 7 March 2021).

12 Jóhann Páll Ástvaldsson, "Mackerel War on the Cards as Iceland Increases Quota?", *Iceland Review* (20 August 2019), www.icelandreview.com/news/mackerel-war-on-the-cards-as-iceland-increases-quota/ (accessed 7 March 2021).

13 Against this view, Hans Morgenthau has argued that "politics is governed by objective laws which have roots in human nature". For Morgenthau, the national interest is necessarily defined as a function of the power that a given state has. See Hans J. Morgenthau, *Politics among Nations: The Struggle for Power and Peace* (New York, 1978).

14 Criteria to define public interest are abundant in the literature of public law and political theory. For a discussion in the context of EU membership, see Andrew Moravcsik and Andrea Sangiovanni, "On Democracy and the 'Public Interest' in the European Union", *CES Working Paper* 93 (2003).

15 The role of these variables has been emphasised by classic realist authors. See, among others, Niccolò Machiavelli, *The Prince* (Oxford, 2008); Thomas Hobbes, *Leviathan*, ed. Noel Malcolm (Oxford, 2012); Morgenthau, *Politics among Nations*; Reinhold Niebuhr, *Moral Man and Immoral Society: A Study in Ethics and Politics* (Louisville, 2013); Henry Kissinger, *Diplomacy* (New York, 1994). For the distinction between hard and soft power, see Joseph S. Nye, *Soft Power: The Means to Success in World Politics* (New York, 2004).

16 Heiko Maas, *Interview with the Welt am Sonntag Newspaper* (19 August 2018), www.auswaertiges-amt.de/en/newsroom/news/maas-welt-am-sonntag/2129042 (accessed 1 March 2021).

17 The conceptual difference between common interest and common good can be drawn in two at least ways. First, there are normatively desirable goods, the provision of which does not serve the interests of all the agents in a group. For instance, universal healthcare access funded through progressive taxes does not seem to maximise the utility of wealthy citizens. Second, a set of agents may have a common interest that clearly jeopardises the common good. To illustrate the point, consider that all individuals may have an interest in evading taxes, but if they do so, they will jeopardise the common good.

18 This question is formulated by Johannes Pollak, "Political Representation and the Common Good: A Fragile Relationship", in Sonja Puntscher Riekmann, Alexander Somek and Doris Wydra (eds), *Is there a European Common Good?* (Baden-Baden, 2013), pp. 156–173.

19 Marta Pilati, "Brace for a Disappointing EU Budget", *European Policy Centre Commentary* (24 February 2020), www.epc.eu/en/Publications/Brace-for-a-disappointing-EU-budget~2f533c (accessed 11 June 2021).
20 It should be added that similar negotiations take place in federalised states, and even within nation-states.
21 See notably Kenneth N. Waltz, *Man, the State and War: A Theoretical Analysis* (New York, 2001).
22 Kenneth N. Waltz, "Structural Realism After the Cold War", *International Security* 25 (2000), p. 10.
23 For a discussion regarding the role of contextual factors in explaining variation of state behaviour in the international system, see Gary Goertz, *Contexts of International Politics* (Cambridge, 1994).
24 Stuart Jeffries, "Is Germany too Powerful for Europe?", *The Guardian* (31 March 2013), www.theguardian.com/world/2013/mar/31/is-germany-too-powerful-for-europe (accessed 18 February 2021).
25 John J. Mearsheimer, *The Tragedy of Great Power Politics* (New York, 2014).
26 On this argument, see notably Robert Axelrod, *The Evolution of Cooperation* (New York, 1984).
27 Giandomenico Majone, *Regulating Europe* (London/New York, 1996), p. 40.
28 On the role of values and ideas in the process of European integration, see Geoffrey Garrett and Barry R. Weingast, "Ideas, Interests, and Institutions: Constructing the European Community's Internal Market", in Judith Goldstein and Robert O. Keohane (eds), *Ideas and Foreign Policy: Beliefs, Institutions and Political Change* (Ithaca, 1993).
29 A number of philosophers and social scientists have claimed that altruistic behaviour is ultimately reducible to self-interest. For instance, in the case of EU membership, it may be argued that any concession made by a member state is expected to pay back in the future. For a discussion on the possibility of altruism in the field of international relations, see Alison Brysk, *Global Good Samaritans: Human Rights as Foreign Policy* (Oxford, 2009).
30 I will discuss this case in greater detail below.
31 An illustrative example is the accession of new member states to the EU. For instance, Greece long blocked the accession of North Macedonia due to a bilateral dispute regarding the latter's official name. Greece's position hardly seems justified from the standpoint of the common good.
32 Yuen Foong Khong, *Analogies at War: Korea, Munich, Dien Bien Phu, and the Vietnam Decisions of 1965* (Princeton, 1992).
33 For a comprehensive discussion on the role of perceptions in international politics, see Robert Jervis, *Perception and Misperception in International Politics* (Princeton, 1976).
34 Jutta Weldes, "Constructing National Interests", *European Journal of International Relations* 2 (1996), pp. 275–318.
35 George C. Herring, "The Cold War and Vietnam", *OAH Magazine of History* 18 (2004), p. 18.
36 Consider the following section of the memorandum from Secretary of Defence McNamara to President Lyndon Johnson of 16 March 1964: "Unless we can

achieve this objective in South Vietnam, almost all of Southeast Asia will probably fall under Communist dominance (all of Vietnam, Laos, and Cambodia), accommodate to Communism so as to remove effective US and anti-Communist influence (Burma), or fall under the domination of forces not now explicitly Communist but likely then to become so (Indonesia taking over Malaysia)". See Robert McNamara, "Memorandum of Secretary of Defence (McNamara) to the President: 16 March 1964", in Edward C. Keefer and Charles S. Sampson (eds), *Foreign Relations of the United States 1964–1968. Volume 1: Vietnam 1964* (Washington, 1992). Available at https://history.state.gov/historicaldocuments/frus1964-68v01/d84 (accessed 27 February 2021).
37 See Daniel C. Hallin, *The "Uncensored War": The Media and Vietnam* (Oxford/New York, 1986). More generally, the acceptance by the American public that an intervention in a remote and unfamiliar country such as Vietnam would serve the national interest of the United States would seem to require, to some degree, a process that has been dubbed "manufacturing consent" by Noam Chomsky and Edward S. Herman. See Noam Chomsky and Edward S. Herman, *Manufacturing Consent: The Political Economy of the Mass Media* (London, 1994).
38 Judith Goldstein and Robert O. Keohane, "Ideas and Foreign Policy: An Analytical Framework", in Judith Goldstein and Robert O. Keohane (eds), *Ideas and Foreign Policy: Beliefs, Institutions and Political Change* (Ithaca, 1993), p. 3.
39 I understand public representation as any *organised* and *legitimate* means of voicing an interest with the intention to influence the decisions of public authorities. The adjective "organised" aims to exclude from our analysis loose or ad hoc attempts to voice an interest, putting the emphasis on the recurrent nature of representation. In turn, the caveat "legitimate" aims to exclude certain morally impermissible forms of exercising influence, such as bribing. Note that this definition refers not only to political parties, but also to associations, trade unions, civic platforms and other organised groups that can influence different stages of the policymaking process. For a discussion on alternative formats of public representation, see Philip Pettit, "Varieties of Public Representation", in Ian Shapiro, Susan C. Stokes, Elizabeth Jean Wood, and Alexander S. Kirshner (eds), *Political Representation* (Cambridge, 2009).
40 The claim that representation implies making a group or a cause present in the public space has been influentially advanced by Hanna Fenichel Pitkin, *The Concept of Representation* (Berkeley, 1967).
41 The process of exercising voice has been influentially detailed by Albert O. Hirschman, *Exit, Voice and Loyalty: Responses to Decline in Firms, Organizations, and States* (Cambridge MA, 1970).
42 Edward C. Page, "The European Commission Bureaucracy: Handling Sovereignty through the Back and Front Doors", in Jack Hayward, Rüdiger Wurzel (eds), *European Disunion: Between Sovereignty and Solidarity* (London, 2012).
43 Note that tax competition among member states has the potential to significantly reduce aggregate tax revenue across the EU as a whole.

44 Robert D. Putnam, "Diplomacy and Domestic Politics: The Logic of Two-level Games", *International Organization* 42 (1988), pp. 427–460.
45 Putnam, "Diplomacy and Domestic Politics", p. 434.
46 Putnam, "Diplomacy and Domestic Politics", p. 434.
47 Putnam, "Diplomacy and Domestic Politics", p. 434. Note that Putnam does not deny that second-level players may try to influence the first level. Consider, for instance, the country-specific recommendations of the European Commission under the European Semester. However, he suggests that the prospects of success of these attempts are fundamentally conditioned by the structure of the two-level game and the non-overlapping constituencies involved.
48 Note that the structure of this game is very different from that of a federation. For instance, the federal government of the United States is accountable to all American citizens. Thus, a president that designs policies only for the benefit of his or her state of origin should expect to lose office in the following elections.
49 On the issue of a lack of agency among EU leadership, see Claus Offe, *Europe Entrapped* (Cambridge, 2015).
50 See Giandomenico Majone, "The Rise of the Regulatory State in Europe", *Western European Politics* 17 (1994), pp. 77–101.
51 Andrew Dobson, "Nudging is Anti-democratic and Anti-political", *The Guardian* (2 May 2014), www.theguardian.com/politics/2014/may/02/nudging-anti-democratic-anti-political (accessed 20 April 2023). For a survey of the moral criticism that the project of nudging human behaviour has faced, see Andreas T. Schmidt and Bart Engelen, "The Ethics of Nudging: An Overview", *Philosophy Compass* 15 (2020), pp. 1–13.
52 Note that this argument does not apply, at least along the same lines, to non-EU countries. Consider the case of the Eurozone, where the financial distress of the relatively small Greek economy came close to bringing the single currency to an end. A similar episode of financial instability in, say, Bosnia or Morocco would not have a comparable effect on the member states. Accordingly, the so-called "butterfly effect", according to which *any* action by *any* given agent impacts *all* the other agents, does not necessarily imply that all the interests of all the states in the world should be represented in a given state's political arena. For a discussion, see Robert E. Goodin, "Enfranchising All Affected Interests, and Its Alternatives", *Philosophy & Public Affairs* 35 (2007), pp. 40–68.
53 See Page, "The European Commission Bureaucracy".
54 For a discussion, see, for instance, Bruno Deffains, Olivier d'Ormesson and Thomas Perroud, "Competition Policy and Industrial Policy: For a Reform of European Law", *Fondation Robert Schuman Policy Papers* (2020).
55 Daniel Chandler and Rod Munday (eds), "Impartiality", *A Dictionary of Media and Communication* (Oxford, 2011).
56 Trialogues are informal negotiations involving the Commission, the European Parliament and the Council with a view to achieving an agreement concerning a given legislative proposal.
57 Thomas Risse, *European Public Spheres: Politics Is Back* (Cambridge, 2015), p. 3.
58 Note that two agents equally committed to pursue the ideal of the common good may reach different conclusions as to what it entails. John Rawls

famously referred to this problem as the "burdens of judgment". This issue will be revisited in Chapter 4, where I discuss the institutional design of EU deliberative institutions. See John Rawls, "The Idea of Public Reason Revisited", *The University of Chicago Law Review* 64 (1997), pp. 765–807.

59 In what follows, I refer to *both* the European Council and the Council of the European Union, since the challenges related to the EU decision-making methods apply similarly to both.

60 When the Council of the European Union votes on a policy proposal, a qualified majority is reached when two conditions are met: (i) 55% of member states vote in favour; (ii) the proposal is supported by member states representing at least 65% of the total EU population. See Council of the European Union, "Qualified Majority", www.consilium.europa.eu/en/council-eu/voting-system/qualified-majority/ (accessed 23 April 2021).

61 According to the Council of the European Union, about 80% of all EU legislation is adopted through qualified majority. However, this figure is biased by the fact that it is harder to approve legislation by unanimity that by qualified majority. See Council of the European Union, "Qualified Majority".

62 It may be argued that the adoption of such policies would be undemocratic in the first place. However, as I will argue below, the question to be addressed is who should be the demos to which EU policies are linked. If the EU demos as a whole is taken into account, such policies may be justified from a democratic standpoint. This, in fact, also applies to a number of federal states where certain federal policies may have uneven distributional effects on the constitutive units of the federation.

63 I have presented this proposal in greater length elsewhere. However, an EU tax could assume other modalities, taking into account considerations related to desirability and feasibility. See João Labareda, *Towards a Just Europe: A Theory of Distributive Justice for the European Union* (Manchester, 2021).

64 Note that most EU institutions represent de facto separated national demoi. This applies not only to the Council of the European Union, but also to the European Parliament (elected from national circles), the College of Commissioners (appointed by the national governments), the Committee of Regions and the Economic and Social Committee (designated by the Council following nominations by national authorities).

65 European Commission, "Financial Transactions Tax: Making the Financial Sector Pay Its Fair Share" (28 September 2011), https://ec.europa.eu/commission/presscorner/detail/en/IP_11_1085 (accessed 3 May 2021).

66 European Commission, "European Governance in the European Union", *Eurobarometer* 74 (2011), pp. 13–14.

67 European Commission, "European Governance in the European Union".

68 Note that, at present, there is an ambiguity in the status of MEPs. According to the treaties, MEPs are supposed to represent all EU citizens, but they are accountable to domestic electorates only.

69 On the "no-demos" thesis, see Dieter Grimm, "Does Europe Need a Constitution?", *European Law Journal* 1 (1995), pp. 282–302.

70 An alternative is to conceive the EU political system as a "demoicracy" where multiple demoi decide their future together. Despite its conceptual appeal, this model, as Miriam Ronzoni has argued, does not substitute for a critical institutional choice between federalism and intergovernmentalism. See Miriam Ronzoni, "The European Union as a Demoicracy: Really a Third Way?", *European Journal of Political Theory* 16 (2017), pp. 210–234.
71 See, for instance, Carine Germond, "Preventing Reform: Farm Interest Groups and the Common Agricultural Policy", in Wolfram Kaiser and Jan-Henrik Meyer (eds), *Societal Actors in European Integration: Polity-Building and Policy-Making 1958–1992* (Basingstoke, 2013).
72 Philippe Van Parijs, "First Letter", in John Rawls and Philippe Van Parijs, *Three Letters on The Law of Peoples and the European Union*, https://ethics.harvard.edu/files/center-for-ethics/files/2003.rawlsvanparijs.r.phil_.econ_.pdf (accessed 2 March 2023).
73 The risk that a democratic regime degenerates into a totalitarian majority that oppresses minorities has been raised by a few liberal thinkers. See, for instance, John Stuart Mill, *On Liberty, Utilitarianism and Other Essays*, ed. Mark Philp (Oxford, 2015).
74 See *Charter of Fundamental Rights of the European Union*.
75 *Treaty on European Union*, article 5.

4

EU institutions for the common good

Introduction

This chapter expands the discussion of the previous one, introducing additional proposals that could gear the Brussels-based decision-making apparatus more towards the common good. It addresses the following questions: What institutional reforms at the EU level, if any, could facilitate the pursuit of the common good? Under what conditions would they be feasible? I argue that a revised supranational framework of representative, participatory, and consultative bodies is both desirable and feasible. More specifically, I present the following proposals: (i) enhancing the level of impartiality of the European Commission by clearly separating its legislative and supervisory tasks; (ii) directly electing the presidents of the Commission and the European Council; (iii) adopting transnational lists for the elections for the European Parliament and strengthening the links between the European and the national parliaments; (iv) creating an EU Citizens' Assembly; and (v) launching an advisory body of former presidents of the EU institutions.

I claim that these institutional reforms would further orient the functioning of EU institutions towards the common good in a variety of ways. To begin with, a more impartial bureaucratic apparatus would be less vulnerable to the interests of the national administrations, thus being in a better position to realise the common good. Similarly, directly electing the presidents of the European Commission and European Council would make these officials accountable to all EU citizens, prompting them to put forward agendas that articulate the diversity of interests in a balanced manner. Furthermore, adopting transnational lists for the European Parliament would lead the political parties of the different member states to work together within common political platforms, turning each MEP into a representative of all European citizens rather than a representative of their compatriots. In turn, creating an EU Citizens' Assembly would give EU citizens a meaningful chance to debate common challenges and shape the agenda of the other EU institutions. Finally, a body of former EU leaders could bring valuable expertise and organisational memory to enlighten the present-day choices. This renewed institutional setting would place the common good at the heart of EU policymaking.

Enhancing the European Commission's impartiality

In Chapter 3, I have presented a strategy to strengthen the European Commission's capacity to "promote the general interest of the Union" by upgrading the role of the Representations of the Commission in the member states.[1] Yet, what should be said about the "two levels of action" of the Commission based in Brussels, namely the College of Commissioners and the sectoral Directorates-General, which design and supervise the implementation of EU policies?[2] How should these two levels share the Commission's extensive competences if they are to jointly promote the general interest?

In the previous chapter, I have also suggested that the decisions by the Commission's bureaucratic apparatus should be impartial vis-à-vis the different member states. Yet why exactly is impartiality instrumental to the realisation of the common good in the EU polity? Isn't there a trade-off between promoting impartial decision-making by the Commission, on the one hand, and making the latter more democratically accountable to its citizens, on the other hand? Furthermore, is there a need to change or to expand the Commission's competences, as it has been argued?[3] If so, would this be politically feasible? To sum up, what institutional reforms, if any, could strengthen the Commission's role as an enabler of the common good in the EU?

Let me begin by explaining why impartiality is a core requisite for a Commission that effectively promotes the common good. By *impartial decision-making*, I mean that "official judgements and reports should be based on objective and relevant criteria, without bias or prejudice, and not take sides".[4] Impartiality involves treating every member state as an equal "rather than necessarily treating them in exactly the same way" since certain commonly agreed rules and goals "may be objectively judged to require different treatment".[5] Consider, for example, the uneven distribution of EU structural funds across the member states with a view to promoting social cohesion, as prescribed by the TEU.[6] Ensuring impartiality in this sense is crucial given that, as we have seen in Chapter 3, the EU is a politically, economically and culturally diverse polity. Given that the governments of the EU member states often pursue conflicting national interests and their power to shape EU policy outcomes is asymmetrically distributed, only an impartial body can ensure the implementation of the common rules and policies and can adjudicate conflicting interests in a fair and credible manner. Given its autonomy from the national administrations, the Commission's "second level of action" – that is, the sectoral Directorates-General – is well placed to perform this role.

A question that follows is how this need to promote impartial decision-making by a bureaucratic apparatus can be reconciled with the demands of democracy.[7] To address this issue in the specific EU institutional context, we might find it useful to note that the Commission holds two powers of a very different nature: (i) legislative initiative and (ii) supervision and enforcement of the application of EU rules and policies by the member states. First, the Commission is the only body in the EU institutional framework that can present legislative proposals, even if it often does so at the request of the Council and the European Parliament.[8] This prerogative means that the Commission is presently the leading EU actor as far as agenda-setting is concerned.[9] Second, the Commission is responsible for overseeing the implementation of a wide range of EU laws, policies, and programmes by the national governments, and it can launch measures against non-compliant member states, notably infringement procedures. This supervisory role covers aspects as varied as compliance with the EU anti-trust rules, enforcement of the EU consumer protection standards and the use of EU funds under the Common Agriculture Policy (CAP). Accordingly, the Commission has been described as "the guardian of the EU treaties".[10]

We might then ask to which of these different roles should the requirement of impartiality primarily apply? From the standpoint of the common good, there should be a clear preference for combining the adoption of common rules and policies through democratic processes with an impartial oversight of their implementation. On the one hand, many legislative choices in EU policy fields (such as trade, competition, and data protection) raise difficult moral dilemmas, which leave room for competing views of what the common exactly entails. Consider, for instance, the diverse understandings of the implications of free trade and the use of artificial intelligence. As I will argue in the following sections, this calls for further efforts to democratise policymaking at the EU level. On the other hand, any common law or policy will likely only succeed in advancing the common good if it is systemically applied by all the member states. Given that the distribution of the benefits and burdens of EU policies is often uneven, compliance will likely only be widespread if an impartial supervision mechanism is established. This observation suggests that a division of responsibilities within the Commission comprising the democratic use of legislative initiative by the College of Commissioners and the impartial oversight of the EU laws and policies by the several Directorates-General is desirable.

However, the current allocation of tasks between the "two levels of action" of the Commission fails to fully realise this principle. Indeed, the current mix of legislative and supervisory tasks across both levels has led an author to describe the Commission as a "politicised bureaucracy".[11] This "dualism" may have far-reaching implications for the common good.[12] To illustrate the point, consider the rules put forward by the Stability and Growth Pact and the corresponding mechanism to address noncompliance with them – that is, the excessive deficit procedure. This framework was agreed by all the member states to ensure financial stability in the EU and to prevent negative externalities.[13] Yet, given that, as has been observed, excessive deficit procedures are often exposed to political interference, there is the risk that special treatment may be granted to certain powerful non-compliant states.[14] The same line of reasoning extends to the enforcement of EU competition rules. Given that the Commissioner for Competition is responsible for determining the permissibility of corporate mergers, the results of some merger efforts could be shaped by the sitting commissioner's political ideology and the objectives of the government appointing them.[15]

A more effective use of the powers of legislative initiative and supervision for the common good could be achieved by ensuring simultaneously that (i) the College of Commissioners has a compelling democratic mandate to shape the rules that govern the EU polity but (ii) refrains from interfering in their application. This approach would imply two significant changes in the status quo. First, the Commission's supervisory duties would exclusively be fulfilled by its Directorates-General. Leaving supervisory tasks with the EU bureaucrats rather than the cabinets of EU Commissioners would likely foster impartiality because EU civil servants are functionally and financially independent from the national administrations.[16] Therefore, this would contribute to an impartial oversight of the common rules. It should be added that implementing this reform would not require an EU treaty change since it would merely imply a reallocation of competences *within* the Commission. Second, the College of Commissioners would have a stronger voice vis-à-vis the Commission bureaucracy when *designing* the common rules and policies to be enforced by the Eurocrats. As I will claim below, a more robust mandate granted through the direct election of the Commission's president would facilitate the adoption of more ambitious measures for the common good.

A more difficult issue is whether the expansion of the current competences of the Commission would be desirable from the standpoint of the common good. To address this question, we might find it useful to distinguish two dimensions in which the distribution of competences in the EU polity could be revised. On the one hand, one might increase the fiscal capacity of the EU, namely by launching a supranational tax. As I have argued in Chapter 3, this is a critical condition for the EU to pursue the common good more consistently. Indeed, once equipped with autonomous sources of revenue, EU institutions would not need to undergo lengthy negotiations regarding interstate transfers each time a new EU policy was needed. Consider, for example, the launch of the Recovery and Resilience Facility to address the dramatic social and economic consequences of COVID-19, which required extended intergovernmental negotiations. On the other hand, one could delegate additional competences to the Commission in certain policy areas, including social policy, education and defence. Here, it is difficult to provide a single and categorical answer, particularly given the trade-off between enhancing supranational response capacity and maintaining a desirable degree of national autonomy.[17] In Chapter 5, I will discuss strategies by which a balance between these two concerns could be struck in the three policy areas just mentioned. In any case, an expansion of the Commission's policy competences should go hand in hand with a democratisation agenda, such as the one presented below.

Electing the presidents of the European Commission and the European Council

I have suggested that the Commission's political leadership should have a strong democratic mandate to make use of the power of legislative initiative to advance the common good. However, the College of Commissioners faces important constraints that reduce its ability to pursue this goal. To begin with, the Commission's president is selected through an untransparent bargaining process between the heads of the national governments that is typically conducted behind the scenes.[18] This opaque process has often led to the nomination of individuals who are unknown to the wider public and whose agendas were not publicly scrutinised before their appointment. For this reason, the presidents of the Commission have a relatively weak mandate to pursue the common good, particularly when this implies significant changes in the status quo. Indeed, whatever ambitious proposals they may have will be vulnerable to strong opposition by the national governments, which can claim that such proposals were never consented to by their constituencies. Furthermore, each commissioner is allowed to recruit a limited staff of their choice, thus being largely dependent on the advice and guidance of the Directorates-General.[19] This dependence means that the EU bureaucracy can, to a considerable extent, shape the political action of the College. These constraints are reinforced by the length of the EU legislative process, which leaves the College with a short window of opportunity to push its agenda forward.[20]

At the same time, the lack of EU-wide elections where the political leadership of the Commission could be held accountable for EU policies transfers the task of rewarding and punishing these policies to the national elections, potentially fuelling interstate cleavages.[21] To illustrate the point, consider the debate about austerity measures during the financial crisis of 2008–2012. Thus, the competing views on austerity were represented mainly by national politicians, notably the minister of finance of Germany, Wolfgang Schäuble, and the successive finance ministers of Greece, including Yanis Varoufakis, rather than by elected officials at the EU level and their challengers from other political parties. This model of "politicisation of European integration", characterised by the aggregation of preferences regarding EU policies at the national level, makes transnational political compromises more difficult and reinforces the vacuum of agency described in Chapter 3.[22] Given that *"national* politics are still the crucial arena for the politicisation of European integration", domestic parties have strong incentives to support EU policies that benefit their constituencies.[23] Even the governments that would ideologically be willing to make more significant concessions for the common good have electoral incentives to pursue national interests at the EU level. As a result, there may not be any agent at the EU level with an effective mandate and appropriate resources to pursue the common good.

In view of this landscape, moving to direct elections for the Commission presidency would be a crucial step forward. In fact, candidates aspiring to become Commission president would be expected to present their priorities and policy proposals, which would be subject to public scrutiny. Given the EU demographics, they would likely need to advance a balanced agenda that accommodates different national perspectives to enhance their chances of being elected.[24] Furthermore, a requirement to achieve a majority in a two-round election in a pan-European constituency would give the new president a robust mandate to pursue reforms since the argument of a lack of a democratic basis would no longer be available.[25] The extension of the term of office of any president would now presuppose re-election, thus correcting the current lack of accountability of the Commission's political leadership.[26] This effort to democratise the Commission's leadership should go hand in hand with the allocation of appropriate resources to pursue its mission, namely the ability of EU Commissioners to build their own teams based on criteria of political confidence. Admittedly, launching elections could take some of the pressure to block costly EU policies for the common good away from national governments. National elections would not need to be used to assess the policies of the governments at the EU level because there would be several elections focused on EU affairs.[27]

This line of reasoning extends to the European Council, which brings together the heads of government of all member states to provide "general political directions and priorities" to the Union, which may have a strong impact on the configuration of EU policies.[28] This applies particularly to periods of EU crises, in which the president of the European Council plays a critical role by orchestrating solutions and building consensus at the supranational level.[29] While most leaders sitting in the Council have been elected by their national electorates, its president is selected through the rather untransparent bargaining process mentioned above. If it is true that, since the creation of this public office by the Treaty of Lisbon, the president of the European Council turned out to be regularly selected amongst those elected national leaders, it is also true that the newly appointed presidents were scrutinised only by the constituency of a single member state. Again, by the time of their appointment, they were largely unknown by the European public, and most EU citizens never had the chance to scrutinise their vision for the EU. Therefore, along the lines of what I have argued regarding the Commission, democratic scrutiny would give the presidents of the European Council a stronger mandate to seek the common good.

Yet how would the elections for the presidency of the Commission and the European Council work in practice? Would they be feasible? Elections for Commission president could be held concurrently with the existing European parliamentary elections that select MEPs. Considering their collaborative functions in the EU's legislative framework, it would be logical for the political terms of the Commission and the European Parliament to remain synchronised.[30] In turn, the election for the presidency of the European Council could take place at different times, given that the political cycle of the 27 member states that comprise it is not aligned with the EU's.[31] This division in electoral momentum across the Union would have the advantage of increasing the regularity of democratic scrutiny at the EU level and clearly separating the elections for the bodies that follow a supranational logic from the one that follows an intergovernmental approach. While reforming the procedures to appoint the leadership of EU institutions would require changes in the EU treaties, reforms to enhance the EU's legitimacy could recruit widespread support among EU citizens. In fact, it has been argued that "people support reforms in these areas independently from their stance regarding the political conflict over Europe".[32]

Creating an assembly of EU citizens

As I argued in Chapter 2, the EU member states share a list of EU values that provide a common moral standpoint from which policy options can be assessed. However, as I have also suggested, the policy implications of these values are not always straightforward. Given their abstract nature, competing interpretations of what these public values entail in practice may exist. For instance, while all member states have endorsed the values of solidarity and liberty by ratifying the EU treaties, their citizens may have different views on how EU institutions should apply those values in practice. These differences may have significant policy implications in fields such as cohesion policy and trade policy. Furthermore, as Chapter 1 emphasised, many public choices are made under considerable epistemic uncertainty. For example, it is not known for a fact what specific set of public policies would effectively promote affordable housing in political communities where real estate markets are highly speculative.[33] Thus, it is not always clear which course of action would advance the common good. In light of these uncertainties, any agenda for the common good that is both effective and able to recruit widespread public support will need to incorporate multiple perspectives of ordinary citizens and identify paths to reconcile some of their disagreements.

These goals could be at least partially achieved by creating a permanent assembly of EU citizens that would bring citizens of the diverse EU polity together to "overcome their differences and find solutions that serve the greater good, including on politically sensitive and technical issues".[34] This new body would facilitate the pursuit of the common good in at least three ways. To begin with, it would give EU citizens a meaningful chance to discuss their perspectives on what the common good entails in terms of concrete EU policies. While directly electing the presidents of the Commission and the European Council would be an important step towards generating pan-European debates between different candidates, EU citizens should also have much more say in the Union's day-to-day policymaking processes.[35] Second, this body could challenge policy dogmas that are hard to contest and abandon, even when their shortcomings are apparent.[36] A case in order is arguably the governance and functioning of the Eurozone.[37] Persistent political dogmas and taboos could be broken by giving the floor to citizens beyond the Brussels bubble, thus opening the way to pursue the common good. Finally, an EU Citizens' Assembly "would force EU policymakers to be exposed on a regular basis to public input from all corners of Europe".[38]

How would the Citizens Assembly work in practice? The mandate of this body would be to deliberate on transnational issues that national bodies of deliberative democracy cannot effectively cover.[39] Such matters typically arise in areas with high cross-national interdependencies, such as energy supply, migration and international security. More specifically, the functioning of this body could be conceived as follows. The members of the Citizens' Assembly would propose topics for discussion to the chair and vice-chairs, who would be elected among them.[40] Once an issue is selected for debate in the plenary, the Citizens' Assembly could ask the European

Commission to present background information with a view to facilitating an informed debate.[41] While this body would not have the power to adopt new legislation, it could cast a vote on whether to insert a particular discussion item in the agenda of meetings of the Council of the European Union at the ministerial level, where high-level political dialogues take place. This agenda-setting power would establish a direct link between the Citizens' Assembly and the Council, thus allowing citizens to call EU ministers to address issues that they consider relevant. In turn, the Council would be required to report in writing on the outcome of its discussions, which could comprise a decision to ask the Commission to present a legislative proposal regarding the issues at stake.

Why would this configuration be desirable? As has been suggested, the ability to set the agenda is one of the most significant powers in representative democracies.[42] Note that the power to set the agendas of the several thematic configurations of the Council of the European Union lies currently with the member states – more specifically, with the government that holds its rotating presidency. Now, the fact that political parties are exposed to lobbying by well-organised interest groups implies that the views and concerns of large but fragmented groups of citizens may eventually fail to be mirrored in the political agenda.[43] As Chapter 3 suggested, this is particularly the case in the EU political system, given the mediating role of national governments and the incentives to pursue their definitions of national interest. Therefore, giving the EU Citizens' Assembly the power to add agenda items would have two advantages. First, it could lead to the discussion of certain proposals that are instrumental to the common good of the Union, but national governments fail to put forward given the political costs at stake.[44] Citizens could more easily advance important proposals that jeopardise the agenda of certain interest groups because, unlike national governments, they do not have to worry about recruiting support and securing funding for being re-elected.[45] Second, leaving the power to adopt legislation with the other EU institutions would avoid the charge of simply bypassing those elected bodies.

A question that follows is whether it would be feasible to launch a body of this sort. Admittedly, creating an EU institution with a role in EU decision-making would require treaty change. Yet this goal would likely be possible to achieve. To begin with, despite being conceived as a temporary initiative, the Conference on the Future of Europe has established a precedent of citizens' participation at the EU level. To enhance its feasibility prospects, the Citizens' Assembly could be granted the right to insert only a limited number of items in the Council's agenda, which could be increased in the future. Furthermore, the specific details regarding the functioning of the Citizens' Assembly, including the number of members, the duration of their membership, the work modalities (e.g., the frequency and format of the meetings) and the funding model to be adopted could be negotiated between the member states with the intention to maximise their support for the proposal. Similarly, the method to select the participants could be chosen within a range of possibilities, provided that it ensured political equality.[46] While obtaining appropriate follow-ups by the Council could be challenging, this could be gradually achieved as the Citizens' Assembly consolidated its position in the EU political scene.[47]

Reforming the European Parliament

Another set of reforms that could contribute to the pursuit of the common good is linked to the composition and functioning of the European Parliament. While the Treaty of Lisbon significantly increased the political weight of this EU institution, the question of how the common good of all EU citizens should be politically represented in the EU political system remains to be addressed.[48] Even if one conceives EU democracy as a union of democratic and sovereign peoples along the lines of the so-called *demoicratic* approach, this does not automatically do away with the claim that the EU demos *as a whole* should be given better representation.[49] Indeed, as Philippe Van Parijs has argued, the critical factual question for the EU is not only whether a common people currently exists, but "whether the circumstances (mobility, contact, interdependencies, etc.) are such that there *should* be a common demos".[50] In what follows, I will claim that the problem of political representation in the EU should be addressed at two levels: the link between EU citizens and the MEPs and the relations between it and the national parliaments. Accordingly, I will present two proposals: (i) reforming the 1976 European Electoral Act to create a pan-European constituency and (ii) upgrading the relations between the national and the European parliaments.

Let us begin with the first proposal. The logic underpinning the proposal of electing candidates through a transnational constituency is that the MEPs would then represent all Europeans, not just their compatriots. This would offer a categorical answer to the question of who are "the people or institutions that can speak 'on behalf of Europe'".[51] Furthermore, as I have argued in relation to the election of the presidents of the Commission and the European Council, transnational lists would significantly increase the incentives faced by political actors to present agendas oriented towards the common good, as opposed to national interests. Note that the idea of creating a pan-European constituency has gained some traction among policymakers in recent years. Following earlier attempts (in 2018) in the context of the debate about the redistribution of the parliamentary seats vacated by the withdrawal of the United Kingdom from the EU, a new proposal to create transnational lists was put forward.[52] While the European Parliament eventually rejected the 2018 proposal, it recruited considerable support across political parties.[53] In turn, despite failing to endorse this proposal in the European Council, the EU heads of government showed some openness to reconsider the issue in the future.[54]

What could explain these mixed signals? More than an intense normative disagreement about the desirability of transnational lists, there are relevant practical concerns regarding its implementation. These concerns were addressed by a new proposal put forward in 2022, which remains the subject of difficult negotiations at the time of writing.[55] More specifically, there was a legitimate fear that small and medium-sized states would be underrepresented. For instance, by relying on transnational lists, the European parties could, in theory, obtain majorities in the Parliament by including only candidates from the most populated states in electable positions. Additionally, apprehensions were raised about rapidly transitioning to a unified constituency without incrementally assessing its effects on the operations of EU institutions.

The more detailed and nuanced proposal presented in 2022 addresses these issues in a compelling manner. First, it establishes the requirement of geographical balance within transnational lists.[56] Second, it creates a small pan-European constituency without replacing the existing national constituencies.[57] Thus, the Parliament would have *both* EU-wide and national constituencies. If successful, this mixed model could be adjusted in the future, notably by increasing the relative size of the pan-European constituency. Creating transnational lists along these lines would be a significant step towards more common-good-oriented policies.

A complementary institutional reform that could foster the pursuit of the common good focuses on strengthening the link between the European Parliament and the national parliaments.[58] In Chapter 3, I argued that the EU should play a more active role in the process of national interest formation through the Representations of the Commission in the member state capitals. Yet the European Parliament should also take part in this process, notably by providing inputs to the debates within the national legislatures. Given the level of interdependence between the member states, their parliaments make a few decisions that shape the future of the Union as a whole and bring about significant externalities. That they do so suggests that it is reasonable to expect them to take a European perspective into account throughout their decision-making processes. To illustrate the point, consider that the decisions on whether to assist financially distressed member states during the Eurozone crisis had to be voted by the parliaments of the member states. Note that a few parliaments had threatened to veto these bailouts, which could have led to the collapse of the Eurozone. However, a critical question that remains to be addressed is how to stimulate a greater weighting of criteria linked to the common good of the whole EU in the deliberation processes of national parliaments without jeopardising their democratic mandates.

A strategy for achieving this goal would be upgrading one of the existing interparliamentary forums at the EU level. While a few structures for cooperation already exist, their ambition is very limited. For instance, the Conference of the Speakers of the European Union Parliaments meets annually. The Conference of Parliamentary Committees for Union Affairs of the Parliaments of the European Union meets every six months in the country, holding the rotating presidency of the Council of the European Union. A permanent structure of cooperation based in Brussels convening regular meetings between national and European parliamentarians would allow for higher coordination and frequent exchanges of views. As it has been argued, such a forum "should not duplicate the legislative work of the European Parliament" but instead "ask questions about, and write reports on, those aspects of EU and Eurozone governance that involve unanimous decision-making and in which the Parliament plays no significant role".[59] For in-depth collaboration to occur in this body, it could be organised according to policy areas, bringing together parliamentarians working in similar parliamentary committees. While the conclusions of this interparliamentary body would not be binding, they would likely be fed into the national policy processes by their co-authors.

In the opposite direction, the existing early warning mechanism – the so-called "yellow card system" – could be adjusted with a view to strengthening the role of national parliaments in EU policymaking.[60] Introduced by the Treaty of Lisbon, this instrument allows a group of at least one-third of all national legislatures to request that the Commission amend or withdraw a legislative proposal if they deem it violates the principle of subsidiarity. However, this mechanism has been invoked on just three occasions.[61] One of the reasons seems to be the short timescales national parliaments are given to invoke the measure, which can be particularly problematic in proposals with great technical detail. Accordingly, the European Parliament has called the Commission to grant additional time for national parliaments to respond to new legislative proposals.[62] Another barrier may be linked to the fact that each national parliament is required to submit its own reasoned opinion to trigger the yellow card system without knowing whether the others will do the same. Instead, the upgraded interparliamentary forum could coordinate a single reasoned opinion subscribed by several parliaments. The combination of measures described in this section would contribute to the

"Europeanisation of parliamentary democracy",[63] facilitating the pursuit of the common good.

Creating an advisory body of former presidents of the EU institutions

The last proposal of this chapter is the creation of a new EU advisory board. Let me begin by outlining its main features. This body would be composed of the former presidents of the Commission, European Parliament and European Council and would have a consultative role. Building on their experience as EU leaders, the board members would provide advice regarding challenging EU political choices and political visibility to the agenda for the common good. They would meet periodically for strategic debates about the future of the EU, as well as thematic debates organised at the request of other EU institutions. Their input could be presented in the format of opinions and reports drafted with the assistance of a secretariat and possibly through meetings with the incumbent EU leadership. The composition of this board would surely be multinational and politically diverse, given that EU leaders are chosen across different EU member states and political parties. To avoid conflicts of interest, membership in this advisory board would be suspended if a member were to become the head of a national government. Note that the political weight of this body could be considerable, at least if the proposal for directly electing the presidents of the Commission and the European Council presented above was adopted. In this scenario, the board members would have formerly been elected through pan-European elections, making them widely known by the EU public.[64]

Yet, how would this body contribute to the pursuit of the common good in the EU? Keeping track of the political dilemmas and choices of the past may help to make informed decisions in the present.[65] Indeed, nurturing the institutional memory of the EU would be a means to explore effective ways to implement EU policies for the common good that face persistent feasibility constraints.[66] Consider, for instance, the crucial lessons that can be learnt from the failed attempts to create a mechanism to ensure compliance with EU values, as discussed in Chapter 2. Maintaining links across different political cycles is challenging in the EU political system. This challenge is not only due to the far-reaching effects of the "New Public Administration" agenda, which reportedly led most modern bureaucracies to be increasingly unable to perform the role of preserving institutional memory but also to the fact that most presidents of EU institutions virtually disappear from the European public space once their mandates are completed.[67] This retreat is at odds with the practice of several democracies, which foresee formal and informal roles for former leaders.[68] Indeed, former EU leaders are in a privileged position to "tell the story" of how critical decisions were made during their terms of office and to provide nuanced recommendations to incumbent decision-makers based on their first-hand knowledge of the challenges underpinning EU policymaking.[69]

In addition to providing valuable inputs to current decision-makers, former EU leaders could actively participate in constructing a European public space geared towards the common good. All over the world, former leaders have used their political capital to draw public attention to important causes and to push for much-needed policies and reforms that remain deadlocked due to adverse political and economic incentives. For example, in a recent meeting of the former leaders of the Commonwealth countries, a public statement was issued calling on their governments to equip the Global Fund to Fight AIDS, tuberculosis and malaria with appropriate financial resources to pursue its goals.[70] Similarly, in the context of the spread of COVID-19, a group of former heads of state has pressed the US government to commit US$5 billion to the global fight against pandemics.[71] In turn, the 2022 meeting of the Clinton Global Initiative, led by former US president Bill Clinton, brought together key actors to agree on 144 concrete commitments to action on climate change, health equity, inclusive economic growth, and the global refugee crisis.[72] These examples illustrate how former EU leaders could put political pressure on the current ones to adopt bold measures for the common good.

It should be noted that creating a board of former presidents of EU institutions would not be a very demanding task under the current institutional setting. Given that this body would essentially have an advisory role, it would not change the EU legislative process and would, therefore, not require an amendment of the EU treaties. More specifically, the board could be set up under the existing rules for creating expert groups of the European Commission. Indeed, the Commission's Directorates-General often launch panels of academics and policy experts to advise on specific policy matters. Given its cross-cutting nature, the advisory board could then be set up by the secretariat-general of the Commission, which would provide logistical support to the meetings and activities of the board. Within this framework, formal opinions and recommendations could be produced, and ad hoc informal consultations with the current EU leaders on specific policy issues could be organised upon request. Furthermore, a yearly high-level conference of former presidents of EU institutions could be set up in order to create momentum and mobilise resources in key areas linked to the European and global common goods. In this way, former leaders could actively participate in the EU public sphere.

Conclusion

I have argued that the EU institutional framework should be reformed to seek the common good more effectively. A combination of adjustments and upgrades in the existing institutions and the launch of new institutional forums could serve this purpose. First, splitting the legislative and supervisory roles of the Commission more clearly would enhance the latter's impartiality. Second, electing the presidents of the Commission and the European Council would empower the EU's political leadership to pursue ambitious reforms for the common good. Third, creating an EU Citizens' Assembly would give citizens a stronger voice regarding issues that concern them all. Fourth, launching transnational lists for the European Parliament would generate a pan-European public debate and trigger the construction of common political agendas. At the same time, increasing the level of collaboration between the European and the national parliaments would allow for a better understanding of the rationale behind legislative proposals and potentially a higher legislative alignment. Finally, a new board of former presidents of the EU institutions could bring valuable expertise informing difficult public choices linked to the common good. I have argued that these proposals would be feasible if the concerns of member states could be accommodated throughout their design stage.

Notes

1 *Treaty on European Union*, article 17.
2 Emmanuelle Schön-Quinlivan, *Reforming the European Commission* (London, 2011), pp. 1–12.
3 Andrew Duff, *Constitutional Change in the European Union: Towards a Federal Union* (Cham, 2022).
4 Daniel Chandler and Rod Munday (eds), "Impartiality", *A Dictionary of Media and Communication* (Oxford, 2011). There has been some controversy amongst moral theorists about the philosophical meaning of impartiality. For simplicity, I adopt Chandler and Munday's definition, which is useful for our discussion due to its policy-oriented character. For an overview of the ongoing debate, see Brian Feltham and John Cottingham (eds), *Partiality and Impartiality: Morality, Special Relationships, and the Wider World* (Oxford, 2010).
5 Chandler and Munday, "Impartiality". Note that this assessment presupposes distributional principles to determine how much of each national interest should be fulfilled and how much of it should be sacrificed to realise a meaningful understanding of impartiality. I offer guidelines to address this problem in João Labareda, *Towards a Just Europe: A Theory of Distributive Justice for the European Union* (Manchester, 2021).
6 *Treaty on European Union*, article 3.

7 This question arises not only in relation to the EU, but also to every modern democracy. See Kenneth J. Meier and Laurence J. O'Toole Jr, *Bureaucracy in a Democratic State: A Governance Perspective* (Baltimore, 2006).
8 According to article 17 of the TEU, "Union legislative acts may only be adopted on the basis of a Commission proposal, except where the Treaties provide otherwise". In recent years, the Council and Parliament's right to invite the Commission to present a legislative proposal has been described as an indirect right of legislative initiative. However, it should be emphasised that such right does not create an obligation for the Commission to follow up with a concrete proposal. For a discussion, see Henning Deters and Gerda Falkner, "Remapping the European Agenda-Setting Landscape", *Public Administration* 99 (2021), pp. 290–303.
9 See M.A. Pollack, *The Engines of Integration: Delegation, Agency, and Agenda Setting in the EU* (Oxford, 2003). It has recently been argued that the Commission should not be treated as a unitary actor as far as agenda-setting is concerned, since its Directorates-General have shown different degrees of success in seeing their legislative proposals through. However, this observation does not challenge the thesis that the Commission has a monopoly of agenda-setting vis-à-vis the other EU institutions. See Christian Rauh, "One Agenda-Setter or Many? The Varying Success of Policy Initiatives by Individual Directorates-General of the European Commission 1994–2016", *European Union Politics* 22 (2020), pp. 3–24.
10 EUR-Lex, "Enforcement of EU Law", https://eur-lex.europa.eu/EN/legal-content/glossary/enforcement-of-eu-law.html (accessed 21 August 2023).
11 Thomas Christiansen, "Tensions of European Governance: Politicized Bureaucracy and Multiple Accountability in the European Commission", *Journal of European Public Policy* 4 (1997), pp. 73–90.
12 This dualism of roles also helps explaining why the existing assessments of the political character of the Commission are so diverse. While a few authors regard the latter as a predominantly bureaucratic body, others have stressed the political nature of its activities. For a discussion, see Neill Nugent and Mark Rhinard, "The 'Political' Roles of the European Commission", *Journal of European Integration* 41 (2019), pp. 203–220.
13 These negative externalities are linked to the fact that, in the context of a single currency area, a high budgetary deficit in a particular member state may affect all the others by means of creating financial instability.
14 See, for instance, Aline Robert, "Excessive Deficit Fine Looms over France", *Euroactiv* (22 September 2014), www.euractiv.com/section/euro-finance/news/excessive-deficit-fine-looms-over-france/ (accessed 6 February 2023).
15 Consider, for instance, the Commission's decision to veto the merger of two rail companies, France's Alstom and Germany's Siemens. The intense debate that followed this decision exposed the contrasting national interests and ideological perspectives regarding the application of EU competition law. See Elisa Braun, Thibault Larger and Simon Van Dorpe, "EU Big Four Press Vestager to Clear Path for Champions", *Politico* (6 February 2020), www.politico.eu/article/eu-big-four-france-germany-italy-poland-press-executive-vice-president-margrethe-vestager-to-clear-path-for-champions/ (accessed 19 March 2023).

16 An exception is the seconded national experts, who are appointed and at least partially funded by the national administrations. However, this category constitutes a small percentage of the Commission's workforce. See Göran Sundström, "Seconded National Experts as Part of Early Mover Strategies in the European Union: The Case of Sweden", *Journal of European Integration* 38 (2015), pp. 1–15.

17 In the policy areas where the EU does not have exclusive competence, this trade-off is typically solved by referring to the subsidiarity principle. However, the preliminary question at stake is whether the areas of EU exclusive competence should be expanded. For a discussion, see Andreas Follesdal, "Subsidiarity", *Journal of Political Philosophy* 6 (1998), pp. 231–259.

18 The president of the Commission is formally elected by the European Parliament, but the candidate presented before the Parliament does not need to be an MEP. In practice, this allows the EU heads of government to appoint whomever they want for the job. While the European Parliament could in principle reject the candidate proposed by the heads of government, this does not typically happen as it could lead to a political deadlock.

19 As a general rule, each commissioner is allowed to recruit six members for their cabinet, to whom several constrains apply, including the following: (i) at least three members should already be working in the EU civil service; (ii) the six members should cover at least three nationalities; (iii) the head of cabinet or the deputy head of cabinet should be of the same nationality as the commissioner; (iv) at least 50% of the commissioner's staff should be women. Altogether, these rules seriously constrain commissioners' ability to select teams to implement their agendas. Note that these rules vary slightly concerning the cabinets of the president and vice-presidents of the Commission. See European Commission, *Communication from the President to the Commission: Rules Governing the Composition of the Cabinets of the Members of the Commission and of the Spokesperson's Service* (2019).

20 For instance, in the parliamentary term initiated in July 2014 the average duration of the ordinary legislative proceeding was between 17 months (if only the proposal was approved by the Parliament and Council in the first reading) and more than 30 months (if a second reading by any of these institutions was required). For this reason, it has been rightly noted that "a vital characteristic of the Commission's ability to influence any policy sector is its ability to respond rapidly to any 'windows of opportunity'". For the figures, see European Parliamentary Research Service, "Average Duration and Number of Concluded Ordinary Legislative Procedures", https://epthinktank.eu/2022/03/11/european-parliament-facts-and-figures/ep-facts-and-figures-fig-19/ (accessed 14 March 2023). For the quote, see Laura Cram, "The European Commission as a Multi-Organization: Social Policy and IT Policy in the EU", *Journal of European Public Policy* 1 (1994), pp. 195–217.

21 On this point, see Karlheinz Reif and Hermann Schmitt, "Nine Second-Order National Elections – A Conceptual Framework for the Analysis of European Election Results", *European Journal of Political Research* 8 (1980), pp. 3–44.

22 Hanspeter Kriesi, "The Politicization of European Integration", *Journal of Common Market Studies* 54 (2016).
23 Kriesi, "The Politicization of European Integration", p. 32.
24 Note that the five most populous EU member states – Germany, France, Italy, Spain and Poland – have significantly different socioeconomic profiles. This would give any aspirant to the Commission's presidency incentives to build a political agenda that negotiates the interests of north and south, west and east.
25 In an EU polity with 27 member states and nearly 450 million citizens, the number of candidates to become presidents of the Commission would potentially be high. Accordingly, the results of the first round could be very scattered. Therefore, a second round between the most voted candidates would be advisable to ensure a strong mandate.
26 Note that this increase of political weight would at least partially be extended to the other commissioners who, despite being appointed by the national governments, receive their specific portfolios and mission letters from the President of the Commission. However, this does not exclude the argument that member states could search for more democratic processes to select their own commissioners than a simple appointment by the national governments, as to include for instance a hearing, or even a vote in the national parliaments.
27 It could be argued that the so-called Spitzenkandidaten ("lead candidate") system, whereby the lead candidate of the most voted party in the European Parliament elections becomes the President of the Commission, is a more desirable alternative. Yet, the experience of the 2014 elections in which this system was tested suggests otherwise. As has been pointed out by Sophia Russack, empirical research indicates that in 2014 "national parties have made little effort to promote EU topics and elections and that the link between national and EU party politics has been weak". As she points out, "[t]he German case is exemplary here: the Christian Democrats posted Angela Merkel's face on the campaign billboards even though she was not a candidate". This would not be possible in a direct election system. See Sophia Russack, "The Problem with the Spitzenkandidaten System", *CEPS Policy Brief* (21 February 2018).
28 *Treaty on European Union,* article 15.
29 For a helpful discussion, see Lucas Schramm and Wolfgang Wessels, "The European Council as a Crisis Manager and Fusion Driver: Assessing the EU's Fiscal Response to the COVID-19 Pandemic", *Journal of European Integration* 45 (2023), pp. 257–273.
30 Yet note that, since the president of the Commission would be directly elected, it would no longer need to be appointed by the Parliament.
31 For example, several heads of government who have a seat in the European Council are replaced during the five-year term of the European Commission and the European Parliament.
32 Constantin Schäfer, Oliver Treib and Bernd Schlipphak, "What Kind of EU Do Citizens Want? Reform Preferences and the Conflict over Europe", *Journal of European Public Policy* 30 (2023), p. 1739.

33 See, for instance, OECD, *Brick by Brick: Building Better Housing Policies* (Paris, 2021).
34 *Manifesto for a European Citizens' Assembly*, https://europeancitizensassembly.eu/ (accessed 2 February 2023). While I will argue that an assembly of EU citizens would be a desirable and effective means to democratise the pursuit of the common good, I will not claim that this is the only institutional model that could be used to achieve such end. For an overview of alternative strategies, see Kathe Callahan, "Citizen Participation: Models and Methods", *International Journal of Public Administration* 30 (2007), pp. 1179–1196.
35 I shall return to this issue in Chapter 5, where I discuss ways in which more opportunities for citizens' participation could enhance civic friendship among EU citizens.
36 This is what Brainard Peters and Lennart Nagel have dubbed "zombie ideas". See Brainard Guy Peters and Lennart Nagel, *Zombie Ideas: Why Failed Policy Ideas Persist* (Cambridge, 2020).
37 See Miguel Otero-Iglesias, "The Eurozone: Victim of its Own Success and Dogmas", *The European Financial Review* (10 February 2015), www.europeanfinancialreview.com/the-eurozone-victim-of-its-own-success-and-dogmas/ (accessed 2 February 2023).
38 Alberto Alemanno, "Europe's Democracy Challenge: Citizen Participation in and Beyond Elections", *German Law Journal* 21 (2020), p. 39.
39 For instance, a town hall meeting with local citizens can hardly deliberate effectively on the problem of international tax evasion, since this issue must be tackled at the supranational level of government. Note that 52% of the deliberative initiatives to date have taken place at the local level; 30% at the regional level; 15% at the national level; and only 3% at the international level. See OECD, *Innovative Citizen Participation and New Democratic Institutions: Catching the Deliberative Wave* (Paris, 2020) p. 70.
40 The chair and vice-chairs would have the power to accept or to exclude proposals by referring to the Citizens' Assembly's mandate to address issues with transnational relevance and would structure the debates in order to ensure manageability. The objection that this could arbitrarily prevent certain important issues from being discussed would not hold if, as I will suggest, the chair and the vice-chairs were required to rotate regularly.
41 The so-called "deliberative turn" in democratic theory has rightly put an emphasis on promoting informed choices by citizens. As has been noted, the list of things that people may need to know in order to arrive to an informed judgment is extensive: "policy relevant facts on all sides of the issue, logic and evidence behind conjectures about the probability of success of various alternatives, potential implications of the policy for oneself and others, the policy preferences of others and the reasons for their preferences, opportunity costs of adopting one policy as opposed to another – and much, much more" [Ian O'Flynn, *Deliberative Democracy* (Cambridge, 2022), pp. 64–65]. However, deliberative accounts do not regard the complexity of information as a definitive barrier against their approach. For a discussion, see Simon Burall,

"Deliberative Engagement with Complex Policies", in Henry Tam (ed.), *Whose Government Is It? The Renewal of State–Citizen Cooperation* (Bristol, 2019).
42 See Peter Bachrach and Morton S. Baratz, "Two Faces of Power", *American Political Science Review* 56 (1962), pp. 947–952.
43 Indeed, it has been rightly argued that ordinary citizens have a very limited control of the political agenda. On this point, see William R. Riker, *Liberalism against Populism: A Confrontation Between the Theory of Democracy and Social Choice* (Long Grove, 1982).
44 Consider, for instance, the discussion of more progressive measures to protect the environment in sectors which are traditionally well organised and politically represented, such as the automobile industries and energy operators.
45 However, it could be argued that citizens may not be committed to pursuing the common good of the EU. For instance, an assembly composed mainly by citizens with a nationalist mindset might refuse to put forward much-needed proposals that would bring about significant political or economic costs for their member states. This suggests that the effective pursuit of the common good at the EU level presupposes the existence of transnational bonds of civic friendship. In Chapter 5, I will discuss this issue in depth.
46 For a helpful discussion, see Bailey Flanigan, Paul Gölz, Anupam Gupta, Brett Hennig and Ariel D. Procaccia, "Fair Algorithms for Selecting Citizens' Assemblies", *Nature* 596 (2021), pp. 548–552.
47 A similar process has taken place regarding the Committee of the Regions, which since its creation in 1994 has gradually won its own space in EU policymaking. See, for instance, European Parliamentary Research Service, "Understanding the European Committee of the Regions" (2021).
48 For an overview of the changes introduced by the Lisbon treaty regarding the role of the European and the national parliaments, see Richard Corbett, "The Evolving Roles of the European Parliament and of National Parliaments", in Andrea Biondi, Piet Eeckhout and Stefanie Ripley (eds), *EU Law After Lisbon* (Oxford, 2012).
49 For influential statements of the demoicratic approach, see Kalypso Nicolaidis, "The Idea of European Demoicracy", in Julie Dickson and Pavlos Eleftheriadis, *Philosophical Foundations of European Law* (Oxford, 2012); and F. Cheneval and F. Schimmelfennig, "The Case for Demoicracy in the European Union", *Journal of Common Market Studies* 51 (2013), pp. 334–350.
50 Philippe Van Parijs, "First Letter", in John Rawls and Philippe Van Parijs, *Three Letters on The Law of Peoples and the European Union*, https://ethics.harvard.edu/files/center-for-ethics/files/2003.rawlsvanparijs.r.phil_.econ_.pdf (accessed 2 March 2023), p. 5.
51 Luuk van Middelaar, *The Passage to Europe: How a Continent Became a Union* (New Haven, 2013), p. 25.
52 For a historical overview, see Philippe Van Parijs, "Transnational Lists in the European Parliament: Soon a Reality?", *The Brussels Times* (16 October 2022), www.brusselstimes.com/307268/transnational-lists-in-the-european-parliament-soon-a-reality (accessed 24 August 2023).

53 A total of 368 MEPs voted against it and 274 voted in favour, while 34 abstained.
54 See European Council, "Informal Meeting of the 27 Heads of State or Government: Main Results" (23 February 2018), www.consilium.europa.eu/en/meetings/european-council/2018/02/23/ (accessed 2 March 2023).
55 By early 2023, the European Parliament had approved the new proposal to reform the European Electoral Act, but a difficult bargaining process was foreseen in the European Council where unanimity is required to pass the proposal.
56 More specifically, "member states would be divided into three groups depending on the size of their population. The lists would be filled with candidates coming from these groups in a proportional way". See European Parliament, "MEPs Begin Revising Rules on EU elections, Calling for Pan-European Constituency" (3 May 2022), www.europarl.europa.eu/news/en/press-room/20220429IPR28242/meps-begin-revising-rules-on-eu-elections-calling-for-pan-european-constituency (accessed 3 March 2023).
57 Under this system, "each voter would have two votes: one to elect members of the European Parliament in national constituencies, and one in an EU-wide constituency, composed by 28 additional seats". See European Parliament, "MEPs Begin Revising Rules on EU Elections, Calling for Pan-European Constituency".
58 This link has been a subject of increasing interest in the specialised literature. For an overview, see Afke Groen and Thomas Christiansen, "National Parliaments in the European Union: Conceptual Choices in the European Union's Constitutional Debate", in Claudia Hefftler, Christine Neuhold, Olivier Rozenberg and Julie Smith (eds), *The Palgrave Handbook of National Parliaments and the European Union* (Basingstoke, 2015).
59 Charles Grant, "Can National Parliaments Make the EU more Legitimate?", *Center for European Reform* (10 June 2013), www.cer.eu/insights/can-national-parliaments-make-eu-more-legitimate (accessed 3 March 2023).
60 For a normative defence of a more active involvement of the national parliaments in EU policymaking, see Richard Bellamy, *A Republican Europe of States: Cosmopolitanism, Intergovernmentalism, and Democracy in the EU* (Cambridge, 2019), chapter 4.
61 European Parliament, "European Parliament: Relations with the National Parliaments", www.europarl.europa.eu/factsheets/en/sheet/22/european-parliament-relations-with-the-national-parliaments (accessed 3 March 2023).
62 European Parliament, *Resolution of 19 April 2018 on the Implementation of the Treaty Provisions concerning National Parliaments* (2018).
63 Katrin Auel, "Introduction: The Europeanisation of Parliamentary Democracy", *The Journal of Legislative Studies* 11 (2005), pp. 303–318.
64 If one of them were to become the head of a national government, their membership of this advisory board would be suspended until the end of their term in office to prevent conflicts of interests. Albeit rare, this is not only a theoretical possibility. Consider, for instance, the cases of Romano Prodi and Mario Monti, who after serving as presidents of the European Commission became prime ministers of Italy.

65 R. Wettenhall, "Organisational Amnesia: A Serious Public Sector Reform Issue", *International Journal of Public Sector Management* 24 (2011), pp. 80–96.
66 For a discussion of the concept of institutional memory, see James P. Walsh and Gerardo Rivera Ungson, "Organisational Memory", *The Academy of Management Review* 16 (1991), pp. 57–91.
67 For an overview of the New Public Administration agenda and its impacts on institutional memory, see Christopher Pollitt, "Bureaucracies Remember, Post-Bureaucratic Organisations Forget?" *Public Administration* 87 (2009), pp. 198–218.
68 Consider, for instance, the role played by the former presidents of the United States and the former chancellors of Germany, who have political offices and dedicated staffs and remain active in the public debate.
69 See J. Corbett, D. Christian Grube, H. Caroline Lovell and R. James Scott, *Institutional Memory as Storytelling: How Networked Government Remembers* (Cambridge, 2020).
70 One, "Former Commonwealth Heads of Government Call for the Successful Replenishment of the Global Fund", 20 June 2022, www.one.org/internatio nal/press/former-commonwealth-heads-of-government-call-for-the-successful-replenishment-of-the-global-fund/ (accessed 7 March 2023).
71 Sheryl Gay Stolberg, "Former Heads of State Urge U.S. to Commit $5 Billion to Global Covid Fight", *The New York Times* (9 May 2022), www.nytimes.com/2022/05/09/us/politics/biden-covd-aid.html (accessed 7 March 2023).
72 Clinton Foundation, "Clinton Global Initiative", www.clintonfoundation. org/programs/leadership-public-service/clinton-global-initiative#meetings/ (accessed 8 March 2023).

5

Building civic friendship in the European Union

Introduction

This chapter addresses the following question: How can civic friendship be strengthened in the EU? I claim that EU citizens will only be willing to mobilise ample resources and endorse significant sacrifices for the common good of the whole EU if they develop extensive bonds of "civic friendship". However, I argue that this goal is within the reach of the EU institutions and national governments. Civic friendship, I claim, should be regarded as the outcome of certain public choices rather than as a stable feature of political communities to be taken as given. Accordingly, I argue that civic friendship could be boosted in the EU if adequate public policies were adopted.

More specifically, I present the following proposals to strengthen transnational bonds: (i) establishing a robust social level playing field to moderate competition among EU workers, notably by launching an EU labour code; (ii) reducing socioeconomic inequalities in the EU; (iii) increasing the opportunities for participation by EU citizens in shared political institutions, namely through the EU Citizens' Assembly previously discussed; (iv) reducing pervasive administrative, legal and economic barriers against freedom of movement; (v) launching a transnational curriculum on EU citizenship education to be offered in all EU schools; and (vi) increasing defence cooperation in the EU, notably by upgrading the EU mutual defence clause and scaling up the Permanent Structured Cooperation and the European Defence Fund.

I begin by defining the notion of civic friendship and explaining the sense in which it shapes the prospects of the common good in the EU. Subsequently, I challenge two assumptions frequently held by the existing literature on this topic – namely, that (i) civic friendship is closely or even intrinsically linked to *national* communities and that (ii) civic friendship is a *stable* feature of these political communities. Then, I sketch the ways in which EU institutions have attempted to promote civic friendship and present reasons why their efforts have been unfruitful. Subsequently, I discuss the six policy proposals mentioned above in depth, explaining what specific problems they aim to address and how they could contribute to strengthening civic friendship in the EU. I also explore ways in which their feasibility could be increased.

The problem of civic friendship in the EU

Civic friendship defined

The preamble of the TEU famously set the goal of "creating an ever closer union among the peoples of Europe".[1] This purpose has been equated with a telos of ever-increasing economic and political integration. In anticipation of Francis Fukuyama's influential "end of history" thesis, many EU leaders seemed to conceive the future of Europe as a one-way road towards a transnational democracy.[2] According to the Schuman Declaration of 1950, a "united Europe" would not be achieved "all at once" but through "concrete achievements", notably the construction of a common market.[3] This gradual integration process, we were told, would bring about a "de facto solidarity" between Europeans.[4] Moreover, the successive and increasingly far-reaching EU treaties, as well as several rounds of enlargement that extended the original group of six member states to 28 (before Brexit), seemed to corroborate the optimism of the EU's founders. While the Union has faced a number of crises and political deadlocks since its founding, these have generally been regarded as opportunities to expand EU competences and to upgrade the EU supranational apparatus.[5]

However, as Chapter 2 has discussed, critical developments such as Brexit and the consolidation of nationalist platforms in several member states have challenged this narrative. This process of fragmentation – the so-called "return of history" – has called into question Robert Schuman's prediction that by committing to the construction of a shared institutional setting, Europeans would develop social and civic bonds.[6] Despite decades of "Europeanisation" of domestic institutions and policies, as well as continued efforts to promote socioeconomic convergence, notably through the launch of EU structural funds, the social and civic bonds between EU citizens seem to remain weak. Among other episodes, this became particularly apparent in the intra-EU cleavages regarding the concession of financial assistance to distressed Eurozone countries and the coordinated response to the refugee crisis. In these cases, the sharp divides within the EU suggest that many EU citizens regard these as national rather than common challenges. This apparent lack of willingness to share the burdens of European integration casts doubt on whether they would be ready to mobilise for the common good of the EU.

This issue is particularly relevant for our discussion since the adoption of ambitious policies for the common good of the EU may, indeed, imply significant sacrifices for certain groups of EU citizens and member states. As I claimed in Chapter 3, given that the EU political system consists of a two-level game, national governments will only be willing to accept the potentially high costs of these policies if their constituencies accept them as well. However, such agreement may be difficult to secure in the face of the current levels of Euroscepticism. Indeed, even if most EU citizens support EU membership, large swathes of national electorates regard the EU integration process with much distrust. For instance, in Italy, Greece, France and Sweden, approximately 30% of the citizens believe their countries would better face the future outside the EU.[7] In six member states – Cyprus, Hungary, Poland, Austria, Slovenia and Romania – this figure is close to 40%.[8] While the institutional reforms proposed in Chapter 4 could improve this landscape by boosting the perceived effectiveness and legitimacy of EU institutions, it remains unclear whether EU citizens would be willing to accept the costs of more ambitious EU policies. What, if anything, could motivate EU citizens to bear the burdens of the common good?

A way to approach this problem is to think of strategies that could strengthen civic friendship in the EU, understood as "a bond of reciprocal good-will between fellow citizens, expressed through norms of civic behaviour, such as mutual recognition of moral equality, mutual concern and mutual defence and support".[9] How are the common good and civic friendship linked? In a nutshell, individuals bound by civic friendship are more willing to act on "a concern for the whole, a dedication to the common good".[10] Civic friendship creates a background in which citizens "wish one other well for their own sake, do things for fellow citizens both individually and as a citizen body".[11] This willingness to sacrifice one's individual interest for the sake of others facilitates the adoption of demanding policies for the common good. To illustrate the point, consider the launch of the Beveridge welfare programme in the UK. Against what rational choice theory would have predicted, this very costly scheme recruited widespread support even among those not expected to become its beneficiaries.[12] As it has been argued, the collective war effort during World War II led British citizens to recognise one another as equal members of the demos and to care about one another's fate.[13] This collective wartime spirit prompted overwhelming support for the welfare programme after the war, regardless of the distribution of costs and benefits at stake.

This example, to which others could be added, suggests that the adoption of policies for the common good is likely more feasible in the presence of civic friendship. Accordingly, "[a]mong the tasks of modern political philosophy is to develop a favoured conception of the relations among modern citizens, among people who can know little or nothing of one another individually and yet are reciprocally dependent".[14] Despite the significance of this research agenda, the conditions that trigger civic friendship have received limited attention in the specialised literature. While some conceptual research has been conducted to investigate the meaning and significance of civic friendship, little has been said about *how* this bond develops in the first place.[15] Therefore, the following questions remain to be addressed: What are the preconditions of civic friendship? What, if anything, can a given polity do to increase civic friendship? This lack of answers has led Mihaela Georgieva to conclude that civic friendship is "a forgotten ideal" in modern political theory.[16] Yet, the relevance of these questions for this book cannot be understated. If civic friendship and the common good are closely linked, then the question of how EU citizens could develop stronger civic bonds deserves careful treatment.[17]

Is civic friendship feasible in the EU?

In recent years, a few authors have suggested that the EU polity does not offer an appropriate context for civic friendship to emerge. Since Aristotle's pioneering account came to light, the notion of civic friendship has typically been linked to clearly delimited sovereign communities, notably the city-state and the nation-state. Accordingly, scholars such as Martha Nussbaum and Michael Sandel have suggested that the limited levels of social interaction and political participation at the supranational level are incompatible with the development of thick civic bonds beyond borders.[18] In the words of Kerry Hoods, "[i]f we consider the practicalities of civic friendship, we find that cosmopolitan friendship is an even more difficult and demanding project than we might have imagined".[19] Although a few scholarly accounts have identified a range of emerging citizenship practices at the European level, EU citizenship is frequently regarded as a somewhat empty legal status.[20] Hence, David Miller has concluded that large conglomerates such as the EU "are divided in such a way that citizens' primary loyalties are *inevitably* directed toward their compatriots".[21] The primacy of national loyalty casts doubt on whether any strategy to increase civic friendship in the EU would be effective.

Yet is the arguably low level of civic citizenship in the EU indeed *inevitable*, as Miller claims? This view neglects the role of public policy in shaping the nature and quality of civic relations within any political community. Indeed, many nation-states and federations have adopted policies specifically aimed at enriching civic life and building a sense of community at some stage in their history.[22] Note that these measures did not always imply morally objectionable forms of social engineering. In fact, a few political institutions have *democratically* enacted policies that have created favourable conditions for individuals to recognise one another as fellow citizens and to seek the common good. Consider, for example, the redistributive policies adopted after German reunification, which allowed individuals with highly contrasting economic resources to become citizens on equal footing in the new demos.[23] In the opposite direction, certain policies may jeopardise civic bonds or prevent them from emerging. For example, Michael Sandel has argued that a set of governmental policies dramatically increasing socio-economic inequalities has put civic life in the United States at risk.[24] This outcome suggests that public policies have the potential to either enhance or jeopardise civic friendship.

This connection between certain types of public policies and the quality of civic relations also applies to the EU. For example, it has been argued that freedom of movement has had a positive impact on citizens' attitudes towards the EU and their fellow EU citizens.[25] Therefore, increasing the financial support to mobility and student exchange programmes, such as Erasmus, and reducing the administrative barriers against working abroad has the potential to strengthen civic friendship in the EU polity. In opposition, the failure to promote a constructive democratic dialogue about social cohesion and to pursue effective strategies to achieve this goal may compromise the civic relations between Europeans. For instance, Jean Tirole has argued that the "bitterness" of the talks between the Greek and the German governments in the context of the sovereign debt crisis is incompatible with the pursuit of the common good.[26] Along the same lines, Claudia Sternberg, Kira Gartzou-Katsouyanni and Kalypso Nicolaidis have argued that the demanding conditions imposed on the Greek people as a precondition to receiving financial assistance have eroded the mutual recognition of Europeans as fellow citizens.[27] The persistence of such impediments raises the question: What specific policies could boost civic friendship in the EU polity?

Why civic friendship remains limited in the EU

Before addressing this question, it should be noted that throughout its history, the EU has taken some measures to increase civic friendship, albeit with limited success. For example, the EU has launched a few symbolic actions intended to create a sense of membership in a shared political community, including the standardisation of EU passports and the proclamation of Europe Day (9 May). A more substantive step towards making an EU demos in a proper sense was the creation of the EU citizenship status by the Maastricht Treaty. Despite being acquired through the citizenship of any of the member states, EU citizenship translates into a distinctive set of citizenship practices, including the right to participate in the elections for the European Parliament to move and reside freely within the EU territory. Furthermore, in line with the strategy put forward by the Schuman Declaration, EU policymakers expected that a wide range of measures targeting the completion of the single market would help connect EU citizens to one another.[28] Consider, for instance, the abolition of border controls and the launch of the single currency. However, these efforts seem to have achieved limited success, at least if we consider the current levels of Euroscepticism.[29]

Why have EU institutions so far failed to promote a stronger civic friendship in the EU, then? One reason may be the apparent failure to agree on a long-term strategy to pursue this goal. Indeed, the strategies to bring EU citizens "ever closer" have changed significantly according to the political priorities of the different leaderships of the European Commission. For instance, the Barroso Commission called for the implementation of a "Plan D for Democracy", which included visits by the commissioners to the member states and national parliaments and more openness over meetings of the Council.[30] However, this plan has been mostly forgotten in the EU policy circles. In turn, the Juncker Commission strongly emphasised increasing the number of citizens' consultations about EU legislative proposals. Yet, this instrument lost much of its earlier prominence once the Von der Leyen Commission prioritised its new deliberative conference concerning the future of Europe. While each of these initiatives had its merits, they were rather short-lived and implemented at the expense of a more stable approach to constructing thicker civic bonds in the EU. In this regard, the Conference on the Future of Europe is telling. From the outset, this initiative sought to conduct a deliberative experiment in a limited time span rather than build the deliberative infrastructure that would allow for permanent citizen participation in shaping the EU's future.[31]

Another reason behind the lack of more satisfactory results may be the limited political will of the national governments to adopt a systemic, rather than modular, approach to transnational civic bonds. As I will claim below, civic friendship is not contingent on a single, miraculous policy but on a cross-cutting policy package that covers a variety of areas and is potentially very ambitious. Undoubtedly, the limited political appetite to engage with this type of programme is at least partially linked to recent developments in the domestic politics of the member states. Given that the nationalist platforms have recruited a high number of voters in several member states, the mainstream political parties increasingly have incentives to seek to recover some of the lost votes by making concessions in their European and global agendas.[32] This development has jeopardised the much-needed support to certain common policies that have the potential to enhance civic friendship from a wide range of policy areas, namely social, education and defence policy, where, as I shall claim below, a systemic approach and an intensified political commitment by the member states are crucial to enhance civic friendship in the EU. While this may be difficult to change in the current political context, a few nuanced policy proposals could enable more effective political action, as I will argue in the following sections.

Measures to increase civic friendship in the EU

In what follows, I shall discuss a few social, economic and political conditions that could strengthen civic friendship in the EU, as well as a set of EU policies to bring them forward. My goal is to apply a systemic approach to address this problem. Accordingly, my proposals should be regarded as a policy package to promote civic friendship in the EU in multiple but complementary ways. Given the obstacles listed above, I will explore ways of improving the feasibility prospects of my proposals. While the measures which will unfold cover several dimensions, ranging from distributive justice to education to defence cooperation, they do not intend to be exhaustive. I shall explain below why I deem these policies particularly important, but there may be others worth considering. Furthermore, note that I do not claim that my proposals would *necessarily* give rise to civic friendship. While I rely on normative and empirical arguments to claim that certain social, economic and political environments are more conducive to civic friendship than others, my proposals are not comparable to the laws of natural science. Finally, I should underscore that each of the proposals presented below merits much more extensive discussion than the space here allows. Therefore, I can only hope to provide a few plausible and feasible *guidelines* on how the problem of civic friendship in the EU could be addressed.

Strengthening the social level playing field in the EU

My first proposal is the creation of a stronger social level playing field in the EU, understood as a set of common rules and practices concerning the social protection of workers. The key insight behind this proposal is that individuals embedded in extremely competitive environments may fail to connect to one another and lose sight of the common good. Indeed, research in the field of social psychology has shown that the high level of competition resulting from neoliberal policies has created a sense of social disconnection between individuals.[33] This fragmentation arises from policies of market liberalisation that place a disproportional emphasis on individual performance at the expense of the collective achievements of social groups and political institutions. As self-reliance and entrepreneurship became a widespread ethos of the "homo neoliberalus", the concern for the community gradually erodes.[34] This "neoliberal incitement to manage oneself as an enterprise" and to prioritise individual rather than collective interests is hardly a background in which bonds of civic friendship will emerge.[35] Therefore, pursuing comprehensive liberalisation agendas comes with a cost in terms of social and civic bonds.

This recent tendency to regard "competition as the defining characteristic of human relations" and to treat any attempts to restrain it as "inimical to freedom" is not exclusive to any state or region.[36] Yet, it is particularly visible in the EU because the common market actively encourages competition between member states. While the EU has effectively reduced barriers against international trade and investment (through the so-called "negative integration"), it has created very few mechanisms to contain (through "positive integration") the imbalances that liberalisation brings about.[37] As a result, firms can readily relocate within the EU to wherever production costs are lower without considering the social dimension.[38] Given this competitive pressure, it should not come as surprise that many Europeans regard one other as rivals rather than fellow citizens. Indeed, fierce competition undermines social empathy and generates fear and anxiety.[39] This cross-border distrust is apparent in the attitudes of certain groups of EU workers towards each other. For example, it is telling that an arguable influx of Polish plumbers into the United Kingdom became one of the main themes of the Brexit debates.

The key question is whether these negative social impacts of competition could be contained without fundamentally changing the economic and political system of the EU.[40] As a few authors have argued, it would be feasible to temper the developments described above by creating a fair transnational competitive environment, particularly in domains such as taxation, labour conditions and social rights.[41] However, it should be noted that the EU has had a dual face in this regard. On the one hand, EU competition policy is "perhaps the most supranational of all EU policies and has become something of a flagship for the EU".[42] Competition policy's prominence has translated into extensive efforts to create a *level playing field* – that is, "a set of common rules and standards that are used primarily to prevent businesses in one country undercutting their rivals in other countries".[43] On the other hand, the EU's understanding of a level playing field has failed to include a robust social dimension. While in areas such as state aid monitoring, cartel prohibition and environment protection, the EU has set common principles that effectively regulate interstate competition, national governments are still allowed to independently adopt their labour laws, including minimum wages and severance payments. This prerogative leaves room for the member states to seek to increase their competitiveness by cutting social rights and benefits, thus reinforcing the competitive behaviour of workers within the common market.

Now, if the EU aims at comprehensively levelling the playing field, it should bring the social dimension into play. This step would be fundamental in creating a fair competitive environment among member states with contrasting fiscal capacities and different competitive advantages in the global value chain. A *social* level playing field, understood as a set of common standards in the domains of labour and social policy, would significantly contribute to alleviating the competitive pressure within the EU. For example, establishing this "social minimum" across the EU would no longer allow transnational companies "to playoff member states against each other when it comes to their investment decisions".[44] By containing predatory behaviour between member states, the EU would leave its citizens less exposed to the volatility of trade and investment, potentially making them less distrustful of one other.[45] Prioritising the development of more cooperative economic relations (rather than competitive ones) could also help address the resentment of those who feel left behind by the processes of economic integration.[46] If combined with appropriate measures to reduce socioeconomic inequalities, as described in the next section, such developments could pave the way to the creation of stronger social bonds between EU citizens.

How, then, do we create such a level playing field? As I have argued elsewhere, a key instrument to serve this purpose would be an EU labour code.[47] An EU labour code would set minimum standards regarding the working conditions in the common market, including a coordinated minimum wage and minimum severance payments. To ensure contrasting price levels across the Union are accommodated, the minimum wage could be defined as a percentage of the median national income, and minimum severance payments could be set in terms of a given number of monthly salaries. Despite being significant, the challenges linked to the harmonisation of labour rules would not be markedly more substantial than in other policy areas, such as trade policy, where cross-border diversity had been high before the Europeanisation of policies took place. In fact, other multilevel polities, including Germany and Belgium, have federal labour rules. The current diversity of national labour markets and social welfare regimes within the EU could be accommodated by allowing member states to grant additional rights and benefits to their workers, provided that the common minimum standards are fulfilled. This regulatory diversity suggests that the EU labour code is feasible, depending mainly on political will. In this regard, member states have shown encouraging signs of openness to advance the debate on a coordinated minimum wage.[48]

This policy proposal could strengthen civic friendship in the EU by mitigating the social effects of international competitive pressure.[49] Indeed, an EU labour code would allow member states and their citizens to develop more cooperative economic and social relations instead of taking fierce competition for granted. More specifically, an EU labour code would prevent member states from competing against each other on minimum wages and ease to fire workers, thereby setting moral boundaries to the logic of competition that currently invades "almost all domains of our existence".[50] This proposal would not necessarily adversely affect the productivity in the member states, given that it would likely prompt them to compete on other dimensions beyond labour costs, including innovation and product quality. By acknowledging that competitiveness and human well-being are "rival orders of worth", the EU would step towards creating a socioeconomic environment more akin to developing bonds between citizens and pursuing the common good.[51]

Reducing socioeconomic inequalities in the EU

Creating a social level playing field is crucial, yet insufficient to strengthen the bonds of civic friendship within the EU. To achieve this goal, the EU needs to improve not only the rules of the common market but also its outcomes, notably by reducing socioeconomic inequalities among EU citizens. As has been reported extensively, inequalities have been increasing steadily in several Western democracies.[52] While EU membership has contributed significantly to improving the socioeconomic outlook of the member states, the path towards socioeconomic convergence has slowed since the early 2000s.[53] Thus, according to the Eurostat, "[t]he dispersion in GDP per capita across the EU Member States is quite remarkable".[54] For example, in 2020, Denmark's GDP per capita was twice that of Slovakia.[55] Larger still was the gap between Bulgaria and Luxembourg, the latter's GDP per capita being four times that of the former.[56] At the same time, in 2019, "[s]evere material deprivation rates ranged from 1.3 % in Luxembourg, 1.8 % in Sweden and 2.4 % in Finland, to 14.5 % in Romania, 16.2 % in Greece and 19.9 % in Bulgaria".[57] While the period of economic growth following the sovereign debt crisis has generally improved the welfare indicators within the EU, "the rising tide of the post-crisis recovery has not lifted all citizens equally".[58]

This evolution is not entirely surprising. Since the pioneering works of David Ricardo, most economists have argued that free trade and investment increase the *aggregate wealth* of nations compared to a scenario of protectionism.[59] However, it has also been highlighted that liberalisation has adversely affected income and wealth distributions where it has not been combined with appropriate redistributive policies.[60] While many individuals find new and better jobs in the flourishing sectors of an open economy, others lose theirs since their old businesses struggled in the global markets. This distributional pattern mainly tends to harm the most vulnerable individuals, namely low-skilled workers.[61] To ensure a smooth transition to an increasingly open economy, governments need to invest large sums in assisting unemployed citizens and equipping them with new skills. However, the budgetary capacity to perform this task is highly unequal among member states. This imbalance has only been worsened by the sovereign debt crisis, which affected member states asymmetrically. While it is true that the distressed member states have received structural funds to address these imbalances, it is now clear that the EU convergence instruments will need to be scaled up if they are to temper socioeconomic inequalities.

Yet, we might ask, why is inequality problematic from the standpoint of civic friendship? As has rightly been pointed out, economic inequalities undermine social cohesion.[62] An enlightening explanation of this link can already be found in ancient Greek political theory. For example, Plato illustrated the disruptive effects of inequality by referring to a city-state with sharp class divides. As he put it, "[s]uch a city should of necessity be not one, but two, a city of the rich and a city of the poor, dwelling together, and always plotting against one another".[63] Indeed, the widening gap between the rich and the poor may generate sub-groups in the demos with irreconcilable interests and goals. This fragmentation of civil society makes it harder for citizens to develop a concern for the common good. As inequalities continue to rise, a civic ethos according to which citizens were bound to take care of each other – particularly the most vulnerable – has been replaced by a merit-based paradigm whereby individuals are presented as solely responsible for their own fates.[64] Hence, failing to redistribute may erode the spirit of mutual concern and assistance between the members of the polity. While the issue of how much socioeconomic inequality should be tolerated in an egalitarian society has been a matter of much controversy, there is a growing consensus that the dramatic effects of inequality ought to be addressed.[65]

Another undesirable outcome which has been associated with high levels of inequality is a decline in democratic life. A key explanation for this link is that economic inequality translates into political inequality in a variety of ways.[66] First, privileged citizens have better access to those tools that are instrumental to effective democratic participation. For instance, they typically benefit from better access to education and high-quality sources of information. Second, unequal resources lead to contrasting abilities to influence policymaking. For instance, well-funded interest groups can hire well-connected strategists and lobbyists to shape impactfully the political agenda. Third, wealthy citizens have better chances of exercising fully their democratic rights. For instance, they can hire an experienced lawyer to ensure the fulfilment of a particular civil or social right. In these and similar ways, wealthy citizens are usually in a better position to make their voices heard and to shape the outcomes of the decision-making processes. These contrasting opportunities to take part in democratic life have generated disillusionment and distrust in democratic institutions across the Western world and have prevented citizens from recognising one another as equal members of the demos.[67]

The impact of economic inequality on civic relations is particularly apparent in the EU polity. An extreme but quite revealing case is the interstate negotiations regarding the Greek bailouts between 2010 and 2015. Given the lack of economic resources to address the sovereign debt crisis, the Greek government was forced to accept the harsh conditions imposed by the other member states in exchange for financial assistance. The austerity measures included dramatic cuts in pensions, unemployment benefits and healthcare provision. As a result, material deprivation in Greece skyrocketed "at a time when other countries like Germany continued to prosper".[68] Facing a "humiliating deal" and a "humanitarian crisis", many Greek citizens felt that the EU had left them behind.[69] Furthermore, they thought that they did not have a voice in EU decision-making. Indeed, despite the efforts of the Greek government to negotiate a more balanced deal, most EU governments showed a lack of flexibility to engage with the Greek concerns.[70] Thus, Greece was part of "what is perhaps the most intrusive and demanding contract between an advanced nation and its creditors since the Second World War".[71] Given the pervasive disparities within the EU, both socioeconomic and political inequalities may continue to set EU citizens apart.

How, then, can inequality be addressed in the EU? As I have suggested, the existing instruments of cohesion policy are insufficient. Indeed, the dynamics of "creative destruction", which are inherent to contexts of free trade and investment, recurrently generate a need to assist large groups of workers through demanding economic transitions.[72] Such sectoral restructuring requires policymakers to develop policy instruments with sufficient firepower to act quickly and decisively on emerging inequalities. In recent years, a few promising proposals have been put forward, offering alternative (and possibly complementary) paths to reduce inequalities in the EU. Consider, for example, the following proposals: (i) creating a universal basic income for all EU citizens; (ii) launching a sizeable social investment programme to upgrade EU workers' skills; and (iii) creating an autonomous European Monetary Fund to assist member states in need, which would replace the existing intergovernmental European Stability Mechanism.[73] Despite their relative advantages and shortcomings, which cannot be discussed here, each of these proposals has the potential to promote socioeconomic equality among EU citizens.[74]

How might one (or several) of these proposals be implemented? Perhaps the most critical feasibility question at stake is how to obtain the large sums required to finance proposals of this size. In Chapter 3, I argued that an EU corporate tax should be launched to boost the financial resources available to the Union. An EU corporate tax would give the EU an appropriate budgetary capacity to fight inequalities.[75] Part of the funds collected could be allocated to redistributive programmes at the EU level. Moreover, it would be normatively desirable because it would be linked to the wealth generated by the common market.[76] Furthermore, an EU corporate tax would seem more politically feasible than other alternatives that imply direct taxation of EU citizens. The prospects of the proposal would likely be boosted if the tax were initially set at a very low rate (it could always be increased at a later stage, political conditions permitting). In sum, with enhanced fiscal autonomy, EU institutions would have the means to engage with ambitious policies to promote social cohesion and ensure that all EU citizens stand on equal footing. Policy in this direction would strengthen the bonds of civic friendship within the Union.

Creating more opportunities for citizens' participation

Redistributing the gains of the common market is crucial to equip citizens with the necessary resources to be equal members of the EU demos. However, citizens will only be able to take part in the governing of the Union if EU institutions are open to civil society. In this regard, the EU democracy faces at least two structural challenges. First, as I suggested in Chapter 4, the opportunities for citizens to participate in EU institutions are scarce. Except for the European Parliament, none of the EU institutions is directly elected by EU citizens. The instruments to collect the input of citizens throughout the EU policymaking process are equally limited, thus creating a widespread feeling that EU institutions are detached from EU citizens.[77] Second, the opportunities to participate at the EU level that do exist have little effect. For instance, the European Citizens Initiatives (ECI) – an instrument created by the Treaty of Lisbon that allows citizens to present policy proposals to EU institutions – has achieved minimal policy impact. Indeed, by 2018, only four out of the 67 ECIs launched had been successful.[78] These limited chances to be meaningfully involved in shared political institutions translate into a lack of an appropriate context where civic bonds could emerge.

Note that strengthening the opportunities for political participation may foster civic friendship in a variety of ways. First, political participation allows citizens to perceive themselves as equal members of a self-governing demos. For example, many citizens have described the act of voting as an impactful experience that generates a sense of belonging to a political community.[79] Second, participation creates much-needed platforms for citizens to engage with one another and form a common will, particularly when translated into initiatives of deliberative democracy. Indeed, by exchanging ideas and concerns and discussing alternative proposals, citizens frequently develop an understanding of one another's needs as well as mutual concern. To illustrate the point, consider the famous charette (community meeting) organised by the local government in Durham, North Carolina, in 1971, in which a group of black and white citizens agreed on measures to tackle segregation in local schools after ten days of intense discussions, which later became the subject of a book and major motion picture *The Best of Enemies* (2019).[80] Third, participatory initiatives that have a visible follow-up (i.e., that are translated into concrete policy outcomes) empower citizens to achieve real change by acting together as a body of citizens. Consider, for instance, the impact of the participatory budget of Paris on the daily lives of many citizens.[81]

In opposition, the scarcity of opportunities to participate meaningfully may generate two types of political behaviour that undermine civic friendship. On the one hand, the disconnection of citizens from political institutions may produce *political apathy*, understood as a lack of interest in political matters. Indeed, if citizens develop a perception that their preferences and views are recurrently overlooked – either because they lack the chance to express them in the public sphere or because their participation does not impact policymaking in any meaningful way – they may give up on getting involved in public affairs. Any prolonged attenuation in citizen participation will lead steadily to a decline in democratic life and the erosion of civic bonds.[82] At the other extreme, civic disengagement may generate *political radicalism*. Indeed, "there is growing anger among people who feel excluded from influence and decision making".[83] This feeling of disempowerment may lead citizens to adopt radical views and to support extremist political parties that challenge civic and political rights on the grounds of building a "true democracy".[84] Facing an increasingly polarised public sphere, citizens may become increasingly unable to engage with one another and bridge their different positions and worldviews. Both types of behaviour – apathy and radicalism – clearly jeopardise civic friendship.

While participatory citizenship has become a recurrent topic in the discourse of EU officials in recent years, the concrete measures to increase participation in EU institutions have been somewhat disappointing. For example, in 2013, the EU launched the European Year of Citizens, which aimed at raising awareness about "the rights linked to moving to and living in other EU countries".[85] However, the issue of how EU citizens could play a more active role in EU policymaking remained largely unaddressed. In turn, the Juncker Commission put forward new rules for the functioning of the ECIs to increase their impact. Yet the fundamental principle underlying this consultation mechanism, according to which the Commission has discretionary power to decide on whether to follow up on the citizens' proposals, remained unchanged. A few years later, as I mentioned above, the Von der Leyen Commission launched the Conference on the Future of Europe, presenting it as a tool that would turn the EU into a deliberative democracy. However, this initiative committed to achieving a limited degree of policy impact – namely, producing "a report with recommendations for EU institutions".[86] These developments suggest that the rhetoric regarding the improvement of political participation at the EU level has not been matched with appropriate opportunities to participate in EU policymaking.

How could this state of affairs be remedied? Three proposals presented in Chapter 4 could empower EU citizens to participate more actively in the governing of EU institutions. First, by directly electing the presidents of the European Commission and the European Council, EU citizens would have a chance to choose between alternative political visions for the EU polity. While more frequent elections will not be enough to create a vibrant EU democracy, they are certainly one of its indispensable components. Second, upgrading the role of the Commission Representations in the EU capitals could trigger a more engaging debate about EU policies at the local level. Under my proposal, the Representations would regularly launch participatory initiatives aimed at collecting citizens' input regarding the Commission's legislative proposals, and they would be responsible for providing citizens with follow-ups. Third, the creation of an EU Citizens' Assembly would offer EU citizens an opportunity to shape the political debate at the supranational level. This assembly would have significant agenda-setting competences, notably the power to insert discussion points in the agenda of the ministerial meetings of the Council of the European Union. Subsequently, the Council could decide to ask the Commission to present concrete legislative proposals following the citizens' suggestions, and it would be required to report to the Citizens' Assembly on the outcome of its discussions.

These and similar instruments could create a background of civic engagement in which civic friendship and a concern for the common good of the whole EU could more easily flourish. As I have suggested, the EU should explore ambitious democratic innovations, understood as "institutions that have been specifically designed to increase and deepen citizen participation in the political decision-making process".[87] By participating in EU institutions more actively, EU citizens might more easily connect to one another and might feel that they have a real say in EU policymaking. Enhanced participation would also give citizens a chance to engage with different perspectives on EU integration and to develop a better understanding of each other's needs and concerns. This engagement could make the EU more resilient towards the challenges against EU values discussed in Chapter 2. Indeed, "by involving people and empowering them to shape their own futures, we can share responsibility and rediscover the value and pleasure of working and learning together, cooperating in mutual organisations and renewing the bonds of solidarity which make us all stronger".[88] This path could make the idea of a "Citizens' Union" a reality.[89]

Reducing barriers to freedom of movement

As I have argued, a critical condition for civic friendship to flourish in the EU is that citizens interact with each other. Yet this refers not only to political participation through shared institutions but also to daily life. Citizens who live abroad for at least a certain period have the chance to interact regularly with citizens from another nationality and to build transnational ties. As has been pointed out, learning from and engaging with the "Other" reduces the fear of the unknown and generates mutual trust.[90]

Experience of mobility and regular time spent in other European countries is therefore critical for an EU in which a significant degree of prejudice and mistrust exists across borders, undermining the emergence of stronger civic bonds.[91] While the digital transformation has allowed for new forms of remote interaction, studying and working abroad remain unique ways to experience how much individuals have in common. Indeed, interstate mobility contributes to the construction of shared social imaginaries, and it impacts the way in which citizens perceive their own identities. Accordingly, "people who tend to think of themselves as Europeans are people who are more likely to interact with others across Europe".[92] Furthermore, living abroad allows for the development of language skills, which facilitates communication between fellow EU citizens. For these reasons, free movers have been rightly described as "pioneers of European integration".[93]

While the European Commission has made significant efforts to facilitate the mobility of people within the EU in the last decades, the share of mobile EU citizens remains relatively low.[94] Indeed, in 2020, only 3.3 % of EU citizens of working age resided in a member state other than that of their primary citizenship.[95] These figures compare poorly to other multilevel polities, such as the United States, where interstate mobility of workers remains higher than 10% despite the recent downward trend.[96] It should be noted that geographical mobility is considerably higher among university students, where an average of 10% of the students enrolled in degree-awarding programmes of tertiary education in the EU are from another member state.[97] However, the majority of young EU citizens do not pursue a degree in higher education, which reduces the impact of the previous figure.[98] In turn, the renowned Erasmus exchange programme, which Kristine Mitchel has rightly dubbed "a civic experience", covers just 1.1% of tertiary students in the EU.[99] This limited degree of mobility of EU workers and students is somewhat striking, particularly if we take into account that "Europeans consistently rate (in Eurobarometer surveys) their rights of free movement as the most important benefit of EU membership ... and around a third claim to be ready to move abroad if the opportunity and demand arose".[100]

Why is mobility relatively low in a Union where physical borders have for long been removed? There may be strong sociological and psychological reasons, including family ties, cultural distance and language barriers. However, it should also be emphasised that many administrative barriers make the establishment of EU citizens in other member states potentially difficult. For instance, a recent study by the European Union Agency for Fundamental Rights has concluded that "courts in different countries vary in the interpretation of the key EU's provisions regulating EU citizens' rights".[101] For example, narrow interpretations by the national courts of concepts in the EU directives, such as "family member" and "sufficient resources", may hinder workers and their families from moving abroad. Regarding students, several scholarships from national authorities are only available to those pursuing studies in national institutions. Furthermore, there are heavy administrative burdens linked to steps as basic as opening a bank account abroad, enrolling in a local employment centre and registering a foreign car. This is due to demanding legal and evidentiary requirements, inefficient communication between national administrations and lack of information. These barriers seriously restrict free movement.

Many of these barriers could be eliminated, or at least reduced, if appropriate public policies were set in place. In this regard, the EU Agency for Fundamental Rights has listed a number of proposals that could lead to a more consistent implementation of EU legislation on freedom of movement. First, an official and regularly updated handbook on freedom of movement for legal practitioners would help to disseminate significant developments concerning the case law of the CJEU and would provide clear guidance regarding interpretation. Having this information to hand would be crucial given that "the interpretation of certain provisions and terms by national courts differs not only across member states, but sometimes also within the same jurisdiction".[102] Second, the Commission could create a community of practice that shares difficult challenges and workable solutions related to freedom of movement. This policy could be complemented by "strengthening the assistance provided to member states to exchange information on national jurisprudence and approaches between courts and public administration".[103] Finally, in cooperation with the national administrations, the Commission could organise "more intensive and systematic training of legal professionals, in particular judges and public officials responsible for the directive's application in EU member states".[104]

In turn, an EU-wide programme of administrative simplification concerning information exchange could significantly reduce the existing barriers against freedom of movement. For instance, the launch of an EU citizen identification card backed by shared information systems and accepted everywhere in the EU would allow for a swift exchange of data between national administrations. By presenting this ID card, EU citizens could easily demonstrate in any member state that, for example, they are single or married, have a clean criminal record, and have paid taxes in another member state. This policy move would shift the administrative burden from the mobile EU citizen – who presently moves from shop to shop to obtain and validate a variety of documents – to the national administrations, which would communicate directly with one other. An EU citizen card along these lines could be created by an intergovernmental agreement and implemented by the European Union Agency for the Operational Management of Large-Scale IT Systems in the Area of Freedom, Security and Justice. To increase the feasibility of this proposal, national administrations could foresee different stages of information sharing, starting with basic personal data and gradually covering critical areas related to free movement such as taxation, social security coordination, registry of vehicles and criminal records. While this would be a challenging project, successful experiences such as the EU driver's licence and the COVID-19 vaccination pass suggest that it could be realised.

Regarding the mobility of students, a significant step to increase interstate mobility would be granting more financial resources to the European Education Area (EEA). Through effective instruments such as the Bologna process and the European Credit Transfer and Accumulation System, the EEA has contributed significantly to increasing coordination across national educational systems and reducing technical barriers against the mobility of students. However, the resources of the EEA are currently limited. While the overall funding for the Erasmus Plus programme, which provides financial support to mobile students, has increased under the Multiannual Framework 2021–2027, the amount of its individual grants is clearly insufficient to cover the living expenses in many of the destination countries.[105] This shortfall is problematic given that studying abroad is typically a costly endeavour. In addition, the promising "Erasmus Plus Master Degree Loans" – EU-guaranteed loans to pursue a master's degree abroad with favourable repayment terms – are only available to citizens residing in four member states.[106] This limitation means that many students do not have access to appropriate financial resources to study abroad. Hence, increasing the value of Erasmus grants and expanding the scope of the Master Degree

Loans programme would create better conditions for the mobility of students in the EU.

While a few scholars have also drawn attention to some disintegrative effects of freedom of movement, the latter could be remedied by strengthening of the social level playing field and reducing socioeconomic inequalities in the EU, as discussed above. Drawing on the key role played by freedom of movement in the Brexit debates, it has been argued that citizens who do not travel regularly nor emigrate may feel left behind in their countries of origin and may regard free movers as competitors for jobs and social benefits.[107] Yet it should be noted that, according to a 2023 Eurobarometer survey, this segment of citizens is currently relatively small. In fact, 89% of the EU citizens claim to personally benefit from free movement, and 83% recognise its overall benefits for the economy.[108] Regarding the 15% of the EU citizens that consider that free movement is economically harmful, their perception could be changed if appropriate measures were taken to better distribute its benefits. As suggested above, equipping the EU with a stronger social dimension could help address the resentment of those who feel let down by the process of economic integration. Therefore, improving the standards of freedom of movement is certainly preferable than curtailing it.

The potential impact of these measures on the level of civic friendship in the EU should not be underestimated. As Jacques Delors has famously put it, "nobody can fall in love with the single market".[109] Indeed, "cognitive mobilisation" towards the EU, understood as a "rational" endorsement of the process of EU integration on the grounds of the mutual benefits that it generates, is hardly sufficient to enhance transnational bonds.[110] In this regard, the mobility of people has the potential to promote gradually the "Europeanisation of everyday life".[111] It has a transformational effect not only on those who cross national borders but also on their families and friends who indirectly share their experiences. Furthermore, free movement impacts all those who "may have seriously considered the matter, plan to do so in the future or see mobility as an option for their children".[112] As has been noted, "[t]he impact of such a high share of individuals potentially imagining futures that transcend national borders should not be underestimated as a factor influencing what EU citizenship currently is and what it will be in the future".[113] Combined with enhanced participation in EU institutions, free movement could make the experience of being an EU citizen essentially about engaging with social and civic relations beyond member states borders.

Launching a common curriculum on EU citizenship

An additional strategy to promote civic friendship in the EU would be launching a transnational course on EU citizenship to be offered in every school in the EU. To understand the logic behind this proposal, I should begin by mentioning that many EU citizens possess limited knowledge of the functioning of EU institutions and the opportunities to participate in EU decision-making. For example, some EU citizens have never heard of the European Council or the European Commission.[114] More strikingly, nearly half (44%) of Europeans claim not to understand how the EU works.[115] Undoubtedly, such a state of affairs is at least partially explained by the complexity of the EU political system. The constellation of institutional arrangements at the supranational and intergovernmental level is not always easy to grasp, even for experts. Consider, for instance, the diversity of rules and procedures underpinning the single market, the Eurozone and the Schengen Area. However, the fact that what member states "teach about Europe continues to vary" and that "this variation is not just superficial" but rather "fundamental" undermines the development of a shared and solid understanding of EU citizenship and interest among citizens to participate jointly in EU institutions.[116]

This state of affairs is only aggravated by the "menace of nationalism in education".[117] While all EU member states "provide some level of education about Europe and European integration", it has been argued that the existing educational materials have a bias towards nationalist narratives.[118] For example, many history textbooks glorify national heroes and achievements at the expense of adopting a transnational or global approach to historical developments.[119] Similarly, in the field of citizenship education, "the way in which citizenship in and of Europe is portrayed in educational texts tends to reflect *national* priorities and *national* understandings of citizenship".[120] Thus, the predominance of nation-states vis-à-vis other political communities is presented in many schools not simply as a significant historical fact but as an ultimate telos which is not to be challenged. This social reproduction of a Westphalian imaginary whereby EU citizens are led to regard one another as reluctant "friends" (or even as potential "enemies") seems to be incompatible with the development of transnational civic bonds.[121] Therefore, in the absence of a suitable environment where EU students can discuss their civic links with the citizens of other member states, they may remain detached from one another and from EU institutions.

Note that a common curriculum on EU citizenship might contribute to the emergence of bonds of civic friendship in the EU in at least two ways. First, it would enable citizens to acquire knowledge and develop competences which are crucial for being politically engaged members of the EU polity.[122] For instance, EU citizenship education would allow EU citizens to understand better how EU institutions work and to be aware of their rights as EU citizens. Such deep awareness could, in turn, generate a greater interest in EU policy debates at all levels of government while empowering EU citizens to stand up for crucial rights linked to EU citizenship status, such as freedom of movement and non-discrimination.

Second, EU citizenship education might boost civic friendship by promoting the mutual recognition of individuals from different member states as fellow citizens and by encouraging them to shape the future of the Union collaboratively.[123] For instance, the common curriculum could include a simulation of a session of the EU Citizens' Assembly in which each student would be asked to present the policy perspective of a citizen from a given member state.[124] This and similar activities would allow individuals to put themselves in one another's shoes, thus experiencing the diversity of standpoints within the EU and the need to compromise for the sake of the common good.

How could the proposal for a common curriculum on EU citizenship be implemented? A number of practical concerns and objections would undoubtedly be raised. First, it should be noted that education is mainly a national and, in some cases, regional competence.[125] How, then, could a common curriculum be adopted in the current configuration of competences of the EU multilevel polity? Second, how could 27 member states with diverse educational systems and different perspectives on European integration agree on a common curriculum? What body should be responsible for deciding its content and format? Third, what if it were impossible to reach an agreement on this between *all* member states? For instance, the fact that the notion of EU citizenship is contested casts doubt on whether member states would be willing to agree on the content of a transnational curriculum. Should member states nonetheless be forced to adopt the EU curriculum? Finally, it may be argued that a common curriculum would be perceived as social engineering imposed by Brussels seeking to inculcate an attachment to EU institutions among young generations. How could this initiative avoid the charge of arbitrarily replacing the ideology of nationalism with that of federalism?

These are important questions, which I can only address by providing a few general guidelines. To begin with, I should note that the feasibility prospects of this proposal would certainly be higher if member states were allowed to retain control of education policy, as opposed to a scenario which would require delegation of powers to the Commission.[126] Accordingly, this curriculum should be designed and adopted in an intergovernmental format without the need to change the distribution of competences currently foreseen in the EU treaties. Regarding the development of concrete proposals, national governments could jointly set up a panel of teachers, experts, activists and other relevant profiles that would include representatives of all member states.[127] The proposals issued by the panel would be discussed between the national authorities and eventually agreed upon at an intergovernmental conference. Given the intergovernmental character of this process, member states would retain an option to opt out of the common curriculum. In the event of a small group of member states strongly opposing this initiative, it could still be adopted by a majority of the member states, similarly to what has applied to the Schengen area and the Eurozone. The remaining member states would be allowed to join at a later stage if they so wished. Member states would retain full autonomy regarding the contents and format of all other subjects of their curricula.

The question of whether an EU curriculum would recruit a sufficient level of support among national governments and EU citizens would most likely depend on its specific shape. To begin with, the idea of citizenship education should not be controversial as such. While curricula feature much diversity within the Union, most member states already offer some sort of citizenship education, even if not in the specific format of a compulsory separate subject.[128] In turn, the fact that the meaning of EU citizenship has not been crystallised would not necessarily raise a challenge, at least if the common curriculum aimed at stimulating an open debate among students. In this sense, EU citizenship education should not be merely informative; rather, it should allow for critical approaches.[129] Indeed, a curriculum fostering critical thinking about EU affairs could not be fairly charged with merely fabricating support for the EU. In fact, if framed as part of a broader agenda to address the democratic deficit in the EU, this initiative could recruit support from a broad range of national stakeholders. While this proposal would not automatically bring EU citizens closer to one another, it would constitute a step forward, particularly if it could be linked to other relevant experiences for young citizens, such as the European Solidarity Corps and the Erasmus programme.

Increasing defence cooperation in the EU

The last proposal presented in this chapter consists of increasing defence cooperation in the EU, more specifically by developing a legal framework and military capabilities which would allow member states to react together effectively to an attack against any member state. Yet, in what sense can readiness for battle be regarded as a component of civic friendship? Recall that the definition of civic friendship that I presented at the beginning of this chapter included a reference to "mutual defence and support". This link between civic ties and the defence domain might raise justifiable concerns if we conceive "defence" broadly to include, for instance, military operations aimed at expanding a country's territory. Yet the connection seems far more apparent when we narrow it down to cases of "defence from external aggression". Consider, for example, an unjust military strike against an EU member state.[130] If EU citizens care about one another's fate, they will perceive an attack against any member state as an offensive against the whole EU polity. They would not be mere bystanders of such aggression but promptly assist their fellow citizens. This observation suggests that civic friendship and collective security are connected.[131]

Yet how exactly is this link generated? What seems to trigger civic friendship is not so much the experience of taking up arms together, which hardly takes place in a politically stable region, but the (more or less explicit) commitment by citizens to defend one another from hypothetical threats.[132] While early nationalist movements drew heavily on warfare and national defence rituals such as military conscription to advance their agenda, modern democracies tend to regard the bond of mutual assistance rather as a pledge to act together in difficult times.[133] This *willingness* to assist others and the *expectation* of receiving assistance may indeed create mutual trust and a sense of reciprocity between fellow citizens. Note that the fact that a particular region is politically stable and that citizens do not perceive security threats as imminent does not imply that they are indifferent to the prospect of being assisted in case of need. While there has been some scepticism in the West regarding the pursuit of defence activities since the end of the Cold War, public support for security tends to increase whenever a serious threat presents itself. Such a concern with security is clear in the EU, where Eurobarometer surveys have shown that "the majority of the EU's citizens want more security, stability and a coordinated EU response to current threats".[134]

Yet would bonds of mutual assistance along these lines be feasible in the EU polity? In fact, this variety of transnational solidarity has been recurrent in European history. Unlike other policy domains where the resistance against multilateralism has been strong, nations have frequently sought military alliances beyond national borders. Indeed, the creation of "security communities" preceded that of many other forms of regional integration.[135] While it is true that many presumable allies behave opportunistically, several alliances have remained remarkably stable in time.[136] Note that the belief that a given group of states will stand united in dangerous times may create lasting bonds between peoples, even if they are politically and culturally very diverse. Consider, for instance, the North Atlantic Treaty Organization (NATO), which has been the main framework to promote security in Europe in the last decades. Incidentally, the formation of alliances such as NATO has proved to be an effective deterrent to armed conflict.[137] While a commitment to mutual assistance may not be enough to generate civic friendship between EU citizens, it seems hard to conceive of civic friendship in the EU in the absence of such a reciprocal commitment, particularly given the security challenges faced by the Union.

Indeed, the EU faces "multiple security threats".[138] To begin with, the unpredictable behaviour of Russia in recent years has cast a shadow of uncertainty along the EU's eastern border. Despite the diplomatic efforts by the EU institutions and its member states, Russia unlawfully occupied large parts of the Donbas region and annexed Crimea in 2014, and it launched a full-scale invasion of Ukraine in 2022. Furthermore, its armed forces have conducted large-scale military drills next to the borders of the Baltic states and Poland. This activity has raised the fear that one or a few of these member states could be Russia's next target.[139] At the same time, the political instability in northern Africa and the Middle East, particularly in Libya and Syria, has triggered not only a dramatic migration crisis but also a pervasive terrorist threat against the EU. In fact, in 2019, the EU was the target of 21 jihadist attacks, after 24 attacks in 2018 and 33 attacks in 2017.[140] Several member states have suffered significant civilian casualties, which generated a climate of fear and insecurity among citizens. Furthermore, the steady militarisation of several non-EU states and the emergence of new forms of warfare, notably cyberterrorism, has only increased the level of uncertainty. Therefore, "[t]he evolving international stage spells worrying scenarios for the EU, with dark clouds of insecurity and geostrategic competition building on many fronts".[141]

While NATO has been a critical framework to address security challenges in Europe, this key defence alliance is not enough to ensure that EU citizens mutually assist one other in case of need. First, it should be noted that, at the time of writing, five EU member states are not NATO members.[142] This means that millions of EU citizens are not formally bound to aid one other. Second, the retreat of the United States from global security during Donald Trump's presidency revealed the extent of the EU's exposure to policy shifts in Washington. While President Biden has restored close cooperation with America's Western allies, the fact that the security of EU citizens relies to a large extent on the armed forces of the United States remains a serious liability. Third, not all non-EU NATO members have good relations with the EU member states. Consider, for instance, the tensions between Turkey and Cyprus. Conflict between them could lead to a scenario in which NATO would not be able to provide a military response or even in which EU states would find themselves on opposite sides of a conflict.[143] It should be added that EU enlargement in the Balkans may further complicate this puzzle. All this suggests that, even if the NATO framework is crucial to ensure Europe's security, the member states should enhance defence cooperation at the EU level.

How, then, could EU defence cooperation be increased? This goal could be achieved in two ways: (i) by adopting a more ambitious EU legal framework for mutual defence and (ii) by strengthening the joint capabilities of the armed forces of the member states, enabling them to respond together to serious threats. Regarding the EU legal framework, it should be acknowledged that a clause of the TEU asserts that member states are obliged to assist a fellow member state that has been "a victim of armed aggression on its territory".[144] However, the article does not specify that *military* assistance is required in such cases. More strikingly, the EU lacks a formal procedure to activate this article, meaning that any assistance would need to be agreed bilaterally between member states. Therefore, creating a formal procedure to implement the mutual defence clause provides the guarantee that EU citizens will assist one another in the event of external aggression. While this proposal would likely face resistance from the traditionally "neutral" member states, the efforts to bring it to light would have a chance to succeed given the deteriorating context of EU security mentioned above and the increasing openness expressed by key EU security actors to work together in the field of defence.[145]

In terms of enhancing the joint defence capabilities, an essential step forward would be reducing the fragmentation of the EU defence landscape, thus allowing national armed forces to work together more effectively. This point can be illustrated by comparing a few figures concerning the equipment of the US armed forces to that of the EU polity as a whole. For example, while the US Army operates only one main type of battle tank, the EU operates 17; while the US Navy uses four types of destroyers and frigates, the EU uses 29; while the US Air Force employs six types of fighter planes, the EU employs 20.[146] This wide range of equipment in the EU limits dramatically interoperability – that is, the ability of the armed forces of the member states to operate together on the battlefield in case of need. This state of affairs not only reflects the lack of alignment of strategic priorities but is also linked to the fact that "around 80% of defence procurement is run on a purely national basis".[147] Note that the inefficiency resulting from the "lack of cooperation between member states in the field of security and defence is estimated to cost between €25 billion and €100 billion every year".[148] These resources should be allocated to joint initiatives, thus promoting higher efficiency of the defence budgets.

These challenges could be at least partially addressed by scaling up the existing EU programmes in defence cooperation. To begin with, the Permanent Structured Cooperation programme (PESCO) has set 20 binding commitments for participatory member states, which include coordinating the levels and categories of defence investments, developing joint defence capabilities, promoting the interoperability of their armed forces and conducting military procurement jointly.[149] While the implementation of these commitments is reviewed on a yearly basis, there has been a "lack of compliance with binding commitments and a limited embedding of PESCO in national defence-planning processes".[150] This gap has emerged because the level of transnational cooperation envisioned by PESCO implies a significant change in the organisational culture of the national administrations and armed forces. Therefore, the move towards a more collaborative defence landscape requires a close and constant involvement of the political leadership at the national and EU levels. This requirement suggests that "PESCO implementation will falter unless the agenda of the European Council regularly addresses security and defence issues".[151]

In turn, the budget of the European Defence Fund (EDF) could be expanded to support defence cooperation projects at a much higher scale. The main purpose of the EDF is to support research and development of defence technology and equipment to be used jointly by the armed forces of several member states, boosting their ability to operate together in case of need. Accordingly, projects to be funded under the EDF should be highly collaborative and must involve several member states. While the architecture of the EDF creates good incentives for defence cooperation, its current budget is rather limited. Indeed, the EDF's budget for the period 2021–2027 is only €8 billion – that is, an average of approximately €1 billion per year. This sum is the equivalent of the defence budget of Lithuania in 2020 and is almost 60 times less than Russia's budget in the same year.[152] By pooling resources at the EU level and increasing the firepower of the EDF, member states would have a stronger incentive to collaborate and strengthen their defence capabilities. Altogether, the measures presented in this section would allow EU citizens to regard themselves as part of an emerging "defence Union".

Conclusion

I have claimed that civic friendship could be boosted in the EU if appropriate public policies are adopted. I presented six proposals to achieve this end: (i) strengthening the social level playing field in the EU, namely by launching an EU labour code; (ii) reducing socioeconomic inequalities in the EU by distributing more fairly the gains of European integration; (iii) improving the opportunities for citizens' political participation, through the creation of an EU Citizens Assembly, the launch of direct elections for the presidency of the European Commission and the European Council and by enhancing the role of the Representations of the Commission; (iv) reducing barriers against freedom of movement by eliminating significant administrative, legal and economic burdens; (v) launching a transnational curriculum on EU citizenship education, which would be offered in all EU schools; and (vi) increasing defence cooperation, notably by upgrading the mutual defence clause between member states and scaling up the Permanent Structured Cooperation and the EDF. These "concrete achievements", to apply Robert Schuman's words, could generate a "de facto solidarity between EU citizens".[153]

Notes

1. *Treaty on European Union*, Preamble.
2. Francis Fukuyama, *The End of History and the Last Man* (New York, 1992).
3. Robert Schuman, *The Schuman Declaration* (9 May 1950).
4. Schuman, *The Schuman Declaration* (9 May 1950).
5. In her discussion of how crisis can be regarded as an opportunity to expand EU competences, Paola Gosio cites West German Chancellor Helmut Schmidt's observation in the 1970s that the European Community thrives on crises. See Paola Gosio, "Covid-19 Crisis: An Opportunity for the EU to Expand its Competences in Public Health?", *The Euroculturer: European Culture, Politics and Society in Focus* (25 February 2021), https://euroculturer.eu/2021/02/25/covid-19-crisis-an-opportunity-for-the-eu-to-expand-its-competences-in-public-health/ (accessed 5 November 2021).
6. See Jennifer Welsh, *The Return of History: Conflict, Migration and Geopolitics in the Twenty-First Century* (Toronto, 2016).
7. European Commission, *Standard Eurobarometer 94: Public Opinion in the European Union* (2021), p. 88.
8. European Commission, *Standard Eurobarometer 94: Public Opinion in the European Union* (2021), p. 88.
9. Jason A. Scorza, "Civic Friendship", *The International Encyclopaedia of Ethics* (2013).
10. Michael J. Sandel, *Justice: What's the Right Thing to Do?* (London, 2010), p. 263.
11. Sibyl A. Schwarzenbach, "On Civic Friendship", *Ethics* 107 (1996), p. 97.
12. Note that standard models of rational choice theory would typically portray this setting as a conflict of interests between prospective net beneficiaries and net funders in which citizens would support whatever option maximises their individual utility. Against this view, I claim that citizens also take into account motives other than self-interest when deciding which policy option they wish to support. For a study that discusses the role of altruism in voting behaviour, see James H. Fowler, "Altruism and Turnout", *The Journal of Politics* 68 (2006), pp. 674–683.
13. As has been argued, the launch of the comprehensive welfare programme in the United Kingdom following the Beveridge Report was only possible due to the spirit of mutual recognition and concern that participation in World War II generated among British citizens. Before the war, such a programme would likely have been politically unfeasible. For a detailed discussion of the context and development of the Beveridge Report, see Jose Harris, *William Beveridge: A Biography* (Oxford, 1997).

14 Daniel Brudney, "Two Types of Civic Friendship", *Ethical Theory and Moral Practice* 16 (2013), p. 730.
15 Contemporary discussions of civic friendship have typically taken Aristotle's seminal account as a starting point, seeking either to revive, modernise or emulate it. For Aristotle's original account, see Aristotle, *The Nicomachean Ethics*, ed. Lesley Brown (Oxford, 2009). For a contemporary theory of civic friendship drawing heavily on Aristotle's, see Sibyl A. Schwarzenbach, *On Civic Friendship: Including Women in the State* (New York, 2009). For the view that any contemporary conception of civic friendship should break with Aristotle's account to avoid licensing "illiberal interventions in the lives of citizens in service of some idea of moral improvement", see R.K. Bentley, "Civic Friendship and Thin Citizenship", *Res Publica* 19 (2013), pp. 5–19.
16 Mihaela Georgieva, "The Forgotten Ideal of Friendship in Modern Political Theory", *Res Publica* 19 (2013), pp. 95–102.
17 Note that, in this chapter I assume that it is preferable to think of civic friendship as a matter of degree (i.e., citizens may have *stronger* or *weaker* bonds of civic friendship), rather than in "either-or" terms (i.e., citizens either have or do not have at all bonds of civic friendship). This is consistent with empirical evidence that certain polities have a more vibrant civic life than others. For an influential discussion, see Robert D. Putnam, *Making Democracy Work: Civic Traditions in Modern Italy* (Princeton, 1994).
18 See, for instance, Martha C. Nussbaum, *The Cosmopolitan Tradition: A Noble but Flawed Ideal* (Cambridge MA, 2019) and Michael Sandel, "The Energy of the Brexiteers and Trump Is Born of the Failure of the Elites", *New Statesman* (13 June 2016), www.newstatesman.com/politics/2016/06/michael-sandel-the-energy-of-the-brexiteers-and-trump-is-born-of-the-failure-of-elites (accessed 3 March 2022).
19 Kerry Hoods, "Civic and Cosmopolitan Friendship", *Res Publica* (2013), p. 81. While cosmopolitan ideals have forcefully challenged the statist conception of civic friendship, many of the existing cosmopolitan accounts leave the critical question of *how* transnational bonds of civic friendship could be created largely unaddressed. A remarkable exception is Hauke Brunkhorst, *Solidarity: From Civic Friendship to a Global Legal Community* (Cambridge MA, 2005).
20 For example, Antje Wiener has argued that EU citizenship is a status under construction, in line with the "historical variability of context and contents of citizenship". However, as William Maas has rightly pointed out, the view that citizenship is "a unitary and homogeneous legal status granted to an individual by a sovereign state" remains dominant. See Antje Wiener, "Assessing the Constructive Potential of Union Citizenship: A Socio-Historical Perspective", *European Integration Online Papers* 1 (1997) and Willem Maas, "Varieties of Multilevel Citizenship", in William Maas (ed.), *Multilevel Citizenship* (Philadelphia, 2013).
21 David Miller, "Republicanism, National Identity and Europe", in Cécile Laborde and John Maynor (eds), *Republicanism and Political Theory* (Malden, 2008) p. 155. Italics added.

22 For an illustrative discussion focused on the French case, see Eugene Weber, *Peasants into Frenchmen: The Modernization of Rural France 1870–1914* (Stanford, 1976).
23 As I will claim below, socioeconomic inequality may jeopardise democratic life because it usually translates into power inequality.
24 See Michael Sandel, *The Tyranny of Merit: What's Become of the Common Good?* (New York, 2020).
25 Neil Fligstein, "Who are the Europeans and How Does this Matter for Politics", in Jeffrey T. Checkel and Peter J. Katzenstein (eds), *European Identity* (Cambridge, 2009). As I will explain bellow, a few scholars have also made a case for certain disintegrative effects of freedom of movement. However, as I will argue, these effects could be remedied through appropriate social policies.
26 Jean Tirole, *Economics for the Common Good* (Princeton, 2017), p. 282.
27 Claudia Sternberg, Kira Gartzou-Katsouyanni and Kalypso Nicolaidis, *The Greco-German Affair in the Eurocrisis: Mutual Recognition Lost?* (London, 2018).
28 It has indeed been argued that a sense of membership of a people is typically built by sharing common everyday life experiences. See Michael Billig, *Banal Nationalism* (London, 2014).
29 This raises the important question of what an appropriate test for the degree of civic friendship would be. I claim that, in the EU case, indicators of Euroscepticism are acceptable proxies to assess whether EU citizens meet a basic standard of civic friendship. By definition, citizens who do not want to be part of the EU polity clearly lack bonds of civic friendship with one other.
30 European Commission, *Communication to the Council, the European Parliament, the European Economic and Social Committee and the Committee of the Regions: The Commission's Contribution to the Period of Reflection and Beyond: Plan-D for Democracy, Dialogue and Debate* (2005).
31 See Alberto Alemanno, "EU Citizen Participation 'in the Union's Democratic Life': A Policy and Legal Analysis", in O. Costa and S. Van Hecke (eds), *The EU Political System After the 2019 European Elections* (Cham, 2023).
32 Consider, for instance, Emmanuel Macron's veto against the opening of EU accession negotiations with Albania and North Macedonia, clearly targeting the support of conservative voters in France. Macron's decision has been described as "a historic mistake" from a European perspective. See Financial Times Editorial Board, "Emmanuel Macron's EU Accession Veto Is a Historic Mistake", *Financial Times* (21 October 2019), www.ft.com/content/eda39e1e-f3eb-11e9-b018-3ef8794b17c6 (accessed 17 November 2012).
33 For an overview, see Julia C. Becker, Lea Hartwich and S. Alexander Haslam, "Neoliberalism Can Reduce Well-Being by Promoting a Sense of Social Disconnection, Competition, and Loneliness", *British Journal of Social Psychology* 60 (2021), pp. 947–965.
34 Thomas Teo, "Homo Neoliberalus: From Personality to Forms of Subjectivity", *Theory & Psychology* 28 (2018), pp. 581–599.
35 Christina Scharff, "The Psychic Life of Neoliberalism: Mapping the Contours of Entrepreneurial Subjectivity", *Theory, Culture & Society* 33 (2016), p. 109.

36 George Monbiot, "Neoliberalism – The Ideology at the Root of All Our Problems", *The Guardian* (15 April 2016), www.theguardian.com/books/2016/apr/15/neoliberalism-ideology-problem-george-monbiot (accessed 1 December 2021).

37 See F.W. Scharpf, "The European Social Model: Coping with the Challenges of Diversity", *Journal of Common Market Studies* 40 (2002), pp. 645–670.

38 The effects of business relocation are hardly covered by public programmes. While the European Globalisation Adjustment Fund for Displaced Workers and the European Social Fund aim to address this problem, they have limited resources and they face serious constraints in the types of assistance that can be provided to distressed firms and workers.

39 Richard Sennet, *The Corrosion of Character: The Personal Consequences of Work in the New Capitalism* (New York, 1998).

40 As I explained in the introduction, this book follows a practice-dependence approach – that is, it takes the EU *as it is* as its starting point with the purpose of providing practical guidance to policymakers and increasing the feasibility of its proposals. Accordingly, in this section I discuss strategies to promote *incremental change* (e.g., how to reform capitalism in the EU), as opposed to more *radical alternatives* (e.g., how to replace capitalism by a better system). Of course, an argument could also be made to promote such fundamental transformation.

41 See, for instance, Mathias Risse and Gabriel Wollner, *On Trade Justice: A Philosophical Plea for a New Global Deal* (Oxford, 2019) and Joseph E. Stiglitz, *Making Globalization Work* (London, 2006).

42 Michelle Cini and Lee McGowan, *Competition Policy in the European Union* (Basingstoke, 2009), p. 1.

43 Institute for Government, "UK–EU Future Relationship: Level Playing Field" (16 December 2020), www.instituteforgovernment.org.uk/explainers/future-relationship-level-playing-field (accessed 29 October 2021).

44 Dorothee Bohle, "Race to the Bottom? Transnational Companies and Reinforced Competition in the Enlarged European Union", in B. van Apeldoorn, J. Drahokoupil and L. Horn (eds), *Contradictions and Limits of Neoliberal European Governance* (London, 2009), p. 163.

45 One could rightly point out that a social level playing field at EU level would not be enough to protect EU citizens from the harmful impacts of fierce global competition (i.e., from non-EU states). In this regard, as I argued in Chapter 2, the EU institutions should adopt a stronger stance in global markets with a view to ensuring the necessary conditions to realise EU values. For example, as I have claimed, robust provisions regarding the rights of workers should be included in the EU's trade and investment agreements with the rest of the world and should be duly enforced by a new European Agency for Fair Trade. Therefore, a combination of internal and external EU policies could at least partially contain the competitive pressure facing EU citizens.

46 It should be noted that this resentment is not only linked to EU integration, but also to globalisation more broadly. For an influential study on widespread disenchantment with globalisation, see Joseph E. Stiglitz, *Globalization and Its Discontents Revisited: Anti-Globalization in the Era of Trump* (London, 2017).

47 João Labareda, *Towards a Just Europe: A Theory of Distributive Justice for the European Union* (Manchester, 2021).
48 European Commission, *European Pillar of Social Rights Action Plan* (2021).
49 Note that a few additional measures could help contain intrastate competition by creating a more robust level playing field in the common market. Consider, for instance, the launch of minimum corporate tax rates. My focus on the EU labour code has to do with its strong impact on the labour relations between EU citizens.
50 William Davies, *The Limits of Neoliberalism: Authority, Sovereignty and the Logic of Competition* (London, 2014).
51 William Davies, "Spirits of Neoliberalism: 'Competitiveness' and 'Wellbeing' Indicators as Rival Orders of Worth", in Richard Rottenburg, Sally E. Merry, Sung-Joon Park and Johanna Mugler (eds), *The World of Indicators: The Making of Governmental Knowledge through Quantification* (Cambridge, 2015).
52 See, for instance, Thomas Piketty, *Capital in the Twenty-First Century* (Cambridge MA, 2014).
53 Cristobal Ridao-Cano and Christian Bodewig, *Growing United: Upgrading Europe's Convergence Machine* (Washington, 2018).
54 Eurostat, "GDP per Capita, Consumption per Capita and Price Level Indices" (2020) https://ec.europa.eu/eurostat/statistics-explained/index.php?title=GDP_per_capita,_consumption_per_cap ita_and_price_level_indices#Relative_volumes_of_GDP_per_capita (accessed 25 November 2021).
55 Eurostat, "GDP per Capita, Consumption per Capita and Price Level Indices". These figures are already adjusted to the different level of prices.
56 "GDP per Capita, Consumption per Capita and Price Level Indices".
57 Eurostat, "Living Conditions In Europe – Material Deprivation and Economic Strain" (2019), https://ec.europa.eu/eurostat/statistics-explained/index.php?title=Living_conditions_in_Europe_-_material_deprivation_and_economic_strain#Material_deprivation (accessed 25 November 2021).
58 Eurofund, "Inequality" (23 November 2021), www.eurofound.europa.eu/topic/inequality#:~:text=Reducing%20inequalities%20for%20EU%20citizens%20and%20promoting%20upward,income%2C%20access%20to%20welfare%2C%20health%20and%20education%20services (accessed 25 November 2021).
59 David Ricardo, *On the Principles of Political Economy and Taxation* (Indianapolis, 2004).
60 See Paul R. Krugman, Maurice Obstfeld and Marc J. Melitz, *International Economics: Theory and Policy* (Essex, 2015), pp. 83–115.
61 This result has originally been derived by the Stolper-Samuelson Theorem, which examines the impact of trade liberalisation on the prices of each factor of production. For an overview, see Alan V. Deardorff and Robert M. Stern (eds), *The Stolper-Samuelson Theorem: A Golden Jubilee* (Ann Arbor, 1994).
62 See Kate Pickett and Richard Wilkinson, *The Spirit Level: Why More Equal Societies Almost Always Do Better* (New York, 2009).
63 Plato, *Republic*, ed. Robin Waterfield (Oxford, 2008), Book VIII 551d.

64 This point is forcefully made by Michael Sandel, *The Tyranny of Merit: What's Become of the Common Good?* (London, 2021).
65 Indeed, egalitarian accounts vary significantly regarding the scope of inequalities that they consider permissible. For instance, John Rawls claims that inequalities are justified as long as they benefit the least advantaged individuals in a given society. In turn, Robert Dworkin argues that inequalities are permissible only if they are the outcome of one's choices ("option luck"), but not if they result from factors beyond one's choices ("brute luck"). Gerald Cohen, for his part, claims that inequalities are not acceptable *on principle*. These disagreements cannot be resolved here. See, respectively, John Rawls, *A Theory of Justice: Revised Edition* (Cambridge MA, 1999); Robert Dworkin, *Sovereign Virtue: The Theory and Practice of Equality* (Cambridge MA, 2002); and G.A. Cohen, *Rescuing Justice and Equality* (Cambridge MA, 2008).
66 See David Casassas and Jurgen De Wispelaere, "Republicanism and the Political Economy of Democracy", *European Journal of Social Theory* 19 (2016), pp. 283–300.
67 Joseph E. Stiglitz, *The Price of Inequality: How Today's Divided Society Endangers Our Future* (New York, 2013), pp. 149–182.
68 Marina Prentoulis, "Greece May Still Be Europe's Sick Patient, but the EU is at Death's Door", *The Guardian* (21 August 2018), www.theguardian.com/commentisfree/2018/aug/21/greece-europe-eu-austerity (accessed 27 November 2021).
69 See John Cassidy, "A Humiliating Deal for Greece", *The New Yorker* (13 July 2015), www.newyorker.com/news/john-cassidy/a-humiliating-deal-for-greece (accessed 29 November 2021); and Alex Politaki, "Greece is Facing a Humanitarian Crisis", *The Guardian* (11 February 2013), www.theguardian.com/commentisfree/2013/feb/11/greece-humanitarian-crisis-eu (accessed 29 November 2021).
70 For a detailed description of the discussions between EU leaders regarding one of the Greek bailouts, see Yanis Varoufakis, *Adults in the Room: My Battle with Europe's Deep Establishment* (London, 2017).
71 Cassidy, "A Humiliating Deal for Greece".
72 Note that EU structural funds were conceived to last for a limited period (i.e., until the member state achieved a certain GDP per capita level) and to cover limited categories of public expenditure (i.e., notably the development of infrastructure). This makes them unfit do deal with the current challenges facing many EU member states. For instance, structural funds can be used to fund the modernisation of the building of a given school, but not pay the salaries of teachers in the field of digital skills. For the classical statement of the concept of "creative destruction", see Joseph A. Schumpeter, *Capitalism, Socialism and Democracy* (New York, 2008).
73 See, respectively, Philippe Van Parijs and Yannick Vanderborght, *Basic Income: A Radical Proposal for a Free Society and a Sane Economy* (Cambridge MA, 2017); Frank Vandenbroucke, Anton Hemerijck and Bruno Palier, "The EU Needs a Social Investment Pack", *OSE Opinion Paper 5* (2011); and Daniel

Gros and Thomas Mayer, "A European Monetary Fund: How and Why?", *CEPS Working Document* (2017).
74 An extended exercise in comparative public policy is beyond the scope of this book. My goal is simply to emphasise that a few promising strategies to address socioeconomic inequality in the EU are *already available*. All that is lacking is the political will to implement them.
75 Currently, most EU programmes are funded through direct contributions to the EU budget by the member states. This means that the availability of resources at the EU level depends entirely on the good will of national governments.
76 Note that European firms derive extraordinary benefits from the system of economic cooperation underpinning the common market. Specifically, they may sell freely across a single market of some 450 million consumers without the burden of border checks, tariffs or other customs duties. Additionally, they can leverage the cost advantages and economies of scale that arise in procurement across the vast pool of European suppliers.
77 This has led a few authors to speak of a "democratic deficit" in the EU. See, for instance, Andreas Follesdal and Simon Hix, "Why There is a Democratic Deficit in the EU: A Response to Majone and Moravcsik", *Journal of Common Market Studies* 44 (2006), pp. 533–562. While this concept has been contested, it captures the widespread view that the EU lacks sufficiently robust mechanisms of democratic participation. For an overview of this debate, see Christine Neuhold, "Democratic Deficit in the European Union", *Oxford Research Encyclopedia of Politics* (2020), https://oxfordre.com/politics/view/10.1093/acrefore/9780190228637.001.0001/acrefore-9780190228637-e-1141 (accessed 10 March 2023).
78 Martin Banks, "New Report Highlights Limited Success of Europe Citizens' Initiative", *The Parliament Magazine* (23 April 2018), www.theparliamentmagazine.eu/news/article/new-report-highlights-limited-of-success-of-europe-citizens-initiative#:~:text=Since%20the%20European%20Citizens'%20Initiative,only%20four%20have%20been%20successful (accessed 29 October 2021).
79 Consider, for instance, the well-documented case of citizens voting for the first time. See, for instance, John Harris and Erica Buist, *The Guardian* (27 May 2017), www.theguardian.com/politics/2017/may/27/strangely-optimistic-first-time-voters-8-june (accessed 7 March 2022).
80 For the context and the main lessons of this meeting, see Osha Gray Davidson, *The Best of Enemies: Race and Redemption in the New South* (Chapel Hill, 2007).
81 Mairie de Paris, "Budget Participatif", https://budgetparticipatif.paris.fr/bp/jsp/site/Portal.jsp# (accessed 16 December 2021).
82 Note that the phenomenon of apathy has the character of a vicious circle: the less citizens feel involved in public matters, the less eager they are to participate. This may explain why the turnout in general elections in many western democracies has steadily declined in recent years, despite the call for more opportunities to participate. For a discussion, see Richard Dagger, *Civic Virtues* (Oxford, 1997), pp. 132–153.

83 Hazel Blears and David Blunkett, "The Road to Empowerment", in Henry Tam (ed.), *Whose Government Is It? The Renewal of State–Citizen Cooperation* (Bristol, 2019), p. 74.
84 Indeed, several political parties in the EU which have been charged of challenging basic democratic principles such as the rule of law and equality of status have claimed to give back the voice to the people. For a mapping of these arguments, see Roger Eatwell and Matthew Goodwin, *National Populism: The Revolt Against Liberal Democracy* (London, 2020).
85 European Parliament, "European Year of Citizens: Raising Awareness of EU Citizens' Rights" (23 October 2012), www.europarl.europa.eu/news/en/pressroom/20121019IPR54022/european-year-of-citizens-raising-awareness-of-eu-citizens-rights#:~:text=The%20activities%20organised%20for%20the%20European%20Year%20of,programme%2C%20which%20enables%20young%20people%20to%20study%20abroad (accessed 17 August 2023).
86 This arguably low level of ambition is mentioned in the conference's website. See Conference on the Future of Europe, https://futureu.europa.eu/pages/about (accessed 16 December 2021).
87 Graham Smith, *Democratic Innovations: Designing Institutions for Citizen Participation* (Cambridge, 2009), p. 1.
88 Blears and Blunkett, "The Road to Empowerment", p. 74.
89 Steven Blockmans and Sophia Russack (eds), *Direct Democracy in the EU: The Myth of a Citizens' Union* (London, 2018).
90 The point that European nation-states have been dominated by fear of the "Other" and of the loss of a national identity is forcefully made by Dominique Moïsi, *The Geopolitics of Emotion: How Cultures of Fear, Humiliation, and Hope are Reshaping the World* (New York, 2009).
91 Note that misrepresentation of one another may hinder EU citizens from developing bonds of civic friendship, or from adopting measures that could facilitate its emergence. To illustrate the point, consider the distrust between many northern and southern Europeans throughout the sovereign debt crisis. Jeroen Dijsselbloem, then president of the Eurogroup, made this point clear when he stated that financially distressed member states should not expect to be assisted after having spent all their money "on drinks and women". See Mehreen Khan and Paul McClean, "Dijsselbloem Under Fire after Saying Eurozone Countries Wasted Money on 'Alcohol and Women'", *Financial Times* (21 March 2017), www.ft.com/content/2498740e-b911-3dbf-942d-ecce511a351e (accessed 31 January 2022).
92 Fligstein, "Who are the Europeans and How Does this Matter for Politics", p. 145.
93 Ettore Recchi and Adrian Favell (eds), *Pioneers of European Integration: Citizenship and Mobility in the EU* (Cheltenham, 2009).
94 In this section, I focus on two large categories of free movers: (i) workers (broadly understood as to include job seekers) and (ii) students. For simplicity, I leave aside other important but less specified categories, such as pensioners and tourists. Indeed, the data for pensioners residing in other member states that that of their citizenship is currently limited. In turn, the extent to

which tourism can meaningfully impact European integration is a matter of dispute. As Adrian Favell puts it, "if mobility consists primarily of holidaying with co-nationals in the Costa del Sol, or going on the rampage as a hooligan at a European football championship, European identity will not be the result". For the quote, see Adrian Favell, "Immigration, Migration, and Free Movement", in Jeffrey T. Checkel and Peter J. Katzenstein (eds), *European Identity* (Cambridge, 2009), p. 181. For a typology of free movers in the EU, see Mikkel Barslund and Matthias Busse, "Labour Mobility in the EU: Addressing Challenges and Ensuring Fair Mobility", *CEPS Special Report* 139 (2016).

95 Eurostat, "EU Citizens Living in Another Member State", https://ec.europa.eu/eurostat/statistics-explained/index.php?title=EU_citizens_living_in_another_Member_State_-_statistical_overview#Key_messages (accessed 25 January 2022).

96 See OECD, "The Decline in Labour Mobility in the United States: Insights from New Administrative Data", *Economics Department Working Papers* 1644 (2020).

97 Mabel Sánchez Barrioluengo and Sara Flisi, *JRC Science for Policy Report: Student Mobility in Tertiary Education: Institutional Factors and Regional Attractiveness* (Luxembourg, 2017), p. 18.

98 In 2020, nearly 40% of the citizens between 25 and 34 years old in the EU had completed tertiary education (i.e., they possess a bachelor, a master and/or PhD degree). It should be noted that this share varies considerably across member states. See Eurostat, "Educational attainment Statistics", https://ec.europa.eu/eurostat/statistics-explained/index.php?title=Educational_attainment_statistics (accessed 26 January 2021).

99 For the quote, see Kristine Mitchell, "Student Mobility and European Identity: Erasmus Study as a Civic Experience", *Journal of Contemporary European Research* 8 (2012), pp. 491–518. For the figure on Erasmus students, see Mabel Sánchez Barrioluengo and Sara Flisi, *JRC Science for Policy Report*, p. 19.

100 Adrian Favell, "Immigration, Migration, and Free Movement", in Jeffrey T. Checkel and Peter J. Katzenstein (eds), *European Identity* (Cambridge, 2009), p. 181.

101 European Union Fundamental Rights Agency, *Making EU Citizens' Rights a Reality: National Courts Enforcing Freedom of Movement and Related Rights* (Luxembourg, 2018).

102 European Union Fundamental Rights Agency, *Making EU Citizens' Rights a Reality*, p. 49.

103 European Union Fundamental Rights Agency, *Making EU Citizens' Rights a Reality*, p. 49.

104 European Union Fundamental Rights Agency, *Making EU Citizens' Rights a Reality*, p. 49.

105 For instance, in the academic year 2020–2021 a Portuguese student undertaking Erasmus in Sweden, Luxembourg or Ireland received a monthly grant of €390, while the monthly grant for Germany, Austria or France was €340. See Caixa Geral de Depósitos, "Quanto Custa Fazer Erasmus? Faça Face às Despesas", www.cgd.pt/Site/Saldo-Positivo/formacao-e-tecnologia/Pages/quanto-custa-fazer-erasmus.aspx (accessed 28 January 2022).

106 These are Spain, Italy, Croatia and Romania. See European Commission, "Erasmus Master Degree Loans", https://erasmus-plus.ec.europa.eu/opportunities/individuals/students/erasmus-master-degree-loans (accessed 28 January 2022).
107 See, for instance, Stephen Holmes and Ivan Krastev, *The Light That Failed: Why the West Is Losing the Fight for Democracy* (London, 2020).
108 European Commission, *Flash Eurobarometer 528: Citizenship and Democracy* (2023), p. 19.
109 Jacques Delors, quoted by The Economist, "Why Europe's Single Market Is at Risk" (14 September 2019).
110 See Ronald Inglehart, "Cognitive Mobilization and European Identity", *Comparative Politics* 3 (1970), pp. 45–70.
111 Ettore Recchi (ed.), *The Europeanisation of Everyday Life: Cross-Border Practices and Transnational Identifications among EU and Third-Country Citizens: Final Report* (2014). Available at www.ssoar.info/ssoar/handle/document/39526.
112 Saara Koikkalainen, "Free Movement and EU Citizenship from the Perspective of Intra-European Mobility", in Rainer Bauböck (ed.), *Debating European Citizenship* (Cham, 2018), p. 124.
113 Koikkalainen, "Free Movement and EU Citizenship from the Perspective of Intra-European Mobility", p. 124.
114 European Commission, *Standard Eurobarometer 94: Public Opinion in the European Union* (2021), p. 91.
115 European Parliament, "Teaching about the EU: 44% of Europeans Don't Understand How the EU Works", 11 April 2016, www.europarl.europa.eu/news/en/headlines/society/20160408STO22170/teaching-about-the-eu-44-of-europeans-don-t-understand-how-the-eu-works (accessed 14 February 2022).
116 Avril Keating, *Education for Citizenship in Europe: European Policies, National Adaptations and Young People's Attitudes* (London, 2014), p. 93.
117 As early as in 1926, Jonathan French Scott analysed how the portrayal of England, France, Germany and the United States in one another's textbooks shaped the prospects of nationalism or world peace. See Jonathan French Scott, *The Menace of Nationalism in Education* (New York, 2012).
118 Keating, *Education for Citizenship in Europe*, p. 93.
119 See, for instance, Rachel D. Hutchins, *Nationalism and History Education: Curricula and Textbooks in the United States and France* (London, 2016). On the meaning of a transnational or global approach to history, see Sebastien Conrad, *What is Global History?* (Princeton, 2017).
120 Keating, *Education for Citizenship in Europe*, p. 93.
121 In this regard, it is telling that ancient military victories against neighbouring member states continue to be celebrated in many schools. For an influential discussion of the notions of "friend" and "enemy" in the context of international relations, see Carl Schmidt, *The Concept of the Political* (Chicago, 2007).
122 A study by the Council of Europe has identified 20 competences that are required to create a "culture of democracy" in polities which feature a high level of diversity. These competences can be developed at school through

appropriate curricula. See Council of Europe, *Competences for Democratic Culture: Living Together as Equals in Culturally Diverse Democratic Societies* (Strasbourg, 2016).

123 Indeed, it has been demonstrated that citizenship education in an "open classroom climate" (i.e., where "students are provided with opportunities to wrestle with political and social issues") has a positive impact on the level of political engagement of young citizens. This effect could be replicated at the EU level. See David E. Campbell, "Voice in the Classroom: How an Open Classroom Climate Fosters Political Engagement among Adolescents", *Political Behaviour* 30 (2008), pp. 437–454.

124 A similar initiative – the so-called "Model UN" – has been successfully conducted by the United Nations. See United Nations, "Model United Nations", www.un.org/en/mun (accessed 10 February 2022).

125 According to article 6 of the TFEU, in the field of education, the European Commission's competences are limited to supporting, coordinating and supplementing the actions of the member states.

126 National administrations have indeed evinced a concerted lack of appetite for delegating competences in the field of education. While this may change in the future, it suggests that successful proposals will need to be built in a decentralised manner.

127 This panel would discuss different possible formats for the course, alternative content to be covered and desirable pedagogical approaches. Therefore, it would address questions such as the following: Should the course be taught at primary, elementary and/or secondary level? Should it be mandatory or elective? Should it be a separate subject, or could it be a flexible module to be plugged into other existing courses at the national level? How many hours of weekly teaching should it entail? What specific topics, problems and questions should it cover? What supporting materials would be required? What knowledge, skills and competences should a student have developed by the end of the course?

128 For instance, the curricula of a few member states cover citizenship education as a cross-curricular theme or integrated into other compulsory subjects/learning areas. See European Commission, *Citizenship and Education at School in Europe 2017: Eurydice Report* (Luxembourg, 2017).

129 Laura Johnson and Paul Morris, "Towards a Framework for Critical Citizenship Education", *The Curriculum Journal* 21 (2010), pp. 77–96.

130 The concept of just and unjust wars has been a subject of much debate in the specialised literature. For simplicity, I assume that, in the absence of any compelling self-defence or humanitarian grounds, invading a sovereign state would be unjust. For an influential discussion, see Michael Walzer, *Just and Unjust Wars: A Moral Argument with Historical Illustrations* (New York, 2015).

131 Authors affiliated with the school of pacifism might object that responding to violence by employing violent means would be morally impermissible. However, it may be argued that a swift and coordinated response to an aggression against a member state would be the best means to promote peace in Europe. In fact,

the current territorial configuration and institutional apparatus of the EU and its member states have been able to secure an unprecedentedly long period of peace after centuries of bloodshed. This suggests that defending the current international order is instrumental to achieving a lasting peace. For an overview of the pacifist argument, see Robert Holmes, *Pacifism: A Philosophy of Nonviolence* (London, 2017).
132 The degree to which the bonds of mutual defence have been institutionalised varies across countries. For instance, a few constitutions include provisions regarding the duty to perform military service.
133 See John Hutchinson, *War and Nationalism* (Oxford, 2017).
134 European External Action Service, "A Stronger EU on Security and Defence" (19 November 2018), https://eeas.europa.eu/headquarters/headquarters-home page_en/35285/A%20stronger%20EU%20on%20security%20and%20 defence (accessed 18 February 2022).
135 See Emanuel Adler and Michael Barnett (eds), *Security Communities* (Cambridge, 1998).
136 As an illustrative example, consider the Anglo-Portuguese alliance created by the Treaty of Windsor which has been in force since 1386. This alliance has been used to call for assistance a number of times ever since and it has never been revoked.
137 A study comprising data from 1816 to 2000 has concluded that deterrent alliances contingent upon the adversary's attack decrease the likelihood that a third party will initiate a conflict with an alliance member. See Brett V. Benson, "Unpacking Alliances: Deterrent and Compellent Alliances and Their Relationship with Conflict, 1816–2000", *The Journal of Politics* 73 (2011), pp. 1111–1127.
138 Antonina Bakardjieva Engelbrekt, Anna Michalski, Niklas Nilsson and Lars Oxelheim (eds), *The European Union: Facing the Challenge of Multiple Security Threats* (Cheltenham, 2018).
139 Reuters, "Russian Military in Belarus Threatens Baltics and Poland, Says Lithuanian President" (17 January 2022), www.reuters.com/world/europe/russ ian-military-belarus-threatens-baltics-poland-says-lithuanian-president-2022- 02-17/ (accessed 18 February 2022).
140 European Parliament, "Terrorism in the EU: Terror Attacks, Deaths and Arrests in 2019" (21 September 2021), www.europarl.europa.eu/news/en/headlines/ security/20180703STO07125/terrorism-in-the-eu-terror-attacks-deaths-and- arrests-in-2019 (accessed 18 February 2022).
141 Raluca Csernatoni, "EU Security and Defence Challenges: Toward a European Defence Winter?", *Carnegie Europe* (11 June 2020), https://carnegieeurope.eu/ 2020/06/11/eu-security-and-defense-challenges-toward-european-defense-win ter-pub-82032 (accessed 18 February 2022).
142 These are: Austria, Cyprus, Ireland, Malta and Sweden. However, in July 2022, Sweden's application for accession to the alliance was approved and was quickly ratified by most NATO members. At the time of writing, Sweden's accession is scheduled for final ratification in autumn 2023.

143 In the event of a conflict between Turkey and Cyprus, there could be different readings within the EU of what the legal and political obligations of the member states would be. While some member states might be prompt to assist their fellow member state, others might prioritise their commitment to the NATO framework.
144 *Treaty on European Union*, article 42 (7).
145 An illustrative example is the recent accession to NATO by Finland, which had historically positioned itself as a neutral state. This major policy shift was linked to the invasion of Ukraine by Russia.
146 European Commission, *The European Defence Fund: Stepping up the EU's Role as a Security and Defence Provider*, https://ec.europa.eu/docsroom/documents/34509 (accessed 22 February 2022).
147 European Commission, *The European Defence Fund*.
148 European Commission, *The European Defence Fund*.
149 For the complete list of 20 commitments, see PESCO, "Binding Commitments", https://pesco.europa.eu/binding-commitments/ (accessed 25 February 2022).
150 European Parliamentary Research Service, *Implementation and Governance of Permanent Structured Cooperation* (2020), www.europarl.europa.eu/RegData/etudes/ATAG/2020/659280/EPRS_ATA(2020)659280EN.pdf (accessed 25 February 2022).
151 Netherlands Institute of International Relations, "PESCO Implementation: The Next Challenge", *Policy Report* (2018), p. 11.
152 For the defence data on EU member states, see European Defence Agency, "Defence Data", https://eda.europa.eu/publications-and-data/defence-data (accessed 25 February 2022). For the data on other global players, see Stockholm International Peace Research Institute, *Trends in the World Military Expenditure 2020*, https://sipri.org/sites/default/files/2021-04/fs_2104_milex_0.pdf (accessed 25 February 2022).
153 Schuman, *The Schuman Declaration* (9 May 1950).

Conclusion

To conclude this discussion, it is worth returning to the three research questions I raised in the introduction. These were: (i) On what grounds, if any, can EU values be regarded as a meaningful and common moral standpoint amongst the member states? (ii) What type of institutional framework could best realise the common good in the EU? and (iii) What conditions can foster, or jeopardise, the development of stronger civic bonds amongst EU citizens? Let me briefly summarise the answers that I have provided.

I have claimed that public values – understood as those endorsed by a given polity through its fundamental legal sources, notably constitutions and international treaties – provide guidelines regarding what fundamental conditions and goals a society considers desirable. Contrary to personal or cultural values, public values are not connected to one's worldview, ethical convictions or religious beliefs. By bridging the substantial moral differences amongst citizens, public values create a common viewpoint in which collective choices can be publicly labelled as "good" or "bad" – that is, the standpoint of the common good. I have further argued that when a group of states explicitly endorses common public values through international treaties, it is possible to derive a transnational conception of the common good.

This possibility, I have suggested, applies in the case of the EU member states. I have claimed that the values outlined in the EU treaties allow for the mapping of conditions and goals that member states jointly consider desirable, thus translating a shared understanding of the common good. These notably include maintaining liberal democracy, enabling decent standards of social welfare and ensuring a high level of environmental protection. Against what I have dubbed the cultural approach to European values, I have claimed that EU values are not European by definition. Indeed, they have been endorsed by a few non-European like-minded states. Furthermore, EU values are not set in stone. Indeed, they are subject to a gradual interpretation through EU policymaking processes, judicial decisions and public debates and may change more dramatically by means of reforming the EU treaties.

EU values, I have argued, are not just a moral point of reference. They should be promptly put into practice by the EU institutions, which have a duty to seek their enforcement by the member states and to promote an international order that enables their fulfilment. I have claimed that, in its capacity as guardian of EU values, the EU should develop robust safeguards against internal breaches of EU values, notably by better enforcing the provision of the Treaty on European Union regarding the suspension of the voting rights of non-compliant member states, as well as by creating a procedure through which chronically non-compliant member states could be ejected from the Union. At the same time, acting as an enabler of the European Model, the EU should create a set of bodies that would allow its values to be realised in a globalised world where non-state actors are increasingly powerful. I have presented three examples of such institutions: (i) a European Transnational Tax Authority, (ii) a European Credit Rating Agency and (iii) a European Agency for Fair Trade.

To be effective, this institutional framework to pursue EU values would need to be complemented by a few reforms of the EU decision-making process. This need for reform is linked to the fact that the national interests within the EU are highly diverse and must be reconciled for the common good to be realised. To achieve this goal, the member states and the EU should pursue at least two complementary strategies. First, EU actors should play a more active role in the processes of national interest formation at the domestic level. I have suggested that an effective avenue to achieve this goal would be upgrading the role of the Representations of the European Commission in the EU capitals, which would bring issues related to the common good of the EU to the attention of national authorities and citizens. Second, the voice and firepower of EU institutions should be strengthened, notably by becoming more representative of the EU demos as a whole (as opposed to national demoi) and by being granted appropriate resources to realise the common good.

Accordingly, I have put forward a few proposals that could help the EU move beyond tricky political deadlocks and act as a credible broker between the member states. More specifically, I have argued that the unanimity rule in the Council of the European Union is normatively undesirable and should be abolished. Furthermore, I have claimed that the impartiality of the European Commission could be enhanced by clearly separating its legislative and supervisory responsibilities. I have also suggested that the presidents of the Commission and the European Council should be directly elected. I have sustained the creation of a pan-European constituency for the European Parliament and the strengthening of the links between the national and European parliaments. Finally, I have proposed the launch of an EU Citizens' Assembly and an advisory board composed of former presidents of EU institutions. Altogether, these institutional reforms could gear EU policymaking towards the pursuit of the common good.

Yet, I have argued that these reforms and the sacrifices that they may bring about will likely only be feasible if EU citizens develop stronger bonds of civic friendship among each other. I have claimed that this goal could be achieved if adequate public policies were to be adopted by the EU institutions and national governments. I have presented the following proposals: (i) creating a thicker social level playing field in the EU, namely by means of launching an EU labour code; (ii) reducing socioeconomic inequalities in the EU; (iii) improving the opportunities for political participation by EU citizens; (iv) reducing the barriers against freedom of movement, notably by curtailing administrative, legal and economic burdens currently facing free movers; (v) launching a transnational curriculum on EU citizenship education; and (vi) increasing defence cooperation, notably by upgrading the EU mutual defence clause and scaling up the PESCO programme and the EDF.

Despite the tone of disagreement and polarisation that often characterises the public debates on EU affairs, this book has demonstrated that EU member states share a thick understanding of the fundamental conditions and goals that they consider desirable. What seems to be currently missing is not so much a basic moral consensus but the appropriate institutional setting and sufficiently strong transnational civic bonds to bring these conditions and goals forward. In this regard, while admittedly ambitious, the package of proposals presented above would constitute a significant step towards acting and thinking for the common good.

Bibliography

Books and articles

Ackerman, Bruce, *We the People, Volume 2: Transformations* (Cambridge MA, 2000).
Adler, Emanuel and Michael Barnett (eds), *Security Communities* (Cambridge, 1998).
Akaliyski, Plamen, Christian Welzel and Josef Hien, "A Community of Shared Values? Dimensions and Dynamics of Cultural Integration in the European Union", *Journal of European Integration* 44 (2022), pp. 569–590.
Alba, Pedro, Patricia Bliss-Guest and Laura Tuck, "Reforming the World Bank to Play a Critical Role in Addressing Climate Change", *Center for Global Development Policy Paper* 288 (2023).
Alemano, Alberto, "EU Citizen Participation 'in the Union's Democratic Life': A Policy and Legal Analysis", in O. Costa and S. Van Hecke (eds), *The EU Political System After the 2019 European Elections* (Cham, 2023).
Alemano, Alberto, "Europe's Democracy Challenge: Citizen Participation in and Beyond Elections", *German Law Journal* 21 (2020), pp. 35–40.
Alter, Karen J., "Who are the 'Masters of the Treaty'? European Governments and the European Court of Justice", *International Organization* 52 (1998), pp. 121–147.
Anderson, Benedict, *Imagined Communities: Reflections on the Origin and Spread of Nationalism* (London, 2016).
Appiah, Kwame Anthony, *The Honor Code: How Moral Revolutions Happen* (New York, 2010).
Aquinas, *Political Writings*, ed. R. W. Dyson (Cambridge, 2002).
Archibugi, Daniele, *The Global Commonwealth of Citizens: Toward Cosmopolitan Democracy* (Princeton, 2008).
Aristotle, *The Nicomachean Ethics*, ed. Lesley Brown (Oxford, 2009).
Aristotle, *The Politics*, ed. R. F. Stalley (Oxford, 2009).
Ástvaldsson, Jóhann Páll, "Mackerel War on the Cards as Iceland Increases Quota?", *Iceland Review* (20 August 2019), www.icelandreview.com/news/mackerel-war-on-the-cards-as-iceland-increases-quota/ (accessed 7 March 2021).
Axelrod, Robert, *The Evolution of Cooperation* (New York, 1984).
Bachrach, Peter and Morton S. Baratz, "Two Faces of Power", *American Political Science Review* 56 (1962), pp. 947–952.
Banks, Martin, "New Report Highlights Limited Success of Europe Citizens' Initiative", *The Parliament Magazine* (23 April 2018), www.theparliamentmagazine.eu/news/article/new-report-highlights-limited-of-success-of-europe-citizens-initiative#:~:text=Since%20the%20European%20Citizens'%20Initiative,only%20four%20have%20been%20successful (accessed 29 October 2021).

Barak, Aharon, *Proportionality: Constitutional Rights and their Limitations* (Cambridge, 2012).
Barrioluengo, Mabel Sánchez and Sara Flisi, *JRC Science for Policy Report: Student Mobility in Tertiary Education: Institutional Factors and Regional Attractiveness* (Luxembourg, 2017).
Barroso, José Manuel, *State of the Union Speech* (2013). ec.europa.eu/commission/presscorner/detail/en/SPEECH_13_684 (accessed 18 June 2024).
Barslund, Mikkel and Matthias Busse, "Labour Mobility in the EU: Addressing Challenges and Ensuring Fair Mobility", *CEPS Special Report* 139 (2016).
Bauböck, Rainer, "Why European Citizenship? Normative Approaches to Supranational Union", *Theoretical Inquiries in Law* 8 (2007), pp. 453–488.
Bayer, Lili, "Brussels Drops Lockdown Exit Plan after Anger from Capitals", *Politico* (8 April 2020), www.politico.eu/article/commission-to-unveil-exit-strategy-as-countries-push-to-lift-coronameasures/ (accessed 28 August 2020).
BBC, "Europe and Right-Wing Nationalism: A Country-by-Country Guide" (13 November 2019), www.bbc.com/news/world-europe-36130006 (accessed 26 April 2022).
Becker, Julia C., Lea Hartwich and S. Alexander Haslam, "Neoliberalism Can Reduce Well-Being by Promoting a Sense of Social Disconnection, Competition, and Loneliness", *British Journal of Social Psychology* 60 (2021), pp. 947–965.
Beitz, Charles and Robert E. Goodin (eds), *Global Basic Rights* (Oxford, 2011).
Bell, Daniel, *Communitarianism and its Critics* (Oxford, 1993).
Bell, Daniel, "Communitarianism", *The Stanford Encyclopedia of Philosophy* (Fall 2022 Edition), Edward N. Zalta and Uri Nodelman (eds), https://plato.stanford.edu/archives/fall2022/entries/communitarianism/ (accessed 27 July 2023).
Bellah, Robert N., Richard Madsen, William M. Sullivan, Ann Swidler and Steven M. Tipton, *Habits of the Heart: Individualism and Commitment in American Life* (Berkeley, 1985).
Bellamy, Richard and Dario Castiglione, "Between Cosmopolis and Community: Three Models of Rights and Democracy within the European Union", in Daniele Archibugi, David Held and Martin Köhler (eds), *Re-imagining Political Community: Studies in Cosmopolitan Democracy* (Stanford, 1998).
Bellamy, Richard, *A Republican Europe of States: Cosmopolitanism, Intergovernmentalism, and Democracy in the EU* (Cambridge, 2019).
Benhabib, Seyla, *The Rights of Others: Aliens, Residents and Citizens* (Cambridge, 2004).
Benhabib, Seyla, *Another Cosmopolitanism* (Oxford, 2006).
Benson, Brett V., "Unpacking Alliances: Deterrent and Compellent Alliances and Their Relationship with Conflict, 1816–2000", *The Journal of Politics* 73 (2011), pp. 1111–1127.
Bentley, R.K., "Civic Friendship and Thin Citizenship", *Res Publica* 19 (2013), pp. 5–19.
Berger, Stefan, "Remembering the Second World War in Western Europe, 1945–2005", in M. Pakier and B. Stråth (eds), *A European Memory: Contested Histories and Politics of Remembrance* (2010).
Berstein, Serge, *The Republic of de Gaulle 1958–1969* (Cambridge, 2006).
Besselink, Leonard, "The Bite, the Bark and the Howl: Article 7 TEU and the Rule of Law Initiatives", in András Jakab and Dimitry Kochenov (eds), *The Enforcement of EU Law and Values: Ensuring Member States' Compliance* (Oxford, 2017).
Bieber, Florian, "Is Nationalism on the Rise? Assessing Global Trends", *Ethnopolitics* 17 (2018), pp. 519–540.

Billig, Michael, *Banal Nationalism* (London, 2014).

Birnbaum, Michael and Craig Timberg, "EU: Russians Interfered in Our Elections, Too", *The Washington Post* (14 June 2019), www.washingtonpost.com/technology/2019/06/14/eu-russians-interfered-our-elections-too/ (accessed 6 April 2022).

Blears, Hazel and David Blunkett, "The Road to Empowerment", in Henry Tam (ed.), *Whose Government Is It? The Renewal of State–Citizen Cooperation* (Bristol, 2019).

Blockmans, Steven and Sophia Russack (eds), *Direct Democracy in the* ohle, Dorothee, "Race to the Bottom? Transnational Companies and Reinforced Competition in the Enlarged European Union", in B. van Apeldoorn, J. Drahokoupil and L. Horn (eds), *Contradictions and Limits of Neoliberal European Governance* (London, 2009).

Bozeman, Barry, *Public Values and Public Interest: Counterbalancing Economic Individualism* (Washington, 2007).

Brand, Oliver, "Conceptual Comparisons: Towards a Coherent Methodology of Comparative Legal Studies", *Brooklyn Journal of International Law* 32 (2007), pp. 405–466.

Braun, Elisa, Thibault Larger and Simon Van Dorpe, "EU Big Four Press Vestager to Clear Path for Champions", *Politico* (6 February 2020), www.politico.eu/article/eu-big-four-france-germany-italy-poland-press-executive-vice-president-margrethe-vestager-to-clear-path-for-champions/ (accessed 19 March 2023).

Brudney, Daniel, "Two Types of Civic Friendship", *Ethical Theory and Moral Practice* 16 (2013), pp. 729–743.

Brunkhorst, Hauke, *Solidarity: From Civic Friendship to a Global Legal Community* (Cambridge MA, 2005).

Brunnermeier, Markus K., Harold James and Jean-Pierre Landau, *The Euro and the Battle of Ideas* (Princeton, 2018).

Brysk, Alison, *Global Good Samaritans: Human Rights as Foreign Policy* (Oxford, 2009).

Burall, Simon, "Deliberative Engagement with Complex Policies", in Henry Tam (ed.), *Whose Government Is It? The Renewal of State–Citizen Cooperation* (Bristol, 2019).

Bush, George W., *State of the Union Address* (2002), https://georgewbush-whitehouse.archives.gov/news/releases/2002/01/20020129-11.html (accessed 6 October 2022).

Caixa Geral de Depósitos, "Quanto Custa Fazer Erasmus? Faça Face às Despesas", www.cgd.pt/Site/Saldo-Positivo/formacao-e-tecnologia/Pages/quanto-custa-fazer-erasmus.aspx (accessed 28 January 2022).

Callahan, Kathe, "Citizen Participation: Models and Methods", *International Journal of Public Administration* 30 (2007), pp. 1179–1196.

Campbell, David E., "Voice in the Classroom: How an Open Classroom Climate Fosters Political Engagement among Adolescents", *Political Behaviour* 30 (2008), pp. 437–454.

Canovan, Margaret, *The People* (Cambridge, 2005).

Casassas, David and Jurgen De Wispelaere, "Republicanism and the Political Economy of Democracy", *European Journal of Social Theory* 19 (2016), pp. 283–300.

Cassidy, John, "A Humiliating Deal for Greece", *The New Yorker* (13 July 2015), www.newyorker.com/news/john-cassidy/a-humiliating-deal-for-greece (accessed 29 November 2021).

Castiglione, Dario, "Political Identity in a Community of Strangers", in Jeffrey T. Checkel and Peter J. Katzenstein (eds), *European Identity* (Cambridge, 2009).
Chakrabarty, Dipesh, *Provincializing Europe: Postcolonial Thought and Historical Difference* (Princeton, 2008).
Chandler, Daniel and Rod Munday (eds), "Impartiality", *A Dictionary of Media and Communication* (Oxford, 2011).
Cheneval, F. and F. Schimmelfennig, "The Case for Demoicracy in the European Union", *Journal of Common Market Studies* 51 (2013), pp. 334–350.
Chomsky, Noam and Edward S. Herman, *Manufacturing Consent: The Political Economy of the Mass Media* (London, 1994).
Chung, Joseph H., "Human Rights Violations by Multinational Corporations: Corruption, Lawlessness and the 'Global Value Chain'", *Centre for Research on Globalisation*, www.globalresearch.ca/human-rights-violation-multinational-corporations-global-value-chain-corruption-lawlessness/5779160 (accessed 26 July 2023).
Cini, Michelle and Lee McGowan, *Competition Policy in the European Union* (Basingstoke, 2009).
Clinton Foundation, "Clinton Global Initiative", www.clintonfoundation.org/progrıams/leadership-public-service/clinton-global-initiative#meetings/ (accessed 8 March 2023).
Closa, Carlos and Dimitri Kochenov (eds), *Reinforcing Rule of Law Oversight in the European Union* (Cambridge, 2016).
Closa, Carlos, Dimitry Kochenov and J.H.H. Weiler, "Reinforcing Rule of Law Oversight in the European Union", *RSCAS Working Papers* (2014).
Cohen, G.A., *Rescuing Justice and Equality* (Cambridge MA, 2008).
Cohen, Joshua, "An Epistemic Conception of Democracy", *Ethics* 97 (1986), pp. 26–38.
Cohen, Joshua, "Is there a Human Right to Democracy?", in Christine Sypnowich (ed.), *The Egalitarian Conscience: Essays in Honour of G. A. Cohen* (Oxford, 2006).
Conrad, Maximilian, Guðmundur Hálfdanarson, Asimina Michailidou, Charlotte Galpin and Niko Pyrhönen (eds), *Europe in the Age of Post-Truth Politics: Populism, Disinformation, and the Public Sphere* (Cham, 2023).
Conrad, Sebastien, *What is Global History?* (Princeton, 2017).
Corbett, Jessica, "'Not Enough!' Climate Activists Disappointed with New EU Emissions Deal on Eve of Biden Summit", *Common Dreams* (21 April 2021), www.commondreams.org/news/2021/04/21/not-enough-climate-activists-disappointed-new-eu-emissions-deal-eve-biden-summit (accessed 14 June 2022).
Corbett, J., D. Christian Grube, H. Caroline Lovell and R. James Scott, *Institutional Memory as Storytelling: How Networked Government Remembers* (Cambridge, 2020).
Corbett, Richard, "The Evolving Roles of the European Parliament and of National Parliaments", in Andrea Biondi, Piet Eeckhout and Stefanie Ripley (eds), *EU Law after Lisbon* (Oxford, 2012).
Council of Europe, *Competences for Democratic Culture: Living Together as Equals in Culturally Diverse Democratic Societies* (Strasbourg, 2016).
Council of the European Union, "Commission's Communication on a New EU Framework to Strengthen the Rule of Law: Compatibility with the Treaties", *Opinion of the Legal Service* 10296/14 (2014), nr. 28.

Council of the European Union, "Qualified Majority", www.consilium.europa.eu/en/council-eu/voting-system/qualified-majority/ (accessed 23 April 2021).

Council of the European Union, "The Role of the Council in International Agreements", www.consilium.europa.eu/en/council-eu/international-agreements/ (accessed 25 October 2022).

Council of the European Union, *Conference on the Future of Europe* (24 June 2020), www.consilium.europa.eu/media/44679/st09102-en20.pdf (accessed 22 September 2020).

Court of Justice of the European Union, "The Conditions Introduced by Hungary to Enable Foreign Higher Education Institutions to Carry Out their Activities in its Territory are Incompatible with EU Law", *Press Release* 125/20 (2020).

Cram, Laura, "The European Commission as a Multi-Organization: Social Policy and IT Policy in the EU", *Journal of European Public Policy* 1 (1994), pp. 195–217.

Crawford, James, "The Criteria for Statehood in International Law", *British Yearbook of International Law* 48 (1977), pp. 93–182.

Christiansen, Thomas, "Tensions of European Governance: Politicised Bureaucracy and Multiple Accountability in the European Commission", *Journal of European Public Policy* 4 (1997), pp. 73–90.

Crouch, Colin, *Post-Democracy* (Cambridge, 2004).

Csernatoni, Raluca, "EU Security and Defence Challenges: Toward a European Defence Winter?", *Carnegie Europe* (11 June 2020), https://carnegieeurope.eu/2020/06/11/eu-security-and-defense-challenges-toward-european-defense-winter-pub-82032 (accessed 18 February 2022).

Cudd, Ann and Seena Eftekhari, "Contractarianism", *The Stanford Encyclopedia of Philosophy* (Winter 2021 Edition), Edward N. Zalta (ed.), https://plato.stanford.edu/archives/win2021/entries/contractarianism/ (accessed 15 February 2024).

Dagger, Richard, *Civic Virtues* (Oxford, 1997).

Davidson, Osha Gray, *The Best of Enemies: Race and Redemption in the New South* (Chapel Hill, 2007).

Davies, William, *The Limits of Neoliberalism: Authority, Sovereignty and the Logic of Competition* (London, 2014).

Davies, William, "Spirits of Neoliberalism: 'Competitiveness' and 'Wellbeing' Indicators as Rival Orders of Worth", in Richard Rottenburg, Sally E. Merry, Sung-Joon Park and Johanna Mugler (eds), *The World of Indicators: The Making of Governmental Knowledge through Quantification* (Cambridge, 2015).

Duke, George, "The Distinctive Common Good", *The Review of Politics* 78 (2016), pp. 227–250.

De Búrca, Gráinne, "Poland and Hungary's EU Membership: On Not Confronting Authoritarian Governments", *International Journal of Constitutional Law* 20 (2022), pp. 13–34.

De Gruyter, Caroline, "European Values Are Non-Negotiable", *EUObserver* (22 July 2020), https://euobserver.com/opinion/148998 (accessed 28 October 2022).

Deardoff, Alan V. and Robert M. Stern (eds), *The Stolper-Samuelson Theorem: A Golden Jubilee* (Ann Arbor, 1994).

Deffains, Bruno, Olivier d'Ormesson and Thomas Perroud, "Competition Policy and Industrial Policy: For a Reform of European Law", *Fondation Robert Schuman Policy Papers* (2020).

Delors, Jacques, quoted by *The Economist*, "Why Europe's Single Market Is at Risk" (14 September 2019).

Deters, Henning and Gerda Falkner, "Remapping the European Agenda-Setting Landscape", *Public Administration* 99 (2021), pp. 290–303.
Deutsch, Anthony, "Dutch Refugee Council Sues State over 'Inhumane' Asylum Centres", *Reuters* (18 August 2022), www.reuters.com/world/europe/dutch-refugee-council-sues-state-over-inhumane-asylum-centres-2022-08-18/ (accessed 1 January 2023).
Dickson, Julie and Pavlos Eleftheriadis (eds), *Philosophical Foundations of European Union Law* (Oxford, 2012).
Dietsch, Peter, *Catching Capital: The Ethics of Tax Competition* (Oxford, 2015).
Dobson, Andrew, "Nudging is Anti-democratic and Anti-political", *The Guardian* (2 May 2014), www.theguardian.com/politics/2014/may/02/nudging-anti-democratic-anti-political (accessed 20 April 2023).
Downs, George W. and Michael A. Jones, "Reputation, Compliance, and International Law", *Journal of Legal Studies* 31 (2002).
Drieschova, Alena, "Post-Truth Politics in the UK's Brexit Referendum", *New Perspectives* 26 (2018), pp. 89–106.
Duff, Andrew, *Constitutional Change in the European Union: Towards a Federal Union* (Cham, 2022).
Dworkin, Robert, *Sovereign Virtue: The Theory and Practice of Equality* (Cambridge MA, 2002).
Dzehtsiarou, Kanstantsin and Donal K. Coffey, "Suspension and Expulsion of Members of the Council of Europe: Difficult Decisions in Troubled Times", *International and Comparative Law Quarterly* 68 (2019), pp. 443–476.
Eatwell, Roger and Matthew Goodwin, *National Populism: The Revolt Against Liberal Democracy* (London, 2020).
Einarsdóttir, Gréta Sigríður, "EU to Threaten Sanctions Against Iceland and Greenland Over Mackerel Dispute", *Iceland Review* (26 August 2019), www.icelandreview.com/news/eu-to-threaten-sanctions-against-iceland-and-greenland-over-mackerel/ (accessed 7 March 2021).
Engelbrekt, Antonina Bakardjieva, Anna Michalski, Niklas Nilsson and Lars Oxelheim (eds), *The European Union: Facing the Challenge of Multiple Security Threats* (Cheltenham, 2018).
Erman, Eva and Niklas Möller, "What Distinguishes the Practice-Dependent Approach to Justice?", *Philosophy & Social Criticism* 42 (2016), pp. 3–23.
Esping-Anderson, Gøsta, *The Three Worlds of Welfare Capitalism* (Cambridge, 2004).
Etzioni, Amitai, "The EU: The Communitarian Deficit", *European Societies* 15 (2013), pp. 312–330.
Etzioni, Amitai, *The Spirit of Community* (New York, 1993).
Etzioni, Amitai, *The Common Good* (Cambridge, 2007).
EUR-Lex, "Enforcement of EU Law", https://eur-lex.europa.eu/EN/legal-content/glossary/enforcement-of-eu-law.html (accessed 21 August 2023).
Eurofund, "Inequality", www.eurofound.europa.eu/topic/inequality#:~:text=Reducing%20inequalities%20for%20EU%20citizens%20and%20promoting%20upward,income%2C%20access%20to%20welfare%2C%20health%20and%20education%20services (accessed 25 November 2021).
European Commission, "6 Commission Priorities for 2019–2024", https://ec.europa.eu/info/strategy/priorities-2019-2024_en (accessed 21 September 2020).
European Commission, "Erasmus Master Degree Loans", https://erasmus-plus.ec.europa.eu/opportunities/individuals/students/erasmus-master-degree-loans (accessed 28 January 2022).

European Commission, "European Governance in the European Union", *Eurobarometer* 74 (2011).
European Commission, "Financial Transactions Tax: Making the Financial Sector Pay Its Fair Share", 28 September 2011, https://ec.europa.eu/commission/presscorner/detail/en/IP_11_1085 (accessed 3 May 2021).
European Commission, *Citizenship and Education at School in Europe 2017: Eurydice Report* (Luxembourg, 2017).
European Commission, *European Pillar of Social Rights Action Plan* (2021).
European Commission, *Flash Eurobarometer 528: Citizenship and Democracy* (2023).
European Commission, *Joint European Roadmap towards Lifting COVID-19 Containment Measures* (2020).
European Commission, *Standard Eurobarometer 94: Public Opinion in the European Union* (2021).
European Commission, *The European Defence Fund: Stepping up the EU's Role as a Security and Defence Provider*, https://ec.europa.eu/docsroom/documents/34509 (accessed 22 February 2022).
European Commission, *White Paper on Social Policy* (1994).
European Council, "Informal Meeting of the 27 Heads of State or Government: Main Results" (23 February 2018), www.consilium.europa.eu/en/meetings/european-council/2018/02/23/ (accessed 2 March 2023).
European Council, "Promoting EU Values through Trade", www.consilium.europa.eu/en/policies/trade-policy/promoting-eu-values/ (accessed 21 September 2020).
European Defence Agency, "Defence Data", https://eda.europa.eu/publications-and-data/defence-data (accessed 25 February 2022).
European External Action Service, "A Stronger EU on Security and Defence", https://eeas.europa.eu/headquarters/headquarters-homepage_en/35285/A%20stronger%20EU%20on%20security%20and%20defence (accessed 18 February 2022).
European External Action Service, *Special Report Update: Short Assessment of Narratives and Disinformation around the Covid-19/Coronavirus Pandemic* (27 April 2020), www.eeas.europa.eu/delegations/un-geneva/eeas-special-report-update-short-assessment-narratives-and-disinformation_en (accessed 31 July 2023).
European Parliament, "European Parliament: Relations with the National Parliaments", www.europarl.europa.eu/factsheets/en/sheet/22/european-parliament-relations-with-the-national-parliaments (accessed 3 March 2023).
European Parliament, "European Year of Citizens: Raising Awareness of EU Citizens' Rights" (23 October 2012), www.europarl.europa.eu/news/en/press-room/20121019IPR54022/european-year-of-citizens-raising-awareness-of-eu-citizens-rights#:~:text=The%20activities%20organised%20for%20the%20European%20Year%20of,programme%2C%20which%20enables%20young%20people%20to%20study%20abroad (accessed 17 August 2023).
European Parliament, "MEPs Begin Revising Rules on EU elections, Calling for Pan-European Constituency" (3 May 2022), www.europarl.europa.eu/news/en/press-room/20220429IPR28242/meps-begin-revising-rules-on-eu-elections-calling-for-pan-european-constituency (accessed 3 March 2023).
European Parliament, "Teaching about the EU: 44% of Europeans Don't Understand How the EU Works" (11 April 2016), www.europarl.europa.eu/news/en/headlines/society/20160408STO22170/teaching-about-the-eu-44-of-europeans-don-t-understand-how-the-eu-works (accessed 14 February 2022).

European Parliament, "Terrorism in the EU: Terror Attacks, Deaths and Arrests in 2019" (21 September 2021), www.europarl.europa.eu/news/en/headlines/security/20180703STO07125/terrorism-in-the-eu-terror-attacks-deaths-and-arrests-in-2019 (accessed 18 February 2022).

European Parliament, Report on the Situation of Fundamental Rights: Standards and Practices in Hungary (2013).

European Parliamentary Research Service, "Average Duration and Number of Concluded Ordinary Legislative Procedures", https://epthinktank.eu/2022/03/11/european-parliament-facts-and-figures/ep-facts-and-figures-fig-19/ (accessed 14 March 2023).

European Parliamentary Research Service, "Understanding the European Committee of the Regions" (2021).

European Parliamentary Research Service, *Implementation and Governance of Permanent Structured Cooperation* (2020), www.europarl.europa.eu/RegData/etudes/ATAG/2020/659280/EPRS_ATA(2020)659280EN.pdf (accessed 25 February 2022).

European Parliamentary Research Service, *Labour Rights in EU Trade Agreements: Towards Stronger Enforcement* (2022).

European Union Fundamental Rights Agency, Making EU Citizens' Rights a Reality: National Courts Enforcing Freedom of Movement and Related Rights (Luxembourg, 2018).

Favell, Adrian, "Immigration, Migration, and Free Movement", in Jeffrey T. Checkel and Peter J. Katzenstein (eds), *European Identity* (Cambridge, 2009).

Feltham, Brian and John Cottingham (eds), *Partiality and Impartiality: Morality, Special Relationships, and the Wider World* (Oxford, 2010).

Financial Times Editorial Board, "Emmanuel Macron's EU Accession Veto Is a Historic Mistake", *Financial Times* (21 October 2019), www.ft.com/content/eda39e1e-f3eb-11e9-b018-3ef8794b17c6 (accessed 17 November 2012).

Flanigan, Flanigan, Paul Gölz, Anupam Gupta, Brett Hennig and Ariel D. Procaccia, "Fair Algorithms for Selecting Citizens' Assemblies", *Nature* 596 (2021), pp. 548–552.

Fligstein, Neil, "Who are the Europeans and How Does this Matter for Politics", in Jeffrey T. Checkel and Peter J. Katzenstein (eds), *European Identity* (Cambridge, 2009).

Follesdal, Andreas, "Subsidiarity", *Journal of Political Philosophy* 6 (1998), pp. 231–259.

Follesdal, Andreas and Simon Hix, "Why There is a Democratic Deficit in the EU: A Response to Majone and Moravcsik", *Journal of Common Market Studies* 44 (2006), pp. 533–562.

Foret, François and Oriane Calligaro (eds), *European Values: Challenges and Opportunities for EU Governance* (New York, 2018).

Fowler, James H., "Altruism and Turnout", *The Journal of Politics* 68 (2006), pp. 674–683.

Franceinfo, "En Visite en Inde, François Hollande Réussira-t-il à Conclure la Vente de 36 Rafale?" (24 January 2016), www.francetvinfo.fr/economie/aeronautique/rafale/francois-hollande-reussira-t-il-a-vendre-des-rafale-a-l-inde_1283507.html (accessed 7 March 2021).

Franceinfo, "Résultats de l'Élection Présidentielle 2022", www.francetvinfo.fr/elections/resultats/#xtor=SEC-799-BIN[FTVI_Election_Presidentielle_Resultats_Metropole_search_2022_2nd_tour]-[Election_Presidentielle_Resultats_Nationaux]-S-[1143493031073414] (accessed 26 April 2022).

François, Étienne and Thomas Serrier (eds), *Europa: Notre Histoire* (Paris, 2019).
Freedom House, "Democracy Status" (2021), https://freedomhouse.org/explore-the-map?type=nit&year=2022 (accessed 18 May 2022).
Friese, Heidrun and Peter Wagner, "Survey Article: The Nascent Political Philosophy of the European Polity", *Journal of Political Philosophy* 10 (2002), pp. 342–364.
Fry, James D., Bryane Michael and Natasha Pushkarna, *The Values of International Organizations* (Manchester, 2021).
Fukuyama, Francis, *The End of History and the Last Man* (New York, 1992).
Gallie, W.B., "Essentially Contested Concepts", *Proceedings of the Aristotelian Society* 56 (1956), pp. 167–198.
Garrett, Geoffrey and Barry R. Weingast, "Ideas, Interests, and Institutions: Constructing the European Community's Internal Market", in Judith Goldstein and Robert O. Keohane (eds), *Ideas and Foreign Policy: Beliefs, Institutions and Political Change* (Ithaca, 1993).
Gauthier, David, *Morals by Agreement* (Oxford, 1987).
Georgieva, Mihaela, "The Forgotten Ideal of Friendship in Modern Political Theory", *Res Publica* 19 (2013), pp. 95–102.
Germond, Carine, "Preventing Reform: Farm Interest Groups and the Common Agricultural Policy", in Wolfram Kaiser and Jan-Henrik Meyer (eds), *Societal Actors in European Integration: Polity-Building and Policy-Making 1958–1992* (Basingstoke, 2013).
Gillingham, John R., *The EU: An Obituary* (London, 2016).
Ginsburg, Tom and Alberto Simpser (eds), *Constitutions in Authoritarian Regimes* (Cambridge, 2013).
Goertz, Gary, *Contexts of International Politics* (Cambridge, 1994).
Goldstein, Judith and Robert O. Keohane, "Ideas and Foreign Policy: An Analytical Framework", in Judith Goldstein and Robert O. Keohane (eds), *Ideas and Foreign Policy: Beliefs, Institutions and Political Change* (Ithaca, 1993).
Goodin, Robert E., *Utilitarianism as a Public Philosophy* (Cambridge, 1995).
Goodin, Robert E., "Enfranchising All Affected Interests, and Its Alternatives", *Philosophy and Public Affairs* 35 (2007), pp. 40–68.
Gordon, Joy, "Smart Sanctions Revisited", *Ethics & International Affairs* 25 (2011), pp. 315–335.
Gosio, Paola, "Covid-19 Crisis: An Opportunity for the EU to Expand its Competences in Public Health?", *The Euroculturer: European Culture, Politics and Society in Focus* (25 February 2021), https://euroculturer.eu/2021/02/25/covid-19-crisis-an-opportunity-for-the-eu-to-expand-its-competences-in-public-health/ (accessed 5 November 2021).
Grant, Charles, "Can National Parliaments Make the EU more Legitimate?", *Center for European Reform* (10 June 2013), www.cer.eu/insights/can-national-parliaments-make-eu-more-legitimate (accessed 3 March 2023).
Grayling, A.C., *For the Good of the World: Is Global Agreement on Global Challenges Possible?* (London, 2022)
Greenawalt, Kent, *Private Consciences and Public Reasons* (Oxford, 1995).
Greenwood, Justin, *Interest Representation in the European Union* (London, 2017).
Grimm, Dieter, "Does Europe Need a Constitution?", *European Law Journal* 1 (1995), pp. 282–302.
Grimm, Dieter, "The Democratic Costs of Constitutionalisation: The European Case", *European Law Journal* 21 (2015), pp. 460–473.

Groen, Afke and Thomas Christiansen, "National Parliaments in the European Union: Conceptual Choices in the European Union's Constitutional Debate", in Claudia Hefftler, Christine Neuhold, Olivier Rozenberg and Julie Smith (eds), *The Palgrave Handbook of National Parliaments and the European Union* (Basingstoke, 2015).

Gros, Daniel and Thomas Mayer, "A European Monetary Fund: How and Why?", *CEPS Working Document* (2017).

Haas, Ernst B., "Turbulent Fields and the Theory of Regional Integration", *International Organization* 30 (1976), pp. 173–212.

Haas, Tobias and Hendrik Sander, *The European Car Lobby: A Critical Analysis of the Impact of the Automobile Industry* (Brussels, 2019).

Habermas, Jürgen, "Why Europe Needs a Constitution", *New Left Review* 11 (2001), pp. 5–26.

Habermas, Jürgen, *The Postnational Constellation: Political Essays* (Cambridge, 2001).

Hackett, Conrad, "5 Facts about the Muslim Population in Europe", *Pew Research Center* (29 November 2017), www.pewresearch.org/fact-tank/2017/11/29/5-facts-about-the-muslim-population-in-europe/ (accessed 22 September 2022).

Hallin, Daniel C., *The "Uncensored War": The Media and Vietnam* (Oxford/New York, 1986).

Hanhimäki, Jussi M., "Reform and Challenges: The Future of the United Nations", *The United Nations: A Very Short Introduction* (Oxford, 2008).

Harris, John and Erica Buist, *The Guardian* (27 May 2017), www.theguardian.com/politics/2017/may/27/strangely-optimistic-first-time-voters-8-june (accessed 7 March 2022).

Harris, Jose, *William Beveridge: A Biography* (Oxford, 1997).

Harrison, James, Mirela Barbu, Liam Campling, Franz Christian Ebert, Deborah Martens, Axel Marx, Jan Orbie, Ben Richardson and Adrian Smith, "Labour Standards Provisions in EU Free Trade Agreements: Reflections on the European Commission's Reform Agenda", *World Trade Review* 18 (2019), pp. 635–657.

Held, David, *Models of Democracy* (Cambridge, 2006).

Hemerijick, Anton, *Changing Welfare States* (Oxford, 2012).

Herring, George C., "The Cold War and Vietnam", *OAH Magazine of History* 18 (2004), pp. 18–21.

Himmelfarb, Gertrude, *The De-Moralization of Society: From Victorian Virtues to Modern Values* (New York, 1996).

Hirschman, Albert O., *Exit, Voice and Loyalty: Responses to Decline in Firms, Organizations, and States* (Cambridge MA, 1970).

Hix, Simon and Bjørn Høyland, *The Political System of the European Union* (New York, 2011).

Hobbes, Thomas, *Leviathan*, ed. Noel Malcolm (Oxford, 2012).

Hoffmann, Stanley, "Obstinate or Obsolete? The Fate of the Nation-State and the Case of Western Europe", *Daedalus* 95 (1966), pp. 862–915.

Holmes, Robert, *Pacifism: A Philosophy of Nonviolence* (London, 2017).

Holmes, Stephen and Ivan Krastev, *The Light That Failed: Why the West Is Losing the Fight for Democracy* (London, 2020).

Hoods, Kerry, "Civic and Cosmopolitan Friendship", *Res Publica* (2013), pp. 81–94.

Human Rights Watch, *Locked Up Alone: Detention Conditions and Mental Health at Guantanamo* (New York, 2008).

Huntington, Samuel P., *The Clash of Civilizations and the Remaking of World Order* (London, 2002).
Hutchins, Rachel D., *Nationalism and History Education: Curricula and Textbooks in the United States and France* (London, 2016).
Hutchinson, John, *War and Nationalism* (Oxford, 2017).
Inglehart, Ronald, "Cognitive Mobilization and European Identity", *Comparative Politics* 3 (1970), pp. 45–70.
Institute for Government, "UK–EU Future Relationship: Level Playing Field" (16 December 2020), www.instituteforgovernment.org.uk/explainers/future-relationship-level-playing-field (accessed 29 October 2021).
Jacobsohn, Gary Jeffrey, "Constitutional Values and Principles", in Michel Rosenfeld and András Sajó (eds), *The Oxford Handbook of Comparative Constitutional Law* (Oxford, 2012).
Jeffries, Stuart, "Is Germany too Powerful for Europe?", *The Guardian* (31 March 2013), www.theguardian.com/world/2013/mar/31/is-germany-too-powerful-for-europe (accessed 18 February 2021).
Jervis, Robert, *Perception and Misperception in International Politics* (Princeton, 1976).
Johnson, Laura and Paul Morris, "Towards a Framework for Critical Citizenship Education", *The Curriculum Journal* 21 (2010), pp. 77–96.
Josselin, Daphné and William Wallace (eds), *Non-State Actors in World Politics* (New York, 2001).
Juncker, Jean-Claude, *State of the Union Address 2017* (13 September 2017), https://ec.europa.eu/commission/presscorner/detail/en/SPEECH_17_3165 (accessed 27 July 2023).
Juncker, Jean-Claude, "The Hour of European Sovereignty", *State of the Union Address 2018* (12 September 2018), https://ec.europa.eu/commission/sites/beta-political/files/soteu2018-speech_en_0.pdf (accessed 4 January 2021).
Katzenstein, Peter J. (ed.), *The Culture of National Security: Norms and Identity in World Politics* (New York, 1996).
Keating, Avril, *Education for Citizenship in Europe: European Policies, National Adaptations and Young People's Attitudes* (London, 2014).
Keys, Mary M., *Aquinas, Aristotle, and the Promise of the Common Good* (Cambridge, 2008).
Khan, Mehreen and Paul McClean, "Dijsselbloem under Fire after Saying Eurozone Countries Wasted Money on 'Alcohol and Women'", *Financial Times* (21 March 2017), www.ft.com/content/2498740e-b911-3dbf-942d-ecce511a351e (accessed 31 January 2022).
Khomeini, Ruhollah, *American Plots against Iran Speech* (1979), http://emam.com/posts/view/15718/Speech (accessed 6 October 2022).
Khong, Yuen Foong, *Analogies at War: Korea, Munich, Dien Bien Phu, and the Vietnam Decisions of 1965* (Princeton, 1992).
Kissinger, Henry, *Diplomacy* (New York, 1994).
Kochenov, Dimitry, "The Acquis and Its Principles: The Enforcement of the 'Law' versus the Enforcement of 'Values' in the EU", in András Jakab and Dimitry Kochenov (eds), *The Enforcement of EU Law and Values: Ensuring Member States' Compliance* (Oxford, 2017).
Koikkalainen, Saara, "Free Movement and EU Citizenship from the Perspective of Intra-European Mobility", in Rainer Bauböck (ed.), *Debating European Citizenship* (Cham, 2018).

Konstadinides, Theodore, *The Rule of Law in the European Union: The Internal Dimension* (Oxford, 2017).
Kotler, Philip, *Advancing the Common Good: Strategies for Businesses, Governments and Nonprofits* (Santa Barbara, 2019).
Kriesi, Hanspeter, "The Politicization of European Integration", *Journal of Common Market Studies* 54 (2016).
Krugman, Paul R., Maurice Obstfeld and Marc J. Melitz, *International Economics: Theory and Policy* (Essex, 2015), pp. 83–115.
Labareda, João, *Towards a Just Europe: A Theory of Distributive Justice for the European Union* (Manchester, 2021).
Laclau, Ernesto, *On Populist Reason* (London, 2005).
Lacroix, Justine, "French Republicanism and the European Union", in Samantha Besson and José Luis Martí (eds), *Legal Republicanism: National and International Perspectives* (Oxford, 2009).
Leggewie, Claus, "Equally Criminal? Totalitarian Experience and European Memory", *Transit Online* (2007), www.iwm.at/transit-online/equally-criminal-totalitarian-experience-and-european-memory (accessed 28 August 2023).
Listhaug, Ola, Sabrina P. Ramet and Dragana Dulić (eds), *Civic and Uncivic Values: Serbia in the Post-Milošević Era* (Budapest, 2011).
Lovera-Parmo, Domingo, "Protests, Riots, Inequality and a New Constitution for Chile", *Oxford Human Rights Hub* (15 December 2019), https://ohrh.law.ox.ac.uk/protests-riots-inequality-and-a-new-constitution-for-chile/ (accessed 14 December 2022).
Luppi, Roberto (ed.), *John Rawls and the Common Good* (New York, 2021).
Lyons, Kate and Gordon Darroch, "Frexit, Nexit or Oexit? Who Will Be Next to Leave the EU", *The Guardian* (27 June 2016), www.theguardian.com/politics/2016/jun/27/frexit-nexit-or-oexit-who-will-be-next-to-leave-the-eu (accessed 31 August 2018).
Maas, Heiko, *Interview with the Welt am Sonntag Newspaper* (19 August 2018), www.auswaertiges-amt.de/en/newsroom/news/maas-welt-am-sonntag/2129042 (accessed 1 March 2021).
Maas Willem, "Varieties of Multilevel Citizenship", in William Maas (ed.), *Multilevel Citizenship* (Philadelphia, 2013).
Machiavelli, Niccolò, *The Prince* (Oxford, 2008).
Macintyre, Alasdair, *After Virtue* (Notre-Dame, 1984).
Macron, Emmanuel, "Macron Denounces Nationalism as a 'Betrayal of Patriotism' in Rebuke to Trump at WWI Remembrance", *The Washington Post* (11 November 2018), www.washingtonpost.com/world/europe/to-mark-end-of-world-war-i-frances-macron-denounces-nationalism-as-a-betrayal-of-patriotism/2018/11/11/aab65aa4-e1ec-11e8-ba30-a7ded04d8fac_story.html (accessed 4 January 2021).
Macron, Emmanuel, *Discours du Président de la République lors de la Commémoration du Centenaire de L'Armistice* (11 November 2018), www.elysee.fr/emmanuel-macron/2018/11/12/discours-du-president-de-la-republique-emmanuel-macron-a-la-ceremonie-internationale-du-centenaire-de-larmistice-du-11-novembre-1918-a-larc-de-triomphe (accessed 5 October 2022).
Macron, Emmanuel, in Claire Stam, "Europe Is No 'Menu à la Carte', Macron Tells Visegrad Four and Salvini", *Euroactiv* (20 September 2019), www.euractiv.com/section/uk-europe/news/europe-is-no-menu-a-la-carte-macron-tells-visagrad-four-and-salvini/ (accessed 30 March 2022).

Mahoney, Christine, *Brussels versus the Beltway: Advocacy in the United States and the European Union* (Washington, 2008).
Mairie de Paris, "Budget Participatif", https://budgetparticipatif.paris.fr/bp/jsp/site/Portal.jsp# (accessed 16 December 2021).
Majeski, Stephen J., "Generating and Maintaining Cooperation in International Relations: A Model of Repeated Interaction Among Groups in Complex and Uncertain Situations", *International Interactions* 21 (1996), pp. 265–289.
Majone, Giandomenico, "The Rise of the Regulatory State in Europe", *Western European Politics* 17 (1994), pp. 77–101.
Majone, Giandomenico, *Regulating Europe* (London, 1996).
Malešević, Siniša, *Nation-States and Nationalisms: Organization, Ideology and Solidarity* (Cambridge, 2013).
Manifesto for a European Citizens' Assembly, https://europeancitizensassembly.eu/ (accessed 2 February 2023).
Manners, Ian, "The Constitutive Nature of Values, Images and Principles in the European Union", in Sonia Lucarelli and Ian Manners (eds), *Values and Principles in European Union Foreign Policy* (New York, 2006).
Manners, Ian, "The Normative Ethics of the European Union", *International Affairs* 84 (2008), pp. 45–60.
Mansbridge, Jane J., *Beyond Adversarial Democracy* (Chicago, 1983).
Mcnamara, Robert, "Memorandum of Secretary of Defence (McNamara) to the President: 16 March 1964", in Edward C. Keefer and Charles S. Sampson (eds), *Foreign Relations of the United States 1964–1968. Volume 1: Vietnam 1964* (Washington, 1992). Available at https://history.state.gov/historicaldocuments/frus1964-68v01/d84 (accessed 27 February 2021).
Mearsheimer, John J., *The Tragedy of Great Power Politics* (New York, 2014).
Mehta, Uday Singh, *Liberalism and Empire: A Study in Nineteenth-Century British Liberal Thought* (Chicago, 1999).
Merkel, Angela, *Debate on the Future of Europe: Opening Statement by Angela Merkel, German Federal Chancellor* (13 November 2018), https://multimedia.europarl.europa.eu/en/debate-on-the-future-of-europe-opening-statement-by-angela-merkel-german-federal-chancellor-_I162933-V_v (accessed 4 January 2021).
Merkel, Angela, "Merkel: Europe Must Unite to Stand Up to China, Russia and U.S.", *The Guardian* (15 May 2019), www.theguardian.com/world/2019/may/15/angela-merkel-interview-europe-eu-unite-challenge-us-russia-china (accessed 28 February 2021).
Mill, John Stuart, *On Liberty, Utilitarianism and Other Essays*, ed. Mark Philp (Oxford, 2015).
Miller, David, "Republicanism, National Identity and Europe", in Cécile Laborde and John Maynor (eds), *Republicanism and Political Theory* (Malden, 2008).
Mitchell, Kristine, "Student Mobility and European Identity: Erasmus Study as a Civic Experience", *Journal of Contemporary European Research* 8 (2012), pp. 491–518.
Moïsi, Dominique, *The Geopolitics of Emotion: How Cultures of Fear, Humiliation, and Hope are Reshaping the World* (New York, 2009).
Monbiot, George, "Neoliberalism – The Ideology at the Root of All Our Problems", *The Guardian* (15 April 2016), www.theguardian.com/books/2016/apr/15/neoliberalism-ideology-problem-george-monbiot (accessed 1 December 2021).
Montesquieu, *The Spirit of the Laws*, ed. Anne M. Cohler, Basia Carolyn Miller and Harold Samuel Stone (Cambridge, 1989).

Moravcsik, Andrew, "In Defence of the Democratic Deficit: Reassessing Legitimacy in the European Union", *Journal of Common Market Studies* 40 (2002), pp. 603–624.
Moravcsik, Andrew and Andrea Sangiovanni, "On Democracy and the 'Public Interest' in the European Union", *CES Working Paper* 93 (2003).
Moravcsik, Andrew and F. Schimmelfennig, "Liberal Intergovernmentalism", in A. Wiener and T. Diez (eds), *European Integration Theory* (Oxford, 2009), pp. 67–87.
Morgenthau, Hans J., *Politics among Nations: The Struggle for Power and Peace* (New York, 1978).
Müller, Fernando Suárez, "Eurocentrism, Human Rights, and Humanism", *International Journal of Applied Philosophy* 26 (2012), pp. 279–293.
Müller, Jan-Werner, "Why the EU Needs a Democracy and Rule of Law Watchdog", *Aspen Review* (15 March 2017), www.aspen.review/article/2017/why-the-eu-needs-a-democracy-and-rule-of-law-watchdog/ (accessed 19 May 2022).
Müller, Jan-Werner and Kim Lane Scheppele, "Constitutional Patriotism: An Introduction", *International Journal of Constitutional Law* 6 (2008), pp. 67–71.
Murray, Douglas, *The Madness of Crowds: Gender, Race and Identity* (London, 2019).
Neate, Rupert, "12 EU States Reject Move to Expose Companies' Tax Avoidance", *The Guardian* (28 November 2019), www.theguardian.com/business/2019/nov/28/12-eu-states-reject-move-to-expose-companies-tax-avoidance (accessed 18 September 2020).
Netherlands Institute of International Relations, "PESCO Implementation: The Next Challenge", *Policy Report* (2018).
Neuhold, Christine, "Democratic Deficit in the European Union", *Oxford Research Encyclopedia of Politics* (2020), https://oxfordre.com/politics/view/10.1093/acrefore/9780190228637.001.0001/acrefore-9780190228637-e-1141 (accessed 10 March 2023).
Nicolaidis, Kalypso, "The Idea of European Demoicracy", in Julie Dickson and Pavlos Eleftheriadis, *Philosophical Foundations of European Law* (Oxford, 2012).
Nicolaidis, Kalypso, "Democracy and its Critics", *Journal of Common Market Studies* 51 (2013), pp. 351–369.
Niebuhr, Reinhold, *Moral Man and Immoral Society: A Study in Ethics and Politics* (Louisville, 2013).
Nincic, Miroslav, "The National Interest and Its Interpretation", *The Review of Politics* 61 (1999), pp. 29–55.
Nozick, Robert, *Anarchy, State and Utopia* (Malden, 1974).
Nugent, Neill and Mark Rhinard, "The 'Political' Roles of the European Commission", *Journal of European Integration* 41 (2019), pp. 203–220.
Nussbaum, Martha C., *The Cosmopolitan Tradition: A Noble but Flawed Ideal* (Cambridge MA, 2019).
Nye, Joseph S., *Soft Power: The Means to Success in World Politics* (New York, 2004).
O'Flynn, Ian, *Deliberative Democracy* (Medford MA, 2022).
O'Toole Jr, J., *Bureaucracy in a Democratic State: A Governance Perspective* (Baltimore, 2006).
OECD, "The Decline in Labour Mobility in the United States: Insights from New Administrative Data", *Economics Department Working Papers* 1644 (2020).
OECD, *Innovative Citizen Participation and New Democratic Institutions: Catching the Deliberative Wave* (Paris, 2020).

OECD, *Brick by Brick: Building Better Housing Policies* (Paris, 2021).
OECD, *Two-Pillar Solution to Address the Tax Challenges Arising from the Digitalisation of the Economy* (2021), www.oecd.org/tax/beps/brochure-two-pillar-solution-to-address-the-tax-challenges-arising-from-the-digitalisation-of-the-economy-october-2021.pdf#:~:text=Pillar%20Two%20puts%20a%20floor%20on%20tax%20competition,it%20does%20set%20multilaterally%20agreed%20limitations%20on%20it (accessed 20 June 2022).
Offe, Claus, *Europe Entrapped* (Cambridge, 2015).
Office of the High Commissioner for Human Rights, "Status of Ratification Interactive Dashboard", https://indicators.ohchr.org/ (accessed 22 September 2022).
Office of the High Commissioner for Human Rights, Selected Decisions of the Committee on the Elimination of Racial Discrimination (Geneva, 2012).
ONE, "Former Commonwealth Heads of Government Call for the Successful Replenishment of the Global Fund" (20 June 2022), www.one.org/international/press/former-commonwealth-heads-of-government-call-for-the-successful-replenishment-of-the-global-fund/ (accessed 7 March 2023).
Onuf, Nicolas, "Constructivism: A User's Manual", in Vendulka Kubálková, Paul Kowert and Nicholas Onuf (eds), *International Relations in a Constructed World* (New York, 1998).
Otero-Iglesias, Miguel, "The Eurozone: Victim of its Own Success and Dogmas", *The European Financial Review* (10 February 2015), www.europeanfinancialreview.com/the-eurozone-victim-of-its-own-success-and-dogmas/ (accessed 2 February 2023).
Oxford English Dictionary, "Nationalism", www.oed.com/view/Entry/125289 (accessed 8 November 2022).
Page, Edward C., "The European Commission Bureaucracy: Handling Sovereignty through the Back and Front Doors", in Jack Hayward and Rüdiger Wurzel (eds), *European Disunion: Between Sovereignty and Solidarity* (London, 2012).
Pech, Laurent and Kim Lane Scheppele, "Illiberalism Within: Rule of Law Backsliding in the EU", *Cambridge Yearbook of European Legal Studies* 19 (2017), pp. 3–47.
PESCO, "Binding Commitments", https://pesco.europa.eu/binding-commitments/ (accessed 25 February 2022).
Peters, Brainard Guy and Lennart Nagel, *Zombie Ideas: Why Failed Policy Ideas Persist* (Cambridge, 2020).
Pettit, Philip, *Republicanism: A Theory of Freedom and Government* (Oxford, 1997).
Pettit, Philip, "Varieties of Public Representation", in Ian Shapiro, Susan C. Stokes, Elizabeth Jean Wood and Alexander S. Kirshner (eds), *Political Representation* (Cambridge, 2009).
Pettit, Philip, *Just Freedom: A Moral Compass for a Complex World* (New York, 2014).
Pickett, Kate and Richard Wilkinson, *The Spirit Level: Why More Equal Societies Almost Always Do Better* (New York, 2009).
Pierson, Paul, "The Path to European Integration: A Historical-Institutionalist Analysis", in Wayne Sandholtz and Alec Stone Sweet (eds), *European Integration and Supranational Governance* (Oxford, 1998), pp. 28–59.
Piketty, Thomas, *Capital in the Twenty-First Century* (Cambridge MA, 2014).
Pilati, Marta, "Brace for a Disappointing EU Budget", *European Policy Centre Commentary* (24 February 2020), www.epc.eu/en/Publications/Brace-for-a-disappointing-EU-budget~2f533c (accessed 11 June 2021).
Piris, Jean-Claude, *The Future of Europe: Towards a Two-Speed EU?* (Cambridge, 2021).

Pitkin, Hanna Fenichel, *The Concept of Representation* (Berkeley, 1967).
Plato, *Republic*, ed. Robin Waterfield (Oxford, 2008).
Politaki, Alex, "Greece is Facing a Humanitarian Crisis", *The Guardian* (11 February 2013), www.theguardian.com/commentisfree/2013/feb/11/greece-humanitarian-crisis-eu (accessed 29 November 2021).
Pollak, Johannes, "Political Representation and the Common Good: A Fragile Relationship", in Sonja Puntscher Riekmann, Alexander Somek and Doris Wydra (eds), *Is there a European Common Good?* (Baden-Baden, 2013), pp. 156–173.
Pollack, M.A., *The Engines of Integration: Delegation, Agency, and Agenda Setting in the EU* (Oxford, 2003).
Pollitt, Christopher, "Bureaucracies Remember, Post-Bureaucratic Organisations Forget?" *Public Administration* 87 (2009), pp. 198–218.
Pop, Valentina, "Once Scorned, 'Multispeed Europe' Is Back", *The Wall Street Journal* (1 March 2017), www.wsj.com/articles/once-scorned-multispeed-europe-is-back-1488388260 (accessed 4 November 2022).
Prentoulis, Marina, "Greece May Still Be Europe's Sick Patient, but the EU Is at Death's Door", *The Guardian* (21 August 2018), www.theguardian.com/commentisfree/2018/aug/21/greece-europe-eu-austerity (accessed 27 November 2021).
Putnam, Robert D., "Diplomacy and Domestic Politics: The Logic of Two-level Games", *International Organization* 42 (1988), pp. 427–460.
Putnam, Robert D., *Making Democracy Work: Civic Traditions in Modern Italy* (Princeton, 1994).
Putnam, Robert D., *Bowling Alone: The Collapse and Revival of American Community* (New York, 2001).
Rankin, Jennifer and Shaun Walker Orban, "EU Centre-Right Bloc Accused of Sheltering Hungary's Orbán", *The Guardian* (5 April 2018), www.theguardian.com/world/2018/apr/05/eu-centre-right-bloc-accused-of-sheltering-hungarys-orban (accessed 19 May 2022).
Rapier, Robert, "The World's Top Lithium Producers", *Forbes* (13 December 2020), www.forbes.com/sites/rrapier/2020/12/13/the-worlds-top-lithium-producers/ (accessed 2 August 2023).
Rauh, Christian, "One Agenda-Setter or Many? The Varying Success of Policy Initiatives by Individual Directorates-General of the European Commission 1994–2016", *European Union Politics* 22 (2020), pp. 3–24.
Rawls, John, "The Idea of an Overlapping Consensus", *Oxford Journal of Legal Studies* 7 (1987), pp. 1–25.
Rawls, John, "The Idea of Public Reason Revisited", *The University of Chicago Law Review* 64 (1997), pp. 765–807.
Rawls, John, *A Theory of Justice: Revised Edition* (Cambridge MA, 1999).
Rawls, John, *The Law of Peoples* (Cambridge MA, 2001).
Recchi, Ettore (ed.), *The Europeanisation of Everyday Life: Cross-Border Practices and Transnational Identifications among EU and Third-Country Citizens: Final Report* (2014). Available at www.ssoar.info/ssoar/handle/document/39526.
RecchiI, Ettore and Adrian Favell (eds), *Pioneers of European Integration: Citizenship and Mobility in the EU* (Cheltenham, 2009).
Rehg, William, "Solidarity and the Common Good: An Analytic Framework", *Journal of Social Philosophy* 38 (2007), pp. 7–21.
Reich, Robert B., *The Common Good* (New York, 2018).
Reif, Karlheinz and Hermann Schmitt, "Nine Second-Order National Elections – A Conceptual Framework for the Analysis of European Election Results", *European Journal of Political Research* 8 (1980), pp. 3–44.

Reuters, "Marine Le Pen blames Radical Islamism for Charlie Hebdo Attack – Video", *The Guardian* (8 January 2015), www.theguardian.com/world/video/2015/jan/08/marine-le-pen-radical-islamism-charlie-hebdo-attack-video (accessed 21 September 2022).

Reuters, "Russian Military in Belarus Threatens Baltics and Poland, Says Lithuanian President" (17 January 2022), www.reuters.com/world/europe/russian-military-belarus-threatens-baltics-poland-says-lithuanian-president-2022-02-17/ (accessed 18 February 2022).

Reuters, "Viktor Orbán: Our Duty Is to Protect Hungary's Christian Culture", *The Guardian* (7 May 2018), www.theguardian.com/world/2018/may/07/viktor-orban-hungary-preserve-christian-culture (accessed 8 November 2022).

Ricardo, David, *On the Principles of Political Economy and Taxation* (Indianapolis, 2004).

Ridao-Cano, Cristobal and Christian Bodewig, *Growing United: Upgrading Europe's Convergence Machine* (Washington, 2018).

Riekmann, Sonja Puntscher, Alexander Somek and Doris Wydra (eds), *Is there a European Common Good?* (Baden-Baden, 2013).

Riker, William R., *Liberalism against Populism: A Confrontation between the Theory of Democracy and Social Choice* (Long Grove, 1982).

Riordan, Patrick, *A Grammar of the Common Good: Speaking of Globalisation* (London, 2008).

Risse, Mathias and Gabriel Wollner, *On Trade Justice: A Philosophical Plea for a New Global Deal* (Oxford, 2019).

Risse, Thomas, *A Community of Europeans? Transnational Identities and Public Spheres* (Ithaca, 2010).

Risse, Thomas, *European Public Spheres: Politics Is Back* (Cambridge, 2015).

Robert, Aline, "Excessive Deficit Fine Looms over France", *Euroactiv* (22 September 2014), www.euractiv.com/section/euro-finance/news/excessive-deficit-fine-looms-over-france/ (accessed 6 February 2023).

Rolls, Mark G., "Like-Minded States: New Zealand–ASEAN Relations in the Changing Asia-Pacific Strategic Environment", in Anne-Marie Brady (ed.), *Small States and the Changing Global Order: New Zealand Faces the Future* (Cham, 2019).

Ronzoni, Miriam, "The European Union as a Demoicracy: Really a Third Way?", *European Journal of Political Theory* 16 (2017), pp. 210–234.

Rousseau, Jean-Jacques, *The Social Contract and Other Later Political Writings*, ed. Victor Gourevitch (Cambridge, 2018).

Russack, Sophia, "The Problem with the Spitzenkandidaten System", *CEPS Policy Brief* (21 February 2018).

Russet, Bruce M. and John D. Sullivan, "Collective Goods and International Organization", *International Organization* 25 (1971).

Saghaye-Biria, Hakimeh, "Decolonizing the 'Universal' Human Rights Regime: Questioning American Exceptionalism and Orientalism", *ReOrient* 4 (2018), pp. 59–77.

Sandel, Michael J., *Democracy's Discontent: America in Search of a Public Philosophy* (Cambridge MA, 1996).

Sandel, Michael J., *Liberalism and the Limits of Justice* (Cambridge, 1998).

Sandel, Michael J., *Justice: What's the Right Thing to Do?* (London, 2010).

Sandel, Michael J., "The Energy of the Brexiteers and Trump is Born of the Failure of Elites", *The New Statesman* (13 June 2016), www.newstatesman.com/politics/2016/06/michael-sandel-the-energy-of-the-brexiteers-and-trump-is-born-of-the-failure-of-elites (accessed 16 June 2022).
Sandel, Michael J., *The Tyranny of Merit: What's Become of the Common Good?* (London, 2021).
Sangiovanni, Andrea, "How Practices Matter", *Journal of Political Philosophy* (2016), pp. 3–23.
Scanlon, Thomas, *What We Owe to Each Other* (Cambridge MA, 1998).
Schäfer, Constantin, Oliver Treib and Bernd Schlipphak, "What Kind of EU Do Citizens Want? Reform Preferences and the Conflict over Europe", *Journal of European Public Policy* 30 (2023), pp. 1738–1761.
Scharff, Christina, "The Psychic Life of Neoliberalism: Mapping the Contours of Entrepreneurial Subjectivity", *Theory, Culture & Society* 33 (2016), pp. 107–122.
Scharff, Fritz W., "The Joint-Decision Trap: Lessons from German Federalism and European Integration", *Public Administration* 66 (1988), pp. 239–278.
Scharff, Fritz W., "The European Social Model: Coping with the Challenge of Diversity", *Journal of Common Market Studies* 40 (2002), pp. 645–670.
Scharff, Fritz W., "The Joint-Decision Trap Revisited", *Journal of Common Market Studies* 44 (2006), pp. 845–864.
Scheffler, Samuel, "Membership and Political Obligation", *Journal of Political Philosophy* 26 (2018), pp. 3–23.
Scheppele, Kim Lane and R. Daniel Kelemen, "Defending Democracy in EU Member States", in Francesca Bignami (ed.), *EU Law in Populist Times: Crises and Prospects* (Cambridge, 2020).
Scheppele, Kim Lane, Dimitry Vladimirovich Kochenov and Barbara Grabowska-Moroz, "EU Values Are Law, after All: Enforcing EU Values through Systemic Infringement Actions by the European Commission and the Member States of the European Union", *Yearbook of European Law* 39 (2020), pp. 3–121.
Scheuerman, William E., *The Realist Case for Global Reform* (Cambridge, 2011).
Schön-Quinlivan, Emmanuelle, *Reforming the European Commission* (London, 2011).
Schmidt, Andreas T. and Bart Engelen, "The Ethics of Nudging: An Overview", *Philosophy Compass* 15 (2020), pp. 1–13.
Schmidt, Carl, *The Concept of the Political* (Chicago, 2007).
Schneider-Petsinger, Marianne, *Reforming the World Trade Organization: Prospects for Transatlantic Cooperation and the Global Trade System* (London, 2020).
Schramm, Lucas, and Wolfgang Wessels, "The European Council as a Crisis Manager and Fusion Driver: Assessing the EU's Fiscal Response to the COVID-19 Pandemic", *Journal of European Integration* 45 (2023), pp. 257–273.
Schroeder, Werner (ed.), *Strengthening the Rule of Law in Europe: from a Common Concept to Mechanisms of Implementation* (Oxford, 2016).
Schuman, Robert, *The Schuman Declaration* (9 May 1950).
Schumpeter, Joseph A., *Capitalism, Socialism and Democracy* (New York, 2008).
Schwartzberg, Melissa, "Epistemic Democracy and its Challenges" *Annual Review of Political Science* 18 (2015).
Schwarzenbach, Sibyl A., "On Civic Friendship", *Ethics* 107 (1996), pp. 97–128.
Schwarzenbach, Sibyl A., *On Civic Friendship: Including Women in the State* (New York, 2009).

Scorza, Jason A., "Civic Friendship", *The International Encyclopaedia of Ethics* (2013).

Scott, Jonathan French, *The Menace of Nationalism in Education* (New York, 2012).

Sennet, Richard, *The Corrosion of Character: The Personal Consequences of Work in the New Capitalism* (New York, 1998).

Shue, Henry, *Basic Rights: Subsistence, Affluence, and U.S. Foreign Policy* (Princeton, 1996).

Siedentop, Larry, *Democracy in Europe* (New York, 2001).

Singer, Peter, "Famine, Affluence and Morality", *Philosophy & Public Affairs* 1 (1972), pp. 229–243.

Singer, Peter, *The Expanding Circle: Ethics and Sociobiology* (New York, 1981).

Skinner, Quentin, "The Republican Ideal of Political Liberty", in Gisela Bock, Quentin Skinner and Maurizio Viroli (eds), *Machiavelli and Republicanism* (Cambridge, 1991).

Smith, Graham, *Democratic Innovations: Designing Institutions for Citizen Participation* (Cambridge, 2009).

Stasavage, David, *The Decline and Rise of Democracy: A Global History from Antiquity to Today* (Princeton, 2020).

Steber, Martina and Bernhard Gotto (eds), *Visions of Community in Nazi Germany: Social Engineering and Private Lives* (Oxford, 2014).

Steiner, George, *The Idea of Europe: An Essay* (New York/London, 2015).

Sternberg, Claudia, Kira Gartzou-Katsouyanni and Kalypso Nicolaidis, *The Greco-German Affair in the Eurocrisis: Mutual Recognition Lost?* (London, 2018).

Stiglitz, Joseph E., *Making Globalization Work* (London, 2006).

Stiglitz, Joseph E., *The Price of Inequality: How Today's Divided Society Endangers Our Future* (New York, 2013).

Stiglitz, Joseph E., *Globalization and Its Discontents Revisited: Anti-Globalization in the Era of Trump* (London, 2017).

Stilz, Anna, "The Value of Self-Determination", in David Sobel, Peter Vallentyne and Steven Wall (eds), *Oxford Studies in Political Philosophy,* volume 2 (Oxford, 2016).

Stockholm International Peace Research Institute, *Trends in the World Military Expenditure 2020*, https://sipri.org/sites/default/files/2021–04/fs_2104_milex_0.pdf (accessed 25 February 2022).

Stolberg, Sheryl Gay, "Former Heads of State Urge U.S. to Commit $5 Billion to Global Covid Fight", *The New York Times* (9 May 2022), www.nytimes.com/2022/05/09/us/politics/biden-covd-aid.html (accessed 7 March 2023).

Striessnig, Erich and Wolfgang Lutz, "Demographic Strengthening of European Identity", *Population and Development Review* 42 (2016), pp. 305–311.

Sundström, Göran, "Seconded National Experts as Part of Early Mover Strategies in the European Union: The Case of Sweden", *Journal of European Integration* 38 (2015), pp. 1–15.

Tamma, Paola, "EU Leaders Fail to Commit to Climate Neutrality in 2050", *Politico* (22 June 2019), www.politico.eu/article/eu-leaders-fail-to-commit-to-climate-neutrality-by-2050/ (accessed 18 September 2020).

Taylor, Charles, "Atomism", in Shlomo Avineri and Avner de-Shalit (eds), *Communitarianism and Individualism* (Oxford, 1992).

Taylor, Charles, "Irreducibly Social Goods", *Philosophical Arguments* (Cambridge MA, 1997).

Taylor, Kira, "EU Countries Agree World's First Carbon Tariff, but Leave Out Controversial Issues", *Euractiv* (16 March 2022), www.euractiv.com/section/energy-environment/news/eu-countries-agree-worlds-first-carbon-tariff-but-leave-out-controversial-issues/ (accessed 14 June 2022).

TellMAMA, "Anti-Muslim Incidents in France after the Charlie Hebdo Massacre", https://tellmamauk.org/project/anti-muslim-incidents-in-france-after-the-charlie-hebdo-massacre/ (accessed 26 July 2023).

Teo, Thomas, "Homo Neoliberalus: From Personality to Forms of Subjectivity", *Theory & Psychology* 28 (2018), pp. 581–599.

Tetlock, Philip E., *Expert Political Judgment: How Good Is It? How Can We Know?* (Princeton, 2017).

Theuns, Tom, "Is the European Union a Militant Democracy? Democratic Backsliding and EU Disintegration", *Global Constitutionalism* (2023), pp. 1–22.

Thomas, Christopher, "Globalising Sovereignty? Pettit's Neo-Republicanism, International Law and International Institutions", *The Cambridge Law Journal* 74 (2015), pp. 568–591.

Tirole, Jean, *Economics for the Common Good* (Princeton, 2017).

Toqueville, Alexis de, *Democracy in America* (Chicago, 2000).

Transparency Inyernational, "About Lobbying", https://transparency.eu/priority/eu-money-politics/#lobbying (accessed 15 June 2022).

Trilling, Daniel, "Protecting the European Way of Life from Migrants is a Gift to the Far Right", *The Guardian* (13 September 2019), www.theguardian.com/commentisfree/2019/sep/13/protecting-europe-migrants-far-right-eu-nationalism (accessed 7 April 2022).

Trouillet, Julien, "Credit Rating Agencies, Shock and Public Expectations", *AFSE 2015 64th Congress* (2015).

Tuck, Richard, *Natural Rights Theories: Their Origin and Development* (Cambridge, 1981).

Turpin, Colin and Adam Tomkins, *British Government and the Constitution* (Cambridge, 2007).

Tusk, Donald, *Speech by President Donald Tusk at the Athens Democracy Forum 2019* (9 October 2019), www.consilium.europa.eu/en/press/press-releases/2019/10/09/speech-by-president-donald-tusk-at-the-athens-democracy-forum-2019/ (accessed 4 January 2021).

United Nations, "Gender Equality: Women and the Sustainable Development Goals", www.un.org/en/global-issues/gender-equality (accessed 14 December 2022).

United Nations, "Model United Nations", www.un.org/en/mun (accessed 10 February 2022).

United Nations, "Status of the Paris Agreement", https://treaties.un.org/Pages/ViewDetails.aspx?src=TREATY&mtdsg_no=XXVII-7-d&chapter=27&clang=_en#1 (accessed 23 September 2022).

United Nations, "Treaty on the Non-Proliferation of Nuclear Weapons", www.un.org/disarmament/wmd/nuclear/npt/ (accessed 22 September 2022).

United Nations Environment Programme, *Emissions Gap Report 2021: The Heat Is On – A World of Climate Promises Not Yet Delivered* (Nairobi, 2021).

Van Middelaar, Luuk, *The Passage to Europe: How a Continent Became a Union* (New Haven, 2013).

Van Parijs, Philippe and Yannick Vanderborght, *Basic Income: A Radical Proposal for a Free Society and a Sane Economy* (Cambridge MA, 2017).

Van Parijs, Philippe, "First Letter", in John Rawls and Philippe Van Parijs, *Three Letters on The Law of Peoples and the European Union*, https://ethics.harvard.edu/files/center-for-ethics/files/2003.rawlsvanparijs.r.phil_.econ_.pdf (accessed 2 March 2023).

Van Parijs, Philippe, "Transnational Lists in the European Parliament: Soon a Reality?", *The Brussels Times* (16 October 2022), www.brusselstimes.com/307268/transnational-lists-in-the-european-parliament-soon-a-reality (accessed 24 August 2023).

Vandenbroucke, Frank, Anton Hemerijck and Bruno Palier, "The EU Needs a Social Investment Pack", *OSE Opinion Paper 5* (2011).

Varoufakis, Yanis, *Adults in the Room: My Battle with Europe's Deep Establishment* (London, 2017).

Vermuele, Adrian, *Common Good Constitutionalism: Recovering the Classic Legal Tradition* (Cambridge, 2022).

Von Bogdandy, Armin, "Principles and Challenges of a European Doctrine of Systemic Deficiencies", *Common Market Law Review* 57 (2020), pp. 705–740.

Von Bogdandy, Armin and Pál Sonnevend (eds), *Constitutional Crisis in the European Constitutional Area – Theory, Law and Politics in Hungary and Romania* (Oxford, 2015).

Von Bogdandy, Armin, Carlino Antpöhler and Michael Ioannidis, "Protecting EU Values – Reverse Solange and the Rule of Law Framework", in András Jakab and Dimitry Kochenov (eds), *The Enforcement of EU Law and Values, Ensuring Member States' Compliance* (Oxford, 2017).

Von Der Leyen, Ursula, "The World in 2021: Ursula von der Leyen on Teamwork Solving Global Problems", *The Economist* (17 November 2020), www.economist.com/the-world-ahead/2020/11/17/ursula-von-der-leyen-on-teamwork-solving-global-problems (accessed 4 January 2021).

Walker, Shaun, "Orbán Deploys Christianity with a Twist to Tighten Grip in Hungary" *The Guardian* (14 July 2019), www.theguardian.com/world/2019/jul/14/viktor-orban-budapest-hungary-christianity-with-a-twist (accessed 21 September 2022).

Wallaschek, Stefan, "The Framing of Solidarity in the Euro Crisis", *Sheffield Political Economy Research Institute* (22 May 2019), http://speri.dept.shef.ac.uk/2019/05/22/the-framing-of-solidarity-in-the-euro-crisis/ (accessed 4 June 2021).

Walsh, James P. and Gerardo Rivera Ungson, "Organisational Memory", *The Academy of Management Review* 16 (1991), pp. 57–91.

Walt, Stephen M., "Top 10 Warning Signs of Liberal Imperialism", *Foreign Policy* (10 May 2013), https://foreignpolicy.com/2013/05/20/top-10-warning-signs-of-liberal-imperialism/ (accessed 30 September 2022).

Waltz, Kenneth N., "Structural Realism After the Cold War", *International Security* 25 (2000).

Waltz, Kenneth N., *Man, the State and War: A Theoretical Analysis* (New York, 2001).

Walzer, Michael, *Spheres of Justice: A Defence of Pluralism and Equality* (New York, 1983).

Walzer, Michael, "Governing the Globe: What Is the Best We Can Do?", *Dissent* (Fall edition, 2000).

Walzer, Michael, *Just and Unjust Wars: A Moral Argument with Historical Illustrations* (New York, 2015).

Weber, Eugene, *Peasants into Frenchmen: The Modernization of Rural France 1870–1914* (Stanford, 1976).

Weber, Manfred, Iratxe García Pérez, Dacian Cioloș, Ska Keller and Philippe Lamberts, "European Values Are not for Sale", *Politico* (6 October 2020), www.politico.eu/article/european-values-not-for-sale-rule-of-law-eu-budget-and-recovery-plan/ (accessed 27 October 2022).
Weiler, J.H.H., "The Transformation of Europe", *The Yale Law Journal* 100 (1991), pp. 2403–2483.
Weldes, Jutta, "Constructing National Interests", *European Journal of International Relations* 2 (1996), pp. 275–318.
Welsh, Jennifer, *The Return of History: Conflict, Migration and Geopolitics in the Twenty-First Century* (Toronto, 2016).
Wenar, Leif, "Natural Resources", in David Held and Pietro Maffettone (eds), *Global Political Theory* (Cambridge, 2016).
Wendt, Alexander, "Anarchy is What States Make of It: The Social Construction of Power Politics", *International Organization* 46 (1992), pp. 391–425.
Westad, Arne, *The Cold War: A World History* (London, 2018).
Wettenhall, R., "Organisational Amnesia: a Serious Public Sector Reform Issue", *International Journal of Public Sector Management* 24 (2011), pp. 80–96.
White, Lawrence J., "A Brief History of Credit Rating Agencies: How Financial Regulation Entrenched this Industry's Role in the Subprime Mortgage Debacle of 2007–2008", *Mercatus on Policy* 59 (2009).
Wiener, Antje, "Assessing the Constructive Potential of Union Citizenship – A Socio-Historical Perspective", *European Integration Online Papers* 1 (1997).
World Bank, *Minerals for Climate Action: The Mineral Intensity of the Clean Energy Transition* (Washington, 2020).
Zimmermann, Augusto, "Constitutions without Constitutionalism: The Failure of Constitutionalism in Brazil", in Mortimer Sellers and Tadeusz Tomaszewski (eds), *The Rule of Law in Comparative Perspective* (Dordrecht, 2010).
Zuboff, Shoshana, *The Age of Surveillance Capitalism: The Fight for a Human Future at the New Frontier of Power* (London, 2019).

Legal documents, indicators and databases

Charter of Fundamental Rights of the European Union.
Constituição Política da República Portuguesa (1933).
Constitution of the Islamic Republic of Iran.
Constitution of the People's Republic of China.
Elisabeta Dano and Florin Dano v. Jobcenter Leipzig.
European Commission, *Communication from the President to the Commission: Rules Governing the Composition of the Cabinets of the Members of the Commission and of the Spokesperson's Service* (2019).
European Commission, *Communication to the Council, the European Parliament, the European Economic and Social Committee and the Committee of the Regions: The Commission's Contribution to the Period of Reflection and Beyond: Plan-D for Democracy, Dialogue and Debate* (2005).
European Commission, *Communication to the European Parliament and the Council: A new EU Framework to Strengthen the Rule of Law* (2014).
European Commission, *Communication to the European Parliament, the Council, the European Council, the European Economic and Social Committee and the Committee of the Regions: A Union of Equality – Gender Equality Strategy 2020–2025* (2020).

European Commission, *Communication to the European Parliament, the Council, the European Council, the European Economic and Social Committee and the Committee of the Regions: Artificial Intelligence for Europe* (2018).

European Commission, *Communication to the European Parliament, the Council, the European Council, the European Economic and Social Committee and the Committee of the Regions: Union of Equality – LGBTIQ Equality Strategy 2020–2025* (2020).

European Commission, *Communication to the European Parliament, the European Council and the Council: Further Strengthening the Rule of Law within the Union – State of Play and Possible Next Steps* (2019).

European Commission, *Communication to the European Parliament, the European Council, the Council, the European and Social Committee and the Committee of Regions: Strengthening the Rule of Law within the Union – A Blueprint for Action* (2019).

European Commission, Directive 2004/38/EC.

European Commission, *Proposal for a Council Decision on the Determination of a Clear Risk of a Serious Breach by the Republic of Poland of the Rule of Law* (2017).

European Parliament, *Draft Report on a Proposal Calling on the Council to Determine, Pursuant to Article 7(1) of the Treaty on European Union, the Existence of a Clear Risk of a Serious Breach by Hungary of the Values on which the Union is Founded* (11 April 2018).

European Parliament, *Resolution of 12 September 2018 on a Proposal Calling on the Council to Determine, pursuant to Article 7(1) of the Treaty on European Union, the Existence of a Clear Risk of a Serious Breach by Hungary of the Values on which the Union is Founded* (2017).

European Parliament, *Resolution of 14 November 2018 on the Need for a Comprehensive Democracy, Rule of Law and Fundamental Rights Mechanism* (2018).

European Parliament, *Resolution of 19 April 2018 on the Implementation of the Treaty Provisions concerning National Parliaments* (2018).

European Parliament, *Resolution of 25 October 2016 with Recommendations to the Commission on the Establishment of an EU mechanism on Democracy, the Rule of Law and Fundamental Rights* (2016).

European Pillar of Social Rights (2017).

European Social Charter (1961, revised in 1996).

Eurostat, "Educational attainment Statistics", https://ec.europa.eu/eurostat/statistics-explained/index.php?title=Educational_attainment_statistics (accessed 26 January 2021).

Eurostat, "EU Citizens Living in Another Member State", https://ec.europa.eu/eurostat/statistics-explained/index.php?title=EU_citizens_living_in_another_Member_State_-_statistical_overview#Key_messages (accessed 25 January 2022).

Eurostat, "GDP per Capita, Consumption per Capita and Price Level Indices" (2020) https://ec.europa.eu/eurostat/statistics-explained/index.php?title=GDP_per_capita,_consumption_per_capita_and_price_level_indices#Relative_volumes_of_GDP_per_capita (accessed 25 November 2021).

Eurostat, "Living Conditions in Europe – Material Deprivation and Economic Strain" (2019), https://ec.europa.eu/eurostat/statistics-explained/index.php?title=Living_conditions_in_Europe_-_material_deprivation_and_economic_strain#Material_deprivation (accessed 25 November 2021).

International Covenant on Civil and Political Rights (1966).
Protocolo de Asunción sobre compromiso con la promoción y protección de los Derechos Humanos en el MERCOSUR.
Protocolo de Ushuaia sobre Compromiso Democrático en el MERCOSUR, La Republica de Bolivia e la Republica de Chile.
Statute of the Council of Europe (1949).
The ASEAN Charter.
The Convention on the Prevention and Punishment of the Crime of Genocide (1948).
The Convention on the Rights of Persons with Disabilities (2006).
The Convention on the Rights of the Child (1989).
The International Convention for the Protection of All Persons from Enforced Disappearance (2006).
The International Convention on the Suppression and Punishment of the Crime of Apartheid (1973).
The United States Constitution.
Treaty on European Union.
United Nations Charter.
World Values Survey, www.worldvaluessurvey.org/wvs.jsp (accessed 26 July 2023).

Index

accountability 4, 94, *95*, *117*
administrative simplification 14, 151
advisory board of former presidents of EU institutions 13, 125, 126, 175
African Union 50
agenda-setting 13, 73, 114, 120, 127, 148
Albania 63, 78, 162
Aquinas, Thomas 24
Aristotle 5, 23, 24, 137, 161
ASEAN 33, 39, 50
austerity 117, 145
Australia 32
Austria 62, 136, 168, 171

Bangladesh 37
Barroso, José Manuel 64
Belgium 142
Bosnia-Herzegovina 78
Brexit ii, 2, 12, 18, 66, 68, 80, 81, 135, 141, 152
Bulgaria 143
burdens of the common good 38, 62, 136

Charter of Fundamental Rights of the European Union 85, 103
Chile 27, 37
Christianity 2, 9, 30, 54, 58
civic friendship
 defined 5, 60–63, 155, 161
 feasibility of 60–63
 limited in the EU 5, 8, 135, 139
 linked to the common good 27, 136
 as the outcome of public choices 134, 138
 strengthening 134, 136, 140, 143, 149, 153, 159
climate change 4, 10, 12, 17, 21, 24, 37, 38, 57, 69, 71, 89, 125
cohesion policy 119, 145
collective action problem 38
collective memory 9, 54
College of Commissioners 110, 113, 114, 115, 116
Common Agriculture Policy (CAP) 7, 91, 102, 114
communitarianism 8, 18, 24
competition policy 141
conceptions of the common good 21, 22, 28, 35, 40, 59
consumer protection 70, 89, 104, 114
Copenhagen Commission 65, 66, 67, 74, 80
Council of Europe 33, 65, 66, 169
Council of the European Union (the Council)
 agenda of 148
 configurations of 120
 ordinary legislative procedure 128
 relations with the EU Citizens' Assembly 120
 relations with the European Commission 127
 representation of national interests 88
 representation of separate demoi 110
 rotating presidency of 123
 suspension of voting rights 13, 63, 66
 transnational debate 12, 38, 71
 voting rules 5, 80, 85, 104, 110, 174

Court of Justice of the European Union (CJEU) 12, 49, 54, 56, 61, 71, 80, 104, 150
COVID-19 1, 7, 61, 68, 78, 116, 125, 151
Croatia 169
Cuba 32, 35
cultural diversity 2, 9, 24, 40
cyberterrorism 39, 157
Cyprus 136, 157, 171, 172

debt crisis 72, 138, 143, 144, 145, 167
decision-making rules 4, 11, 53
defence cooperation 1, 14, 134, 140, 155, 157, 158, 159, 175
Delors, Jacques 303
democratic iterations 35
democratic mandate 116
democratic scrutiny 65, 73, 118
demoicracy 121
Denmark 21, 25, 90, 143

Economic Community of West African States 50
ejection mechanism 66, 67, 87
environmental protection 10, 12, 23, 33, 52, 59, 67, 69, 70, 73, 86, 89, 173
epistemic uncertainty 4, 25, 119
Erasmus programme 138, 150, 151, 155, 168
essentially contested concept 25
EU Citizens' Assembly 13, 14, 73, 112, 119, 120, 126, 134, 148, 154, 159, 174
EU citizenship 8, 9, 137, 138, 152, 153, 154
EU citizenship education 134, 153, 154, 155, 159, 175
EU corporate tax 101, 146
EU enlargement 89, 135, 157
EU labour code 13, 134, 142, 143, 159, 164, 175
EU values
  as accession criteria 54, 61, 66
  challenges against 59, 60
  commitment to 91
  as a common moral standpoint 10, 118, 173
  defined 5
  as distinct from other values 10, 11, 55, 57, 58, 73
  endorsement of 54, 55
  enforcement of 63, 65, 174
  EU as guardian of 59, 60, 76, 174
  examples of 5, 33
  as grounds for a conception of the common good 4, 57
  as the moral DNA of the Union 2
  noncompliance with 6, 52, 53, 59, 60–63, 64, 65
  not European by definition 12, 173
  realising 2, 6, 57, 76, 87, 174
  thin and thick accounts 53, 55–56, 57
  widely shared 2, 57
Eurogroup 5, 167
European Agency for Fair Trade 71, 72, 74, 163, 174
European Central Bank 72, 87, 97
European Citizens Initiatives 146
European Commission
  accountability 117
  bureaucratic apparatus 13, 97, 113
  citizens' perceptions 153
  delegation of competences to 90, 116
  dependence on the Council 101
  duty to promote the general interest 7, 113
  electing the president of 13, 97, 102, 112, 113–115, 126, 129, 174
  enforcing EU rules 61, 63, 114, 127
  expanding competences 113, 115, 154
  ideational background of 97
  impartiality 97, 112, 113–115, 126
  influence in the domestic spheres 94
  lack of power to adopt legislation 7, 98
  legislative initiative 114, 127
  not a unitary actor 127
  policies 101, 149
  political priorities 139
  political term 118, 129
  relations with the EU Citizens' Assembly 120
  relations with the European Parliament 123, 128
  Spitzenkandidaten system 129
  two levels of action 113, 115
  undemocratic 7
  workforce 128

Index

European Council
  agenda of 159
  citizens' perceptions 153
  divided 62
  electing the president of 13, 102, 112, 113–115, 126, 174
  relations with the European Parliament 122
  suspension of voting rights 63, 65, 80
  voting rules 110, 132
European Court of Human Rights 49
European Credit Rating Agency 13, 71, 72, 74
European Defence Fund 159, 160, 175
European Education Area 151
European Free Trade Association 50
European identity 9, 54, 55, 168
European Model 105
  challenges against 53, 58, 60, 70–71
  as a distinctive model 53, 56, 57, 74
  enabling the 59, 60, 70–71, 76, 174
  feasibility of 59, 69, 73
  political and economic preconditions 68, 71, 74
  realising the 57, 71, 75, 76
  social dimension of 12, 71, 81
  sustainability of 68, 87
  three dimensions of 67, 74
European Parliament
  directly elected 146
  links to national parliaments 13, 112, 126, 174
  ordinary legislative procedure 128
  party politics 62, 64, 76
  political term 118, 129
  reforming the 124, 126, 132, 174
  relations with the European Commission 127
  relations with the European Council 128
  representing separated demoi 110
  transnational debate 12, 38, 71
  transnational lists 13, 112
European public space 124, 125
European Semester 63, 79, 109
European Transnational Tax Authority 13, 52, 71, 74, 174

European Union Agency for Fundamental Rights 150
European way of life 6, 58
Europeanisation 124, 132, 135, 142, 152
Euroscepticism 8, 69, 136, 139, 162
Eurozone 5, 87, 96, 109, 119, 122, 135, 153, 155
ever closer Union 2, 7, 17
externalities 96, 115, 122, 127

Finland 143, 172
France 10, 16, 29, 30, 31, 45, 49, 62, 77, 88, 127, 129, 136, 162, 168, 169
freedom of movement 7, 8, 14, 134, 138, 150, 151, 152, 154, 159, 162, 175
freedom of speech 2, 6, 32, 34, 59, 65
Fukuyama, Francis 135
fundamental rights
  in developing countries 37
  of foreign citizens 39
  fulfilment of 29, 35, 38
  gross and systemic violations of 21, 23, 34, 36, 37
  list of 36
  protection of 37
  respect for 35, 38, 40, 59

gender equality 28, 54, 74
general interest of the Union 17, 113
Germany 25, 45, 48, 62, 87, 89, 90, 93, 117, 127, 129, 133, 142, 145, 168, 169
global challenges 10, 21, 39
global common good 4, 10, 12, 21, 33, 38, 39, 40, 47
globalisation 9, 12, 24, 39, 42, 67, 70, 86, 163
Greece 6, 14, 90, 107, 117, 136, 143, 145
Gulf Cooperation Council 50

Hobbes, Thomas 36, 48
Hollande, François 88
Holy See 34
human rights
  as a EU value 6, 33, 56
  Eurocentric 49

promotion of 33
respect for 56, 61
violations 32
humanitarian intervention 88
Hungary 2, 6, 59, 60, 61, 77, 78, 79, 136

Iceland 88
impermissible harm 3, 22, 23, 34, 37, 41, 103
individualism 8
infringement procedures 114
institutional memory 124
institutional reforms 5, 7, 11, 13, 38, 60, 71, 86, 112, 113, 122, 136, 175
interdependence 10, 24, 59, 122
interest groups 42, 68, 69, 120, 144
internal market 12, 71, 89, 90
International Labour Organization (ILO) 83
international law 21, 34, 36, 40, 48
Iran 21, 34, 47
Ireland 38, 95, 171
Israel 34
Italy 14, 21, 25, 62, 90, 129, 133, 136, 161, 169

Japan 32
Juncker, Jean-Claude 1, 8

Katzenstein, Peter 87
Kosovo 78

Laos 32
legitimacy 9, 65, 118, 136
Le Pen, Marine 30, 62
liberal imperialism 35
Libya 157
like-minded states 9, 32, 33, 70, 173
Lithuania 159
Luxembourg 96, 143, 168

Macron, Emmanuel 1, 30, 162
Malta 171
Manners, Ian 6, 33, 56, 57, 75
maximising utility 3, 100
Members of the European Parliament (MEPs) 102, 110, 112, 118, 121
Mercosur 33, 39, 50

Merkel, Angela 1, 87, 129
Mill, John Stuart 76
Miller, David 137
moral change 28, 29, 35
moral consensus 6, 24, 33, 38, 57, 175
Müller, Jan-Werner 65
Multiannual Financial Framework 89, 151
multinational corporations 12, 37, 68, 69, 72, 83, 86
mutual defence clause 134, 158, 160, 175

national interests
    advancing at any cost 100
    conflict of 13, 26, 39, 91, 101, 113, 127
    convergence of 13, 85, 89, 98, 104
    defined 85, 89–91
    diversity of 87, 89, 174
    formation of 85, 86, 91, 92–94, 122, 174
    going beyond 2, 5, 22, 86–87
    narrow definitions of 100, 102, 120
    negotiating 99
    predominance of 3
    preventing conflicts of 92
    as socially constructed 88, 91
    tensions with the common good 2, 91
nationalism 1, 15, 38, 153, 154, 169
natural resources 35, 50
neighbouring states 10, 59
neoliberalism 10
non-discrimination 6, 32, 33, 56, 104, 154
non-interference 35, 59
non-state actors 12, 35, 52, 53, 60, 67, 68, 69, 70, 74, 86, 174
Nordic Council 50
normative power 6, 54
normative turn in EU studies 9, 19
North Atlantic Treaty Organisation (NATO) 156, 157, 171, 172
North Korea 10, 47
North Macedonia 63, 78, 107, 162
Norway 32

Orbán, Viktor 2, 30, 61, 64

Pakistan 34
pan-European constituency 102, 117, 121, 122, 174
Paris Climate Agreement 34
Permanent Structured Cooperation programme 158, 159, 175
Pettit, Philip 70
Plato 144
pluralism 4, 6, 25, 34, 35, 36, 55, 56, 59
Poland 6, 21, 25, 60, 61, 77, 78, 79, 129, 136, 157
political deadlocks 7, 13, 85, 86, 87, 90, 92, 135, 174
political polarisation 25
political representation 102, 121
Portugal 14, 28, 103
practice-dependence approach 11
proportionality 86, 104
public interest 12, 42, 67, 70, 71, 88, 106
public opinion 93
public reasoning 98–100
public representation 93, 94, 108
public values
  beyond borders 22, 140–143
  change of 28, 29, 34, 44, 76
  clashing conceptions of 34–36
  as a common moral standpoint 4, 21, 26, 27, 29, 31, 38, 40, 53, 173
  defined 4, 21, 22, 26, 53, 173
  as distinct from constitutional values 43
  as distinct from cultural values 30, 173
  endorsement of 11, 25, 31, 44, 52, 173
  examples of 27
  fulfilment of 59
  imposing 35
  interpretation of 27, 28, 29, 119
  morally objectionable 27
  overlap of 4, 10, 21, 28, 32
  priority of 27
  realising 52, 53, 75
  representative of the citizenry 28
Putnam, Robert 13, 85, 94

qualified majority 63, 65, 70, 82, 86, 99, 100, 110

rating agencies 12, 68, 72, 83, 86
rational choice theory 10, 136, 160
Rawls, John 10, 23, 36, 41, 42, 110, 165
refugees 1, 45, 56, 90
regional integration 18, 33, 38, 39, 40, 42, 69, 156
Representations of the Commission 13, 14, 86, 98, 104, 113, 122, 148, 159, 174
Romania 136, 143, 169
Rousseau, Jean-Jacques 23
Russia ii, 1, 5, 25, 32, 37, 157, 159, 172

sacrifices 3, 5, 7, 22, 37, 40, 86, 87, 94, 97, 98, 100, 103, 134, 136, 175
Sandel, Michael 18, 69, 82, 137, 138, 161
Schuman, Robert 135, 160
Schuman Declaration 7, 135, 139
self-determination 35
Serbia 55, 63, 78
Slovenia 136
social construction 31, 87, 91
social engineering 11, 137, 154
social level playing field 13, 134, 140–143, 152, 159, 163, 175
social policy 82, 89, 100, 116, 142
social rights 36, 72, 79, 141
socioeconomic inequalities 8, 13, 22, 60–63, 69, 134, 138, 142, 152, 159, 175
sovereignty 34, 70, 95
Soviet Union 88, 93
Spain 10, 14, 129, 169
Stability and Growth Pact 115
subsidiarity 86, 104, 123, 128
supremacy of EU law 43
Sweden 62, 136, 143, 168, 171
Syria 157

tax evasion 39, 59, 71, 130
trade policy 6, 119, 142
Treaty of Lisbon 63, 66, 82, 118, 121, 123, 131, 146
Treaty of Maastricht 138

Index

Trump, Donald 157
Turkey 157, 172
Tusk, Donald 1
two-level game 13, 85, 95, 98, 102, 104, 109, 136

Ukraine 1, 5, 25, 32, 37, 63, 78, 157, 172
ultimate good 3, 103
unanimity rule 5, 13, 70, 85, 99, 100, 104, 174
United Kingdom 15, 18, 45, 69, 76, 80, 122, 141, 160
United Nations 39, 40, 69, 170
United States 45
   accountability 109
   American Way of Life 76
   armed forces 158
   as distinctive conception of the common good 34
   cleavages 44
   Constitution 29
   culture of national security 88
   distinctive conception of the common good 21, 57
   former Presidents 45
   intervention in Vietnam 92, 93, 108
   mobility of workers 149
   nationalism 69, 169
   relations with Cuba 35, 48
   retreat from global security 1, 157
   socioeconomic inequalities 138
   Supreme Court 45
   weakened sense of community 18

Van Parijs, Philippe 121
Venezuela 32
Visegrad Group 2, 14, 56, 64

World Bank 40
World Trade Organisation 40

www.ingramcontent.com/pod-product-compliance
Ingram Content Group UK Ltd.
Pitfield, Milton Keynes, MK11 3LW, UK
UKHW020449060325
4871UKWH00046B/85